CANADIAN ANNUAL REVIEW OF POLITICS AND PUBLIC AFFAIRS 2007

Canadian Annual Review of politics and public affairs 2007

EDITED BY DAVID MUTIMER

Published with the support of York University by
University of Toronto Press
Toronto Buffalo London

Toronto Buffalo London
www.utppublishing.com
Printed and bound by CPI Group (UK) Ltd, Croydon, CR0 4YY

ISBN 978-1-4426-4855-5

Printed on acid-free paper

A cataloguing record for this publication is available from Library and Archives Canada.

University of Toronto Press acknowledges the financial assistance to its publishing program of the Canada Council for the Arts and the Ontario Arts Council.

Canada Council for the Arts Conseil des Arts du Canada

ONTARIO ARTS COUNCIL
CONSEIL DES ARTS DE L'ONTARIO
50 YEARS OF ONTARIO GOVERNMENT SUPPORT OF THE ARTS
50 ANS DE SOUTIEN DU GOUVERNEMENT DE L'ONTARIO AUX ARTS

University of Toronto Press acknowledges the financial support of the Government of Canada through the Canada Book Fund for its publishing activities.

This book was published with the support of York University.

Copies of the *Canadian Annual Review* published annually for 1989 and 1991–2006 are available.

Contents

Contributors

MELVIN BAKER, Archivist/Historian, President's Office, Memorial University of Newfoundland
RICHARD BISAILLON, Assistant Professor, Department of Political Science, Concordia University, Montreal
EMMANUEL BRUNET-JAILLY, Assistant Professor, School of Public Administration, University of Victoria
PETER EDWARD BUKER, Assistant Professor, Department of Political Studies, University of Prince Edward Island
KRISTIN BURNETT, Associate Professor, Indigenous Learning Department, Lakehead University
KEN COATES, Adjunct Professor of Political Studies, University of Saskatchewan
ROBERT DRUMMOND, Associate Professor, Department of Political Science, York University
ROBERT EVERETT, University Secretariat, York University
ROBERT G. FINBOW, Associate Professor, Department of Political Science, Dalhousie University
JOSEPH GARCEA, Associate Professor, Department of Political Science, University of Saskatchewan
CHRIS HENDERSHOT, Doctoral Candidate, Department of Political Science, York University, Compiler of the calendar and obituaries
CAREY HILL, Independent Researcher, Ottawa, Ontario
HAROLD JANSEN, Assistant Professor, Department of Political Science, University of Lethbridge
SERENA KATAOKA, Doctoral Candidate, Department of Political Science, University of Victoria
GEOFFREY LAMBERT, Professor, Department of Political Studies, University of Manitoba
WARREN MAGNUSSON, Professor, Department of Political Science, University of Victoria

DAVID MUTIMER, Editor of the *Canadian Annual Review of Politics and Public Affairs*; Associate Professor, Political Science, York University; and Director, York Centre for International and Security Studies

PETER NEARY, Professor, Department of History, University of Western Ontario

GREG POELZER, Associate Professor, Department of Political Studies, University of Saskatchewan

DANIEL SALÉE, Professor of Political Science and Principal of the School of Community and Public Affairs, Concordia University

CHRISTOPHER SPEARIN, Assistant Professor, Department of Defence Studies at the Canadian Forces College, Toronto

SHANNON STETTNER, Managing Editor of the *Canadian Annual Review of Politics and Public Affairs*

RICHARD WILBUR, Fundy Promotions, St Andrews, New Brunswick

Canadian calendar 2007

JANUARY

4 John Baird is appointed the new environment minister, replacing Rona Ambrose, as Prime Minister Stephen Harper shuffles Cabinet.

5 The Canadian junior men's hockey team secures its third consecutive world title with 4–2 victory over Russia.

Wajid Khan, a Liberal MP from Ontario, crosses the floor of the House of Commons and joins the Conservatives.

Statistics Canada reports that the unemployment rate decreased 0.2 per cent to 6.1 per cent in December 2006. Employment increased 2.1 per cent or 345,000 jobs in 2006, which represents the highest rate of growth since 2002.

8 The 21,000 members of the Alliance of Canadian Cinema, Television and Radio Artists (ACTRA) go on strike.

9 A report released by a provincial commission in Ontario reports that the SARS outbreak in Toronto could not have been prevented. However, the report also suggests that more could have been done to better protect front-line health-care workers.

10 CanWest Global Communication and Goldman Sachs Capital Partners purchase Alliance Atlantis Communications for $2.3 billion.

12 Statistics Canada reports that according to data from the 2002 Canadian Community Health Survey an estimated 500,000 Canadian workers experienced some form of depression.

15 According to a survey conducted by Léger Marketing 59 per cent of respondents residing in Quebec admitted to being racist to

some degree compared to 47 per cent of non-Quebec Canadian residents.

17 Statistics Canada reports that the number of marriages in Canada totalled 147,391 in 2003 which was down from the 2000 peak of 157,395.

23 An American law requiring all Canadians flying into the United States to have a valid passport goes into effect.

Maher Arar will remain on an American "terrorist" watch list with American officials citing independent information that Arar remains a threat.

Statistics Canada reports that the twelve-month Consumer Price Index (CPI) for December 2006 increased 1.6 per cent.

25 The government of Canada agrees to pay Maher Arar $10 million for its role in the deportation of Arar by the United States to Syria.

Statistics Canada reports that between 2000 and 2006 employment in Canada increased by 1.7 million jobs with 73 per cent or 1.3 million of these jobs being located in Canada's twenty-eight census metropolitan areas.

29 The government of Nova Scotia and the federal government announce a $400 million plan to contain and clean up the Sydney tar ponds.

30 Statistics Canada reports that new immigrants to Canada made little improvement to their economic position between 2002 and 2004. In 2002 low-income rates for new immigrants in their first full year in Canada were 3.5 times higher than rates for people born in Canada. In 2004 this gap closed only slightly, with low-income rates for new immigrants being 3.2 times higher than rates for people born in Canada.

FEBRUARY

5 The House of Commons passes a nonbinding motion that reaffirms Canada's commitment to the Kyoto Protocol.

6 Garth Turner, an independent MP from Ontario, joins the Liberal Party.

8 Statistics Canada reports that the most significant determinants of whether a person attends university in 2003 include the high school attended, parental level of education, and educational expectations and academic performance in high school.

9 Statistics Canada reports that the number of jobs in Canada increased by 89,000 in January, while the unemployment rate increased 0.1 per cent to 6.2 per cent as more people entered the labour market.

11 Conductors and yard service workers for the Canadian National Railway go on strike. The CNR files a complaint attempting to get the strike declared illegal.

14 DaimlerChrysler announces that 2,000 jobs, 13,000 globally, will be cut in Canada as the company begins a massive restructuring effort.

Statistics Canada reports that the 1,666,327 vehicles sold in Canada in 2006 represent the second highest level of annual sales.

16 ACTRA and Canadian screen, radio, and television producers reach a tentative deal bringing an end to a strike by 21,000 Canadian actors.

Statistics Canada reports that 356,000 violent incidents occurred in Canadian workplaces in 2004. This number represents close to one-fifth of all reported incidents of physical assault, sexual assault, and robbery in Canada.

20 Statistics Canada reports that the CPI between January 2006 and January 2007 increased 1.2 per cent.

22 Statistics Canada reports that operating profits for Canadian corporations in 2006 totalled a record high of $231.7 billion.

23 Back-to-work legislation is introduced by the federal Conservatives to end a strike by conductors and yard workers at CNR.

Liberal MP and former minister of foreign affairs Bill Graham announces he will not seek re-election.

Statistics Canada reports that 7.7 per cent of men and 7.6 per cent of women quit their jobs in 2002 compared to 5.5 per cent of men and 7 per cent of women quit their jobs in 1984.

25 The United Transportation Union, representing 2,800 striking workers at CNR, reaches a deal with CNR management ending a two-week strike.

26 Prime Minister Stephen Harper announces that Canada will contribute $200 million for reconstruction aid in Afghanistan.

MARCH

2 Statistics Canada reports that the Canadian economy grew by 2.7 per cent in 2006.

5 Statistics Canada reports that 380,700 people were working for the federal government in March 2006, a slight decrease from the 382,700 employees in March 1995. Scientific and professional employees accounted for 58 per cent of employees, a marked increased from 41 per cent in 1995.

6 Statistics Canada reports that 10 per cent of Canadians over the age of 65 were victims of violent and property crime compared to 31 per cent of Canadians under the age of 65.

11 Daylight saving time goes into effect – three weeks earlier than in 2006.

16 Statistics Canada reports that Canada's net worth increased 2.7 per cent to $4.9 trillion or $150,500 per person during the fourth quarter of 2006.

19 With the federal budget directing $698 million of an estimated $1.5 billion allotted to correcting the fiscal imbalance between the federal government and provinces towards Quebec, the Bloc Québécois announces that it will support the Conservatives' budget, ensuring passage of the budget and preventing an election.

20 Statistics Canada reports that the CPI rose 2 per cent between February 2006 and February 2007.

26 Statistics Canada reports that Canada's GDP per capita in 2005 represented 84.3 per cent of GDP per capita in the United States. This represents a slight improvement from the 1998 low of 81 per cent.

27 Jean Charest and the Liberal Party of Quebec secure a minority government in Quebec's provincial elections. The Liberals win

48 seats, the Action démocratique du Québec win 36 seats, and the Parti Québécois win 36 seats.

With the support of the Bloc Québécois the federal budget easily passes in the House of Commons.

28 Several current and retired members of the RCMP appear before a parliamentary committee and allege fraud, abuse, and a cover-up by senior RCMP officials in the handling of investigations of allegations into further fraud and abuse of the RCMP pension and insurance plans in 2002.

APRIL

8 Six Canadian soldiers are killed when their armoured vehicle strikes a roadside bomb in southern Afghanistan. This is the largest single-day loss of life suffered by Canadian soldiers in Afghanistan.

9 The ninetieth anniversary of the battle for Vimy Ridge is marked with a rededication ceremony for the recently restored Vimy monument.

10 The Canadian women's hockey team secures their ninth world title with a 5–1 victory over perennial rivals the United States.

11 Two Canadian soldiers are killed in two different roadside bomb detonations.

Belinda Stronach, a Liberal MP, announces her immediate resignation from federal politics. Stronach returns to the private sector and accepts a position at Magna International.

Unionized CNR workers are locked out by management with the commencement of rotating strikes across the country following the rejection of a tentative agreement.

Statistics Canada reports that retail sales were up 6.4 per cent to $392.4 billion in 2006.

12 The Liberal Party of Canada announces that for the first time in its history it will not run a full slate of candidates in the next federal election. The Liberals will not be running a candidate against Green Party leader Elizabeth May.

16 Statistics Canada reports that 100,000 persons with PhDs were employed in Canada in 2001. Of these, 57,000 held PhDs in the sciences and/or engineering.

17 Testifying before a parliamentary committee Giuliano Zaccardelli, former RCMP commissioner, denied any wrongdoing in the management of the RCMP pension and insurance fund.

19 Statistics Canada reports that consumers paid 2.3 per cent more for goods and services in March 2007 than in March 2006.

21 A provincial election is called for 22 May in Manitoba.

23 Canada marks the twenty-fifth anniversary of the entrenchment of the Charter of Rights and Freedoms in the Canadian Constitution Act of 1982.

A report published in the *Globe and Mail* reveals that at least thirty Afghan detainees allege experiencing torture after being transferred to the Afghan National Directorate of Security by Canadian Forces.

25 Following allegations of torture of detainees transferred from Canadian to Afghan authority, the Canadian Forces ensures that a monitoring system of how detainees are treated is now in place.

Statistics Canada reports that economic growth in Alberta far outstripped that national average of economic growth in 2006. Alberta's economy expanded 6.8 per cent in 2006.

26 The federal Conservatives announce a plan to require Canadian industry to be 18 per cent more energy efficient by 2010. These new efficiency targets place Canada at least ten years behind fulfilling commitments made under the Kyoto Protocol.

Statistics Canada reports that the population of metropolitan areas increased 45 per cent between 1971 and 2001, whereas rural population increased 13 per cent.

30 Justin Trudeau, the eldest son of Pierre Trudeau, announces his intention to run for the Liberal Party of Canada in the Montreal riding of Papineau in the next federal election.

Statistics Canada reports that 84 per cent of immigrants who had lived in Canada for four years in 2005 indicated they felt positive about moving to Canada. Quality of life in Canada registered as the most prominent reason for immigrating to Canada.

MAY

3 Statistics Canada reports that after adjusting for inflation the median after-tax income for families of two or more people increased 1.6 per cent to $56,000 in 2005 in Canada.

11 Statistics Canada reports that the gap between Canada's wealthiest and poorest families widened considerably between 1989 and 2004. During this time the after-tax income for the top 10 per cent of wealthiest families rose 22 per cent, while after-tax income for families with the lowest 10 per cent of household wealth decreased 11 per cent.

12 Gilles Duceppe announces that he will no longer be seeking the leadership of the Parti Québécois, only twenty-four hours after he announced he was going to run for the position. Duceppe also announced he is backing Pauline Marois for leader of the party.

17 President of the World Bank Paul Wolfowitz announces that he will resign at the end of June.

Consumers paid 2.2 per cent more in April for the goods and services in the CPI basket than they did in April 2006, a slightly slower growth than the 2.3 per cent increase recorded in March. However, excluding energy components, consumer prices increased at their fastest pace (+2.4 per cent) in almost four years.

18 Greyhound bus services west of Ottawa are halted as 1,150 employees go on strike.

Statistics Canada reports that 54 per cent of married people under the age of 35 in 2004 had achieved the same educational level. Furthermore, 24 per cent of wives and 19 per cent of husbands had obtained a university degree in 2001, compared to 4 per cent and 10 per cent in 1971.

Pierre Duchesne is appointed as lieutenant governor of Quebec.

19 Capt. Shawn McCaughey is killed in the crash of the jet he was piloting during practice for a Snowbirds air show in Montana.

22 The New Democratic Party (NDP) secures a third consecutive majority government in Manitoba's thirty-ninth general election. The NDP wins 36 seats, the Conservatives 19 seats, and the Liberals 2 seats.

Prime Minister Stephen Harper makes a surprise visit to Afghanistan.

23 Statistics Canada reports that according to an Organization for Economic Co-operation and Development (OECD) study Canadian teens averaged 9.2 hours of unpaid and paid labour (including school work) on schools days and 3.5 hours of unpaid and paid labour on weekends in 2005. This ranked Canadian teens first in average daily labour hours.

24 Statistics Canada reports that operating profits for Canadian corporations totalled $63.8 billion in the first quarter of 2007, a 2.9 per cent increase from the preceding quarter.

25 Statistics Canada reports that in 2001 an estimated 40 per cent of immigrants to Canada held at least an undergraduate university degree compared to 20 per cent of immigrants to the United States.

Greyhound bus services resumes as 51 per cent of striking Amalgamated Transit Union workers vote to ratify a tentative agreement.

28 Robert Ghiz becomes Prince Edward Island's thirty-first premier as his Liberals win 23 of 27 seats in the provincial legislature. The Progressive Conservatives win the 4 remaining seats.

29 Diane Finely, minister of citizenship and immigration, announces that federal government will restore the citizenship status to people who lost their Canadian citizenship as a result of the enactment of little-known features of the 1947 Citizenship Act.

Statistics Canada reports that the adjusted-for-inflation median total income of two-parent families increased 2.1 per cent to $67,600 in 2005. Median income for single-parent families remained at $30,000.

30 Statistics Canada reports that 3.1 million people were employed in Canada's public sector in 2006. Employment at the provincial level accounted for 51 per cent or 1.5 million workers, municipal employees accounted for 35.3 per cent or 1 million workers, and federal employees accounted for 13.6 per cent or 393,000 workers.

31 Statistics Canada reports that real GDP advanced 0.9 per cent in the first quarter of 2007, double the increase from the previous quarter.

The Parti Québécois announces that the majority of its members will abstain from voting on the provincial budget so as not to trigger another provincial election.

Statistics Canada reports the after-inflation median income of individuals totalled $25,400 in 2005, a 1.9 per cent increase from 2004.

JUNE

4 The World Wildlife Fund releases a report that gives Canada, Russia, and the United States a failing grade on efforts to curb climate change.

5 Bill Casey, a Nova Scotia MP, is expelled from the Conservative caucus after he voted against the bill to implement the federal budget.

7 The Anaheim Ducks defeat the Ottawa Senators 6–2 to win the Stanley Cup for the first time in franchise history.

Quebec announces plans to implement a carbon tax – a first in Canada. The tax, slated to take effect in October, will amount to 0.8 cents a litre of gas sold in the province.

8 In a 6–1 decision the Supreme Court of Canada rules that collective bargaining is protected by the Charter of Rights and Freedoms ruling against sections of British Columbia's Bill 29 that restricted the bargaining rights of BC health-care workers.

Statistics Canada reports that the employment rate for students planning on returning to school in September reached a sixteen-year high in May of 47.2 per cent.

12 Despite suggestions from Nova Scotia premier Rodney MacDonald that MPs from the Atlantic provinces oppose the federal budget, eight Conservative MPs from Atlantic Canada vote to implement the budget.

Statistics Canada reports that the proportion of women aged 25–29 who obtained a university degree increased from 21 per cent in 1991 to 34 per cent in 2001. The proportion for men of similar age rose only slightly from 16 per cent in 1991 to 21 per cent in 2001.

13 Despite all charges being dropped against him, Canada has not yet requested the release of Omar Khadr from Guantánamo Bay.

15 David Brown, the person leading the investigation into how top RCMP officials handled the police forces pension and insurance fund, releases a highly critical report of the management style of former RCMP commissioner Giuliano Zaccardelli.

Statistics Canada reports that single people under the age of 65 represent over a third of people living with low income despite the fact that these people only account for 11 per cent of Canada's total population in 2005.

18 Public Safety Minister Stockwell Day announces that the Conservative government accepts all the recommendations made by the investigation into allegations of fraud and abuse in the management of the RCMP pension and insurance fund.

19 Bill Graham, former interim leader of the Liberal Party of Canada, resigns from federal politics.

Statistics Canada reports that the twelve-month CPI increased 2.2 per cent between May 2006 and May 2007.

Statistics Canada reports that in 2003 one-third of Canadians aged 19–64, particularly university students, participated in non-voting political actions.

20 Three Canadian soldiers are killed by a roadside bomb while on patrol in southern Afghanistan. The number of Canadians killed in Afghanistan now totals sixty.

22 The federal Conservatives announce that Canada's mission in Afghanistan will not be extended beyond February 2009 without parliamentary consensus.

Statistics Canada reports that net worth in Canada totalled $5.3 trillion or $159,000 per capita at the end of the first quarter of 2007.

Statistics Canada reports that spending on social services in Canada for the fiscal year ending March 2007 totalled $172.4 billion or 33 per cent of all program expenditures.

24 Members of the Anglican Church of Canada vote against blessing same-sex marriages.

26 Joe Comuzzi, MP for Thunder Bay–Superior North, joins the Conservative Party of Canada.

27 Jean Lafleur is sentenced to three and a half years in prison for his role in the federal sponsorship scandal.

28 Statistics Canada reports that crime rates in small urban centres were 43 per cent higher than in large urban centres and 58 per cent higher than in rural areas in 2005. However, the 2.5 homicides per 100,000 people in rural areas was higher than the rate of 2 homicides for large urban centres and the rate of 1.7 homicides in small urban centres.

29 Aboriginal groups construct blockades and temporarily close Highway 401 during the Aboriginal national day of action.

Former Liberal prime minister Jean Chretien is named to the Order of Canada.

Statistics Canada reports that 106,000 women and children sought shelter from an abusive relationship between 1 April 2005 and 31 March 2006.

30 Canada's largest telecommunications company, BCE Inc., announces it will be bought by a group led by the Ontario Teachers' Pension Plan. The deal is estimated to be worth $51.7 billion.

JULY

1 Canada celebrates its 140th birthday.

9 The federal Conservatives announce plans to build six to eight new Arctic patrol ships in an effort to reassert Canadian sovereignty in the region.

10 Statistics Canada reports that an estimated 630,000 Canadians sustained an activity-limiting non-fatal work injury in 2003. Almost 75 per cent of those injured were men working blue-collar jobs. An estimated 460,000 men and 170,000 women or 5 per cent of the male workforce and 2 per cent of the female workforce suffered an on-the-job injury.

13 Conrad Black, former head of Hollinger Inc., is found guilty of obstruction of justice and three counts of mail fraud.

Statistics Canada reports that 100,039 induced abortions were performed in 2004, which is down 2.9 per cent from 103,001 in 2003.

16 Senior civil servant William Elliott becomes the first civilian commissioner of the RCMP.

17 Statistics Canada reports that people aged 55–64 represented Canada's fastest growing age group. According to census numbers this age group grew 28.1 per cent between 2001 and 2006, vastly exceeding the average population growth rate of 5.4 per cent.

18 Statistics Canada reports that the national overall crime rate decreased 3 per cent in 2006. The national homicide rate decreased 10 per cent in 2006 after two consecutive annual increases.

19 The Toronto Stock Exchange (TSX) closes the trading day with a record high close of 14,625.76.

20 Vancouver's 1,800 outside workers walk off the job.

21 About 6,000 unionized loggers, truck drivers, and sawmill workers go on strike in British Columbia.

23 Vancouver's 3,500 inside workers join 1,800 outside workers and walk off the job.

Foreign Affairs Minister Peter MacKay announces that Canada will immediately resume aid to the Palestinian Authority.

24 The TSX experiences its largest single-day loss in six years, closing down 400 points.

30 Indian Affairs Minister Jim Prentice and Kashechewan Chief Jonathon Solomon sign a $200 million agreement to rebuild that flood-ravaged reserve. However, the deal does not contain a pledge to move the reserve to higher ground.

Statistics Canada reports that housing prices in Canada rose to an average of $315,332 in June 2007 – the highest average price on record.

31 John Felderhof, the only person charged for his involvement in the Bre-X Minerals scandal, is found not guilty of all charges of insider trading.

AUGUST

1 Conrad Black is refused entry to Canada while he awaits sentencing.

5 Ontario's deputy premier George Smitherman marries his partner Christopher Peloso in Elliot Lake, Ontario.

10 Statistics Canada reports that the unemployment rate decreased 0.1 per cent to 6 per cent in July, which is the lowest rate of unemployment since 1974.

11 Minister of Defence Gordon O'Connor announces plans to build an army training centre in Resolute Bay, refurbish a deep-water port at Nanisivik, and expand the Canadian Rangers by 900 personnel.

14 Prime Minister Stephen Harper shuffles his Cabinet for the second time in 2007. Peter MacKay is made minister of defence, Maxime Bernier moves to foreign affairs, Jim Prentice moves to industry, and Chuck Strahl moves to Indian Affairs.

16 The TSX closes down 200.06 points and is down 1,775 points since its record high close in July.

18 Former Cabinet minister Scott Brison marries his partner Maxime St Pierre, becoming the first federal politician to wed his or her same-sex partner.

19 A ceremony is held in Dieppe, France, to commemorate the fifty-fifth anniversary of the ill-fated Canadian mission during the Second World War.

21 A two-day summit in Quebec among the leaders of Canada, the United States, and Mexico comes to a close with the leaders pledging to work towards more efficient and secure borders.

22 Statistics Canada reports that 48 per cent of Canadians aged 12 and older in 2005, 12.7 million in total, can be considered to be inactive. Furthermore, 25 per cent or 6.6 million Canadians indicated that they sat down for the majority of the day.

23 The Quebec provincial police revealed that three provincial officers were tasked with infiltrating and posing as demonstrators of the Northern American leaders' summit.

Sudan expels a Canadian diplomat in the country, alleging interference in Sudan's affairs.

The Supreme Court of Canada refuses to hear an appeal from eleven homeless people arguing that Ontario's prohibition on panhandling and squeegee kids is unconstitutional.

27 United States Steel Corporation reaches a deal to purchase Canada's last independent steel maker, Stelco Inc., for US$1.1 billion.

28 Steven Truscott is acquitted of murder in the 1959 death of Lynne Harper.

29 The Department of Foreign Affairs announces it is expelling a Sudanese diplomat in retaliation for Sudan's expulsion of a Canadian official.

30 General Motors of Canada announces that 1,200 production jobs at its Oshawa truck factory will be cut.

Statistics Canada reports the average cost, adjusted for inflation, to educate a student in Canada was $9,040 in 2004–5, a 28 per cent increase from 1998–9 when the average was $7,077.

31 Statistics Canada reports that real GDP in Canada advanced 0.8 per cent in the second quarter of 2007.

SEPTEMBER

4 Prime Minister Stephen Harper announces that he will seek to prorogue Parliament until 16 October. The thirty-ninth session was scheduled to resume on 17 September.

Statistics Canada reports that in 2006 women accounted for 55.9 per cent of knowledge-based workers in Canada, up from 43.6 per cent in 1995.

5 David Onley is appointed lieutenant governor of Ontario.

9 Prime Minister Stephen Harper makes it known that he adamantly disagrees with an Elections Canada decision to allow women to have their faces veiled while voting.

10 Statistics Canada reports that the unemployment rate for immigrants who arrived in Canada between 2001and 2006 was

11.5 per cent in 2006 compared to the 4.9 per cent rate for the Canadian-born population. For immigrants who arrived between 1996 and 2001 the unemployment rate was 7.3 per cent.

11 Prime Minister Stephen Harper addresses the Parliament of Australia, becoming the first Canadian prime minister to do so.

12 The price of a barrel of oil tops US$80 for the first time.

13 Canada, the United States, Australia, and New Zealand do not sign the non-binding United Nations Declaration on the Rights of Indigenous Peoples. Nonetheless the Declaration is approved by the UN General Assembly.

14 The United States announces that it will allow the import of older cattle from Canada. Cattle imports resume in November.

17 The Iraqi government announces that it is expelling Blackwater Worldwide, a private security corporation, from the country following the deaths of seventeen Iraqi civilians in a seemingly unprovoked shooting by Blackwater contractors.

Three federal by-elections are held in Quebec, with the Conservatives winning the seat in Roberval, the NDP in Outremont, and the Bloc Québécois in Saint-Hyacinthe.

Statistics Canada reports that net worth in Canada reached $5.3 trillion or $162,200 per capita in the second quarter of 2007.

19 Statistics Canada reports that the twelve-month CPI for August rose 1.7 per cent, a significant decrease from the 2.2 per cent increases in July, June, May, and April.

A $1.9 billion compensation package for the abuse endured by an estimated 80,000 residential school students is formalized. First Nations Chief Phil Fontaine is quoted as saying, "This is an important day. It is a day of celebration. It is a perhaps – and I don't want to overstate this – even a turning point in the history of our nation."

20 The Canadian dollar achieves parity with the US dollar for the first time since 1976.

Statistics Canada reports that in 2003 a full 39 per cent of women aged 19 had attended university, whereas 26 per cent of men aged 19 pursued a university education.

21 Statistics Canada reports that 342,176 babies were born in Canada in 2005, a 1.5 per cent increase from 2004. The national birth rate also increased to 1.54 children per woman. The replacement fertility rate is estimated to be 2.1 children per woman.

24 Statistics Canada reports that in 2004 three-quarters of the 1.2 million Canadians whose annual income exceeds $89,000, 5 per cent of the tax filing population, are men. Statistics Canada also reports that in 2004 the top 5 per cent of the tax filing population accounted for 25 per cent of national income and paid 36 per cent of the national tax base.

25 A Canadian soldier is killed in a mortar attack in southern Afghanistan.

26 Statistics Canada reports that greenhouse gas emission from all industrial sources in Canada increased 18.4 per cent to 573,843 kilotonnes between 1990 and 2002. Export production was the single largest emitter, accounting for 46.1 per cent of total emissions in 2002, up from 36.4 per cent in 1990.

27 The Canadian dollar closes at US$1.0052. This is the first time the Canadian dollar has closed above parity in close to thirty-one years.

Prime Minister Stephen Harper announces that the federal budget surplus for the 2006–7 fiscal year exceeds $13 billion – almost $3 billion more than forecast.

30 John Kelai of Kenya runs the fastest ever time for a marathon on Canadian soil, winning the Scotiabank Toronto Waterfront Marathon Sunday in a time of 2:09:30.

OCTOBER

1 Following an eighteen-month trial four doctors from the Canadian Red Cross Society and Health Canada and Armour Pharmaceutical Co. are found not guilty of charges of criminal negligence and common nuisance brought on by the tainted blood scandal in which thousands of Canadians became infected with HIV and hepatitis C.

Steven Point is appointed lieutenant governor of British Columbia.

3 Statistics Canada reports that in 2006 a total of 476,000 Canadians were receiving regular employment insurance (EI) benefits, which is a 10.3 per cent decline from 2002 when 530,500 Canadians collected EI benefits.

4 Mark Carney becomes the governor of the Bank of Canada.

5 Statistics Canada reports that the unemployment rate for September decreased 0.1 per cent to 5.9 per cent, which is the first time the unemployment rate has dipped below 6 per cent since November 1974.

9 Incumbent Danny Williams and his Progressive Conservative Party secure a landslide victory in provincial elections in Newfoundland-Labrador. The Progressive Conservatives win 43 seats, the Liberals 3 seats, and the NDP 1 seat.

10 Dalton McGuinty's Liberal Party secures a resounding victory in provincial elections in Ontario. The Liberals win 71 seats, the Progressive Conservatives 26 seats, and the NDP 10 seats.

Vancouver's 3,500 full-time and seasonal inside workers ratify an agreement that will see them return to work. Outside workers and librarians reject the offer and remain on strike.

11 Statistics Canada reports that close to 75 per cent of people who commit or attempt to commit spousal homicide do not have a police record of prior incidences of spousal violence; 22 per cent of incidences involve repeat offenders, and 4 per cent of spousal homicide cases involve chronic offenders. Statistics Canada also reports that 82 per cent of spousal homicides are committed by men.

12 Prime Minister Stephen Harper appoints John Manley chair of a five-person committee tasked with investigating the future of Canada's mission in Afghanistan.

13 Bloc Québécois members vote overwhelmingly in favour of the leadership of Gilles Duceppe.

Roger Duguay becomes the new leader of the NDP in New Brunswick.

The University of Toronto Varsity Blues football set a record for the longest losing streak in Canadian Interuniversity with their forty-eighth consecutive loss.

14 Robert Dziekanski of Poland dies after being stunned with a taser by the RCMP at Vancouver International Airport. Dziekanski was in the process of immigrating to Canada.

Vancouver's outside workers ratify an agreement and bring an end to a three-month-long strike.

16 The federal Conservatives announce that their top priorities for the thirty-ninth session of Parliament include major tax cuts, a vote to extend Canada's mission in Afghanistan to until at least 2011, and new crime legislation.

17 Floyd Roland, the member of the Legislative Assembly (MLA) from Inuvik Boot Lake, is elected the tenth premier of the Northwest Territories.

18 Statistics Canada reports that full-time undergraduate students in Canada will pay 2.8 per cent more tuition in 2007–8 then they did in 2006–7. Average tuition for an undergraduate education in Canada for 2007–8 costs $4,524.

19 Statistics Canada reports that the twelve-month CPI for September 2006 and September 2007 rose 2.5 per cent – a marked increase from the 1.7 per cent increase in August.

24 Research in Motion market capitalization – share price multiplied by the number of shares – closes the day at $67.351 billion, surpassing the Royal Bank to become Canada's most valuable corporation.

Statistics Canada reports that in 2001, of the 57,095 people who possessed a PhD in the sciences and engineering, 45,670 were men. These numbers contrast with the fact that women compose 47 per cent of the labour force and constitute 57 per cent of university graduates in Canada.

25 Statistics Canada reports that alcohol sales in Canada for the 2005–6 fiscal year totalled $17.3 billion or $651.50 per person aged 15 and older. Beer sales continue their historic dominance, accounting for 48.6 per cent of sales, with wine accounting for 26.6 per cent and liquor 24.8 per cent.

30 Finance Minister Jim Flaherty tables a motion that will cut personal and corporate taxes by $60 billion over the next five years as well as another 1 per cent cut to the GST, which will come into effect 1 January 2008.

NOVEMBER

1 CAW president Buzz Hargrove announces that 1,100 jobs will be eliminated at Chrysler's Brampton production site in 2008.

2 Statistics Canada reports that the unemployment rate in October fell 0.1 per cent to 5.8 per cent.

6 The value of the Canadian dollar exceeds US$1.09 in after-hours trading.

7 Brad Wall becomes the fourteenth premier of Saskatchewan, following the victory of his Saskatchewan Party in provincial elections. The Saskatchewan Party wins 37 seats and the NDP wins 21 seats in the provincial legislature.

21 Public Safety Minister Stockwell Day announces that Paul Kennedy will review protocols for how the RCMP uses stun guns, in light of the death of Robert Dziekanski after he was shocked by the RCMP at Vancouver International Airport.

Statistics Canada reports that Canada's incarceration rate increased from 107 in 2004–5 to 110 prisoners per 100,000 Canadians in 2005–6. On average 33,123 adults and 1,987 youths were incarcerated in Canada in 2005–6.

25 The Saskatchewan Rough Riders defeat the Winnipeg Blue Bombers 23–19 to win the 95th Grey Cup in Toronto.

29 Statistics Canada reports that the median age of Canadian as of 1 July 2007 is 39 years, up from 37.6 years in 2002.

30 Statistics Canada reports that economic growth in the third quarter of 2007 increased 0.7 per cent, down from 0.9 per cent in the second quarter.

DECEMBER

3 Statistics Canada reports that 14.3 per cent or 4.4 million Canadians reported having a disability in 2006, a 21.2 per cent increase from the 3.6 million people who reported a disability in 2001.

4 Despite being told to leave the country, Canada's ambassador to Iran will stay in Tehran.

7 Statistics Canada reports that the unemployment rate rose 0.1 per cent to 5.9 per cent in November as more people entered the labour force.

9 Robert Pickton is found guilty of six counts of second-degree murder in the deaths of women from Vancouver's lower east side.

10 Conrad Black is sentenced to six and a half years and fined $125,000 after being found guilty of fraud charges in July.

11 Robert Pickton receives a life sentence with no chance of parole for twenty-five years.

14 Michael Burns resigns as chair of Atomic Energy of Canada following the political upheaval caused by the closing of the Chalk River nuclear reactor. The closing of the Chalk River facility created a global shortage of radioactive isotopes used in medical sciences. Prime Minister Stephen Harper appoints Glenna Carr to replace Burns.

Statistics Canada reports that net worth in Canada totalled $5.4 trillion or $163,700 per capita at the end of the third quarter of 2007.

16 The Chalk River nuclear facility resumes operations following the passage of a bill in the House of Commons that bypasses a Canadian Nuclear Safety Commissions order to keep the facility closed until safety concerns could be dealt with.

19 Statistics Canada reports that on 1 October 2007 Canada's population totalled 33,091,200 people.

20 The government of Ontario official cedes control of Ipperwash Provincial Park to the Stoney Point First Nation.

21 According to a report by the federal government, Canada exported $700 million worth of arms in 2003. When weapons sales to the United States are factored in, the total exceeds $2 billion.

27 Former Pakistani prime minister Benazir Bhutto is killed along with at least twenty other Pakistanis in a suicide attack in the city of Rawalpindi.

30 A Canadian soldier is killed by the detonation of a roadside bomb in southern Afghanistan.

CANADIAN ANNUAL REVIEW OF POLITICS AND PUBLIC AFFAIRS 2007

EDITOR'S INTRODUCTION – THE YEAR IN REVIEW

Following a year of remarkable upheaval and political change, 2007 represented a period of relative calm, even stasis. The economy continued on its remarkable run of growth, allowing the new Conservative government to continue its predecessor's tradition of presenting a balanced budget while further reducing Canadians' taxes and increasing government spending. While minority parliaments are not generally considered stable, the Opposition Liberals emerged into the new year with a newly elected, and surprised, Stéphane Dion at the helm and were not looking to engineer a quick election. This is not to say that there were no difficult, indeed controversial issues in the year, but if there was a common theme to them it was their attempted resolution through the creation of independent inquiries.

A minority government, such as that led by Prime Minister Stephen Harper as 2007 began, must work to maintain the support of Commons in a fashion that the more usual Canadian majorities never need to do. Keeping the support of the House, in turn, requires either a heightened level of conversation and compromise or a frightened Opposition. Throughout his political career, the prime minister had shown little appetite for compromise, and so his good fortune was the Liberals' fear of another election – the Grits, we might say, were chicken. The first test of the government came in the spring in a vote on the budget. It was a budget the NDP would never support and that the Liberals could almost certainly not agree to, and so it was left to the Bloc Québécois to save the government, which it did in exchange for an increase in the share of federal payments to Quebec. In November the government faced another compulsory confidence motion, as it opened a new session of Parliament with the traditional Speech from the Throne. In a move unprecedented in Canadian parliamentary history, the Official Opposition Liberals abstained en masse from the vote, and so the Conservative benches were more than able to outvote the combined opposition of the Bloc and NDP.

The Liberals' unwillingness to bring down the government had been reinforced a few weeks before the October throne speech. On 17 September a by-election was held in the riding of Outremont in Montreal. Outremont was a Liberal stronghold, having returned a Liberal in every election since the 1930s, with the exception of the 1988 election where the PCs had won all but 11 of Quebec's seats. Even as the Bloc dominated Quebec, the Liberals retained Outremont: in the 2006 election, Jean Lapierre had been re-elected for the Liberals with a slim but substantial margin over Jacques Leonard of the Bloc. The Liberals nominated a well-known figure in Jocelyn Coulon, who had been hand-picked by the new Liberal leader. Despite all of these advantages, not only did the Liberals not win the by-election, but Coulon was trounced by the similarly high-profile candidate from the NDP, Thomas Mulcair, who won close to 50 per cent of the votes. The race had been seen as an important test of Dion's political judgment and of his ability to deliver seats in his home province. With Mulcair nearly doubling the vote of his Liberal opponent, it seemed a test the Liberal leader failed.

Having survived the rather tepid threat of an election on its throne speech, the government transformed the legal framework for elections in Canada by passing Bill C-16 late in the year. The Westminster system empowers the prime minister in a variety of ways, one of which is the right to request the dissolution of the House and a new election from the Crown. While minority parliaments may trigger elections by denying the government their confidence, the pattern of majorities in Canada has meant that the timing of elections has largely been the first ministers' preserve. Bill C-16 put a legal bar on that power by setting fixed election dates: a general election is to be held on the third Monday in October in the fourth calendar year following the previous election. If Dion's Liberals continue to abstain when presented with the chance to defeat the government, the next federal election will be held on 19 October 2009.

Canada's previous Conservative prime minister returned to the news in significant fashion in 2007. For a number of years there had been rumours and accusations concerning the relationship of Brian Mulroney, when he was prime minister, and Karlheinz Schreiber, a German lobbyist, industrialist, and arms dealer who had long lived in Canada, becoming a Canadian citizen in 1982. Schreiber was wanted in his native Germany on charges of tax evasion and had been fighting extradition for a number of years. In February the Supreme Court cleared the way for his return to Germany, although he remained in Canada pending his final few legal manoeuvers to avoid extradition. With final decisions on

Schreiber's return imminent, the CBC and *Globe and Mail*, which had been investigating the Mulroney-Schreiber relationship doggedly, produced new information in an episode of the Fifth Estate on 31 October and a piece in the *Globe and Mail* the following day. These investigations revealed that despite denying dealings with Schreiber, Mulroney had made a voluntary disclosure to Revenue Canada of cash payments from Schreiber. Prime Minister Harper attempted to distance himself and his government from Mulroney and the affair, announcing on 9 November an independent adviser would be appointed to look into the matter. However, as media and Opposition pressure grew, it was clear that this was insufficient, and so, on 13 November Harper announced the mandate of the independent adviser, University of Waterloo president David Johnston, would expand to include a mandate for a public inquiry and that he would report to Harper in January.

The Opposition parties were not satisfied with this attempt to mute the controversy, particularly given that Schreiber was on the verge of being extradited. The House of Commons Ethics Committee decided to hold hearings into the affair but was faced with the prospect of its key witness being whisked off to Germany within hours of a final determination of the Supreme Court. In response the Speaker of the House of Commons, Peter Milliken, issued a Speaker's Warrant to compel Schreiber's appearance before the committee. Canada was therefore treated to a series of appearances by Schreiber and even by Brian Mulroney throughout the last month of the year. As 2007 ended Schreiber remained in Canada to answer further questions, Johnston was considering the affair and what a public inquiry should probe, and the legacy of Canada's eighteenth prime minister was very much in the balance.

The end of the year also saw the House grappling with a remarkable battle between the government, Atomic Energy of Canada, Ltd. (AECL), and Linda Keen, the nuclear industry regulator. AECL's Chalk River facility produced two-thirds of the world's medical isotopes, the vital ingredient in much medical imaging. In November production was halted for maintenance, but then the shutdown was extended, as the Canadian Nuclear Safety Commission (CNSC) required significant upgrades to prevent possibly dangerous overheating. The government sought to order AECL to resume production, even without the upgrades, so that the radioisotope supply could be maintained and so Canada's market share would not be undermined by others jumping in to fill the gap. Keen, the CNSC head, objected to the government's plan, but they proceeded over her objections. In a remarkable and very unusual procedure the House sat in Committee of the Whole and heard witnesses while considering the government's Bill C-38 which made this order. C-38 was passed on 11 December and then rushed through Senate and on to Rideau Hall the next day.

Internationally the war in Afghanistan continued to dominate the agenda. In 2006 the newly elected Conservative government had made the Afghan war their own, affirming their commitment to the expanded role Canada had agreed to take on in Kandahar Province and gaining a renewed mandate from Parliament. This did not settle matters in Canada, however, as opposition to the war was strong and tended to grow as more and more Canadians were killed. By year's end thirty more Canadians were killed, bringing the total to seventy-four. There was also a growing toll of Afghani civilians being killed, including by NATO actions, further eroding domestic support for the war. The key question that emerged was the length of Canada's enhanced commitment. Initially the government continued to say that the mission in Kandahar would last only until 2009, when Canada would revert to its non-combat contributions to the war. However, external pressure from both NATO allies and the government of President Karzai for Canada to extend the mission grew.

The government was trapped between the twin pressures of mounting domestic opposition, increasingly expressed on the Opposition benches in the minority Parliament, and the desires of its allies. Prime Minister Harper tried to assuage the Opposition by saying that Canada would stick to its 2009 date without consensus in the House, but later as external pressure grew he changed that to majority support. However, that majority was far from certain, with the NDP and Bloc quite resolutely opposed and the Liberals divided. Harper was, therefore, very reluctant to put the question to the House. Finally in October, he pushed the issue off by forming an Independent Panel to advise on the future of Canada's role in Afghanistan. The panel was to examine future roles for Canada, focussing on four in particular: provide army and police training; emphasize reconstruction in Kandahar with other allies taking security responsibility; move to another (presumably less dangerous) region of the country; and withdraw in February 2009.

The creation of the panel effectively ended the discussion on Canada's future in Afghanistan until it delivered its report, which was due in early 2008. More than that however, its make-up posed a difficult political challenge to the Liberals. Prime Minister Harper tapped former Liberal foreign minister John Manley to chair the panel (together with Pamela Wallin, Derek Burney, Paul Tellier, and Jake Epp). This was a typically shrewd political move on Harper's part, as Manley's appointment risked turning the Liberals against themselves. It deferred a decision on which the Liberals might feel forced to defeat the government and trigger an election they were ill-prepared to fight (as they would soon show with their abstention on the throne speech). However, Manley was a leading Liberal and also a supporter of Canada's role in Afghanistan, having been a leading member of the government that had authorized the Kandahar mission.

The mission in Kandahar was not the only controversy surrounding Canada's involvement in Afghanistan in 2007. The issue of the treatment of Afghan detainees transferred by Canada to the Afghan authorities continued to cause the government difficulty. Unlike its allies in Britain and the Netherlands, Canada had no agreement in place with the Afghan government to allow it to monitor the well-being of detainees once they were transferred. In February Canada did sign a new agreement on detainees with Afghanistan, but it fell far short of the UK and Dutch examples, only allowing an Afghan human rights organization (AIHRC) to monitor on Canada's behalf. Defence Minister Gordon O'Connor travelled to Afghanistan to assess the group's capacity and on return got into further political hot water for having said that the International Committee of the Red Cross (ICRC) would monitor the detainees *and report to Canada if abuse was found.* However, ICRC policy is clear, and it only reports to the government holding the prisoners, not to third parties such as, in this instance, Canada. The capacity of the AIHRC, which O'Connor had seemingly vetted, came under suspicion a few weeks later, when reports emerged of alleged torture of detainees which the AIHRC had been prevented from visiting. Under renewed pressure from the Opposition, the government sought to reach a new agreement with Afghanistan to allow the same sort of access as the United Kingdom and the Netherlands.

The defence minister was under consistent pressure from the Opposition in this period, as his bungling on the Afghan detainee file continued, to the point that the prime minister contradicted O'Connor in the House over the status of the new agreement. His position worsened later in the spring, when he sparked controversy with a further incorrect response in the House, this time to a question about the treatment of military personnel killed in Afghanistan. O'Connor asserted that the Department of National Defence (DND) was covering the full cost of dead soldiers' burials, but he was soon contradicted by the parents of Canadian Forces Corporal Matthew Dinning killed by an IED the previous year. The furore resulted in a significant increase in the burial stipend paid to the family of members of the Canadian Forces killed in the line of duty. It also resulted in the shuffling of the hapless defence minister out of the post in a significant reorganization of the government in August, with Peter McKay moving from foreign affairs to defence and upcoming Quebec star Maxime Bernier given McKay's old job in the Pearson Building.

Other lingering issues related to the treatment of those caught up in the various wars of the decade were also important in 2007. In January the government sought to bring the horrifying ordeal of Maher Arar to a conclusion by offering both an official apology and a significant compensation agreement. Arar agreed to drop his $400 million lawsuit but was compensated for the government's role in his gross mistreatment with a $10.5 million settlement, plus an additional $1 million to cover legal fees. On the other hand, the government continued to do nothing helpful in the case of Omar Khadr, the young Canadian held in Guantánamo Bay since his capture in Afghanistan in 2002. Khadr's case was particularly notable, as he was by 2007 the only Western citizen still held at the facility in Cuba, and he had been, at the time of his alleged crimes, only 15 years old! As the year started, it seemed in some ways odd that Khadr was still imprisoned. The charges against him had been thrown out in 2006, but he remained in military custody, and in April new charges were laid. Even these were dismissed in the summer, as the military judge hearing the case determined he did not have jurisdiction, a decision reversed on appeal in September. Khadr faced the prospect of a trial under the widely despised military commissions system, and his government in Ottawa seemed uninterested in doing anything about it.

It should, perhaps, have come as no surprise that the son of an immigrant, Muslim family like Omar Khadr received so little support from the government given the way the year began in Hérouxville, Quebec. In January this tiny town of roughly 1,300, virtually all white francophones, issued a set of standards for immigrants moving to the town. In some ways the standards were unremarkable, other than being issued at all in such a small settlement with absolutely no history of immigration. However, in some of its elements the standards were sufficiently startling to garner global attention. In particular the Hérouxville council found it necessary to counsel potential immigrants that they would not be permitted to perform female circumcision (although presumably its male counterpart would continue to be welcomed), nor could they throw acid into women's faces or stone them to death. The standards prompted outrage, but even when the council "clarified" their statement to try to make it seem more general, it was clear that it was driven by stereotypes of Islamic culture. The controversy joined with several others in Quebec over cultural standards, notably a demand by some in the Orthodox Jewish community in Montreal for a gym to cover its window so they would not have to see women exercising as they walked by! In response the Quebec government appointed a commission to inquire into "reasonable accommodation" of immigrants in Quebec society, headed by two leading Quebec academics, philosopher Charles Taylor and sociologist Gerard Bouchard. They began hearings in the summer and were due to report in 2008, following the year's pattern of commissioning controversy into the next year.

Of course, the desire to push off difficult issues through commissions does mean that there comes a time when they report, and in Ontario a commission on Ipperwash released its report at the end of May. The inquiry had been called by the Ontario government in 2003 to investigate the events surrounding the death of Dudley George, who was shot by the Ontario Provincial Police (OPP) while taking part in the occupation of Ipperwash Provincial Park in 1995. Of the various findings of the inquiry, the most eagerly anticipated surrounded the role, if any, of the government of the day, and particularly the then premier, Mike Harris. Commissioner Sidney Linden found that Harris did not interfere directly in the operation, but he did push for a speedy conclusion to the conflict, in a way that may have contributed to the events that followed. The current premier, Liberal Dalton McGuinty, formally apologized for the province's role in George's death.

The year 2007 also saw the passing of a number of women who had been central to the fight for women's rights in Canada over the previous half century. Doris Anderson had been an early feminist voice, through the vehicle of *Chatelaine*, which she edited for twenty years, through the height of the North American struggle for civil right and the sexual revolution in the 1960s and 1970s. Toronto-based journalist and activist June Callwood, who through her writing and her tireless organizational work promoted justice for women, died. Finally the first female Supreme Court justice, Bertha Wilson, also died in 2007. Justice Wilson was appointed to the court in 1982 and so sat on the court for the first decade of the Canadian Charter of Rights and Freedoms, helping to shape the meaning given to that document.

On balance 2007 seems a year in waiting. Many of the crucial issues to arise were not confronted directly but were pushed off to next year through the time-honoured process of calling a commission of inquiry. Federal politics was both cautious and static, as the government feared defeat and the Opposition feared an election. As the year ended, therefore, the future was uncertain. Commissions' reports and the consequences are hard to predict. Canadian history suggests that minority governments do not endure, although if the Liberals continue with their tactical abstentions, this one might make it to the now-legally mandated election of October 2009.

ROBERT EVERETT

Parliament and politics

To the surprise of many, the minority government of Conservative prime minister Stephen Harper was fast approaching its second anniversary in power as 2007 came to a close. With barely a third of the members in a hostile House of Commons, Harper's right-wing party faced dissent when it came to the weightiest matters on its bold agenda. Chances of survival seemed slim. Yet the campaign that was always in the offing never happened. Friendless but tenacious, the Conservatives withstood two tests of confidence that, had they failed, would have abbreviated their tenure. The Bloc Québécois saved the government when it signed on to a spring budget that enriched Quebec's share of transfer payments from Ottawa. Then, in a scene never witnessed before in Ottawa, the main Opposition party, the Liberals, abstained en masse on a House vote to adopt the Speech from the Throne in November. A combination of careful management, piledriver tactics, ephemeral moments of cooperation, and (largely) Liberal timidity spared Canadians an election they apparently did not want.

More importantly, did citizens get the governance they deserved? Stalemate was the order of the day and, meteorologically, the climate in Ottawa ranged from arid to chilly. The Commons dissolved in frustration, ennui, and bickering as the first session of Canada's thirty-ninth Parliament came to a close in late spring. Campbell Clark of the *Globe and Mail* observed that day-to-day affairs were marred by "filibusters, boycotts, cancelled committees and procedural ploys. Parliament has ... become the scene of a contest of wills between the government and the majority, and their squabbles have stalled proceedings" (18 May). Prorogation held out the promise of a fresh start, but distemper grew chronic, and the brief autumn sitting was little better. Writing in the *Ottawa Citizen*, Don Martin concluded that the year's "legislative lineup was flaccidly disconnected from improving the daily lives of Canadians" (31 Dec.).

At times the dreary deadlock served the Conservatives well. To take one example, Opposition parties goaded the Conservatives on the environment and even passed a bill aimed at requiring the government to live up to commitments made under the Kyoto Protocol. The government responded with legislation and an action plan that other parties deemed feeble. Yet the very absence of substantial legislation provided the Conservatives with cover as they retreated from Kyoto. On other occasions, the Opposition was able to stall and stymie, as was the case with tough law-and-order measures and political reforms coveted by the government. The government was aided, mightily so, by troubles battering the party they unseated in the election of 2006, the Liberals. Saddled with debts and dispirited by bleak polling numbers, the Liberals, led by the earnest if donnish Stéphane Dion, were squeamish about their prospects in the event of an election and concomitantly cautious about defeating the government. Internecine squabbles compounded Dion's dilemmas. Sensing advantage and leaving little to chance, Conservatives subjected him to a pillorying that began almost immediately after Dion's quixotic quest for leadership had ended with an upset victory. Dion threatened on 2 December to precipitate an election in early 2008, but tough talk could not disguise the Liberals' anxieties.

Although hamstrung at times, the government was able to make strides on several fronts. Canada's relationship with the United States thawed as Harper and American president George W. Bush made common cause on environmental strategies, continental security, and international affairs. Decisions about prolonging the country's military commitment in Afghanistan were successfully put off even as the government laid the groundwork for extending the mission. The government had a potent lever available in the budget, and it used it. Financial measures contained in the budget meant that the Conservatives were able to allocate funds to pet projects even when they could not secure full parliamentary approval for more robust regimes.

National institutions

Cabinet

Stephen Harper's Cabinet was relatively stable in 2006, with just one minor change necessitated by the resignation of Michael Chong over the recognition of the Quebecois as a people. Peter Van Loan was lifted from the back benches to takes Chong's place at intergovernmental affairs. Circumstances changed dramatically in 2007, and the prime minister pulled off two managed shuffles.

Only a few days into the new year, Harper made his first move. Insisting that he was fine-tuning rather than girding for an election, the prime minister nevertheless shored up obvious vulnerabilities. The biggest change in symbolic terms involved removing Rona Ambrose as minister of the environment. Inheriting one of the toughest jobs in Cabinet, Ambrose was assigned the task of convincing Canadians of the government's green credibility. Success would have been no mean feat given the Conservatives' enmity to Kyoto. Ambrose did not excel, and gaffes hastened her demotion. Into the breach stepped John Baird, a feisty partisan schooled in the charged atmosphere of Ontario's legislature. Ambrose landed the multiple but less formidable tasks associated with the presidency of the Queen's Privy Council, minister of intergovernmental affairs (an area in which she had worked prior to entering politics), and minister of western economic diversification. Another underperforming minister, Vic Toews, was moved out of justice in favour of Robert Nicholson, the former Government House Leader. Toews was handed the presidency of the Treasury Board, Baird's old job. Monte Solberg and Diane Finley swapped portfolios, with Solberg taking on human resources and social development and Finley moving to citizenship and immigration.

When Harper formed his first government he eschewed an outer ring of secretaries of state, ministers outside the Cabinet proper but with specified responsibilities in conjunction with senior ministers. Now he resorted to a time-honoured way of rewarding backbenchers (and warding off restlessness) by naming a brace of secretaries. Marjory LeBreton, the government leader in the Senate, added the role of secretary of state (seniors). The others in the second circle were:

- Gerry Ritz, small business and tourism;
- Helena Guergis, foreign affairs, international trade, sport;
- Jay Hill, chief government whip and secretary of state without portfolio; and
- Christian Paradis, agriculture.

The changes brought the size of Cabinet up to thirty-one. Although expanded by five, the Cabinet still had proportionally fewer women than Liberal ministries of the recent past.

Verdicts on the moves differed. The *Toronto Star* editorialized that it was "hard to see any evidence in this that Harper is rethinking his broader plans to use Ottawa's $7 billion surplus chiefly to cut taxes, reduce debt and shrink government, rather than invest heavily in health care, the economy and jobs, the environment, poverty reduction or urban renewal." His vision, the *Star* opined, was "a narrow one, by choice" (5 Jan.). The *Vancouver Sun* found it equally difficult to see any fundamental rethinking of approach but praised the prime minister for having the "sense to leave alone the ministers who have been performing well" (5 Jan.). To the *Globe and Mail* the tinkering fell short of the full makeover the government needed, but it concluded that it would "strengthen the Conservative minority government as it enters what many predict will be an election year" (5 Jan.).

Announcing the shuffle gave Harper an opportunity to highlight his government's priorities for the year:

- a budget that would prioritize lower taxes;
- resolve the fiscal balance between Ottawa and the provinces;
- generate more "tough-on-crime" legislation;
- protect the environment and the well-being of Canadians; and
- promote Canadian values in the international arena.

The second shuffle was announced on 15 August. The changes were far weightier this time and they focused on the economy, foreign affairs, and the military. Inevitably Gordon O'Connor was excused from defence. Instantly controversial because of his years as an armaments lobbyist, O'Connor was dogged by Opposition demands for his resignation fuelled by missteps such as erroneous claims that the Red Cross had been monitoring detainees handed over to Afghans by Canadians captors, unpopular bans on media coverage of the return of slain soldiers together with contradictions over the funding of their funerals, and assertions (corrected by Chief of Defence Staff Rick Hillier) that personnel from Quebec would be relieved of front-line duties in order to train Afghan counterparts (*Ottawa Citizen*, 15 Aug.). Harper had stood by O'Connor but now calculated that Peter MacKay could more ably handle the Afghan file in a sideways move from foreign affairs. Maxime Bernier was summoned from industry to take MacKay's place in the hope of persuading doubting fellow Quebecers of the merits of Canada's Afghan cause. O'Connor's consolation was national revenue. Signalling his ascent, Jim Prentice was promoted to industry from Indian affairs. By all accounts he had become a de facto deputy prime minister.

Bev Oda, who had entered the political arena following a career in private broadcasting and a stint with the Canadian Radio-Television and Telecommunications Commission, was reassigned following an underwhelming performance in the Canadian heritage portfolio. She was installed at international cooperation. Josée Verner added Canadian heritage and status of women to her responsibilities for official languages. Lesser moves saw Gary Lunn move to natural resources, Chuck Strahl slide over to Indian affairs and northern development (and federal interlocutor for Métis and non-status Indians), Peter Van Loan rise to Government House Leader and minister for democratic reform, and Jay Hill become a government whip and secretary of state. The lone newcomer was Diane Ablonczy. Surprisingly bypassed in previous Cabinet-making, she entered as secretary of state for small business and tourism.

Editorialists in the *Globe and Mail* detected several trends in the shuffle. Bernier's move from industry to foreign affairs implied that Harper wanted a freer hand to delve into international relations with MacKay out of the picture, while Prentice's new role in industry appeared to signal an emphasis on productivity and competitiveness rather than strict adherence to laissez-faire economics (15 Aug.). The *Toronto Star*'s James Travers was sceptical that a "relatively minor cabinet shuffle that leaves most key players in place [would] provide the momentum the ruling party is missing" but accepted that the new line-up was "sturdier than its predecessors and mercifully unencumbered by embarrassments" (15 Aug.). Two shuffles did not address all of the Conservatives' supposed shortcomings. Chantal Hebert argued that the Cabinet remained "desperately short on strong women and strong Quebecers," deficiencies which, if not remedied "will come back to haunt the Conservatives in the next campaign" (*Toronto Star*, 3 Dec.).

By-elections

A series of resignations by Quebec MPs – all of them prominent in the latter-day history of Quebec nationalist politics at the federal level – resulted in three by-elections grouped together on 17 September. The first to depart was Jean Lapierre, a minister of transportation in the Cabinet of Paul Martin. Lapierre represented the riding of Shefford for the Liberals between 1979 and 1993. His nationalist leanings, enmity towards Jean Chrétien's Trudeau-like federalism, and support for the Meech Lake Accord caused him to bolt the Liberals in 1990 as a founding member of the Bloc Québécois. He eventually repaired to life in radio broadcasting only to make his way back to the Liberal fold when Paul Martin succeeded Chrétien. Lapierre was safely returned to the House as a hand-picked candidate for the riding of Outremont in the 2004.

Next to go was Yvon Loubier, the Bloc Québécois MP for Saint-Hyacinthe–Bagot (21 Feb.). Like Lapierre, Loubier was an early member of the Bloc and had served as the member for Saint-Hyacinthe–Bagot since 1993. A trained economist, Loubier was the Bloc's finance critic

Federal Cabinet in 2007

Minister	Portfolio on January 1	Portfolio as of January 4	Portfolio as of August 14
Stephen Harper	prime minister	prime minister	prime minister
Jim Flaherty	finance	finance	finance
Maxime Bernier	industry	industry	foreign affairs
Stockwell Day	public safety	public safety	public safety
Lawrence Cannon	transport, infrastructure, and communities	transport, infrastructure, and communities	transport, infrastructure, and communities
Jean-Pierre Blackburn	labour and minister for the economic development agency of Canada for the regions of Quebec	labour and minister for the economic development agency of Canada for the regions of Quebec	labour and minister for the economic development agency of Canada for the regions of Quebec
Tony Clement	health and minister for the federal economic development initiative for Northern Ontario	health and minister for the federal economic development initiative for Northern Ontario	health and minister for the federal economic development initiative for Northern Ontario
Robert Nicholson	government leader in the House of Commons and minister for democratic reform	justice and attorney general	justice and attorney general attorney general
David Emerson	international trade, minister for the Pacific Gateway and for the Vancouver-Whistler Olympics	international trade, minister for the Pacific Gateway and for the Vancouver-Whistler Olympics	international trade, minister for the Pacific Gateway and for the Vancouver-Whistler Olympics
Michael Fortier	public works and government services	public works and government services	public works and government services
Lyola Hearn	fisheries and oceans	fisheries and oceans	fisheries and oceans
Greg Thompson	veterans affairs	veterans affairs	veterans affairs
Marjory LeBreton	government leader in the Senate	government leader in the Senate secretary of state (seniors)	government leader in the Senat esecretary of state (seniors)
Gary Lunn	natural resources and minister of state (sport)	natural resources and minister of state (sport)	natural resources and minister of state (sport)

Continued

(Continued)

Minister	Portfolio on January 1	Portfolio as of January 4	Portfolio as of August 14
Rona Ambrose	environment	intergovernmental affairs, western economic diversification and president of the Privy Council	intergovernmental affairs, western economic diversification and president of the Privy Council
Jim Prentice	minister of Indian affairs and northern development and federal interlocutor for Métis and non-status Indians	minister of Indian affairs and northern development and federal interlocutor for Métis and non-status Indians	industry
John Baird	president of the Treasury Board	environment	environment
Vic Toews	justice and attorney general	president of the Treasury Board	president of the Treasury Board
Carol Skelton	national revenue	national revenue	n/a
Josée Verner	official languages, international cooperation, and La Francophonie	official languages, international cooperation, and La Francophonie	official languages, Canadian heritage, and status of women
Chuck Strahl	agriculture and agri-food, and minister for the Canadian Wheat Board	agriculture and agri-food, and minister for the Canadian Wheat Board	minister of Indian affairs and northern development and federal interlocutor for Métis and non-status Indians
Bev Oda	Canadian heritage and minister for the status of women	Canadian heritage and minister for the status of women	international cooperation
Monte Solberg	citizenship and immigration	citizenship and immigration	human resources and social development.
Diane Finley	human resources and skills development	citizenship and immigration	citizenship and immigration
Gordon O'Connor	defence	defence	national revenue
Peter Van Loan	intergovernmental affairs, president of the Queen's Privy Council, and minister for sport	intergovernmental affairs, president of the Queen's Privy Council, and minister for sport	Government House Leader and minister for democratic reform
Helena Guergis	n/a	secretary of state (foreign affairs, international trade, and sport)	secretary of state (foreign affairs, international trade, and sport)

Continued

(Continued)

Minister	Portfolio on January 1	Portfolio as of January 4	Portfolio as of August 14
Christian Paradis	n/a	secretary of state (agriculture)	secretary of state (agriculture)
Jason Kenney	n/a	secretary of state (multiculturalism and Canadian identity)	
Jay Hill	n/a	chief government whip and secretary of state (no portfolio)	
Gerry Ritz	n/a	secretary of state (small business and tourism)	agriculture and agri-food; minister for the Canadian Wheat Board
Diane Ablonczy	n/a	n/a	small business and tourism

for a spell. Although he turned away from federal politics, Loubier retained strong nationalist leanings. He emerged as an unsuccessful candidate for the Parti Québécois in the 2007 provincial election.

The Bloc's Michael Gauthier announced his resignation on 29 July. A past member of the Quebec National Assembly, Gauthier was victorious when he switched to federal politics in the 1993 election. Although uncharismatic, Gauthier defeated Francine Lalonde in the 1996 race to succeed Lucien Bouchard as head of the Bloc and leader of the Opposition. Rising disenchantment in the Bloc's ranks made life difficult for Gauthier, and he surrendered the leadership in 1997. He did remain as the member for the nationalist riding of Roberval–Lac-Saint-Jean and served as House leader for his party. In September he debuted as the host of an eponymous televised public affairs program.

To defend Outremont, a safe seat in the recent past, Stéphane Dion chose Jocelyn Coulon, a prolific author and international affairs analyst. Against him was an erstwhile Liberal and one-time provincial Cabinet minister, Thomas Mulcair of the NDP. Coulon's academic credentials were solid, but his views on the Middle East and other global hotspots led to denunciations by pro-Israeli groups in Montreal. This complicated matters for Dion, who had exercised a leader's prerogative to choose Coulon. As Marcus Townsend observed, "Coulon's success or failure risks being seen as a litmus test for Dion's judgment and his ability to deliver ridings in his home province" (*Montreal Gazette*, 18 July).

In the event, Mulcair pulled off an upset. It was welcome news for the NDP, which had long dreamed of a beachhead in Quebec. It was disastrous for Dion, who was under increasing pressure from within. For good measure, Mulcair had exploited environmental credentials of his own to embarrass Dion in his geographical and ideological backyard.

Roberval–Lac-Saint-Jean was much coveted by the Conservatives. Popular former local mayor Denis Lebel ran under their banner and wrestled the riding from the Bloc thanks to a pronounced swing towards federalism. The result went according to script in Saint-Hyacinthe–Bagot, where the Bloc held on. The successful candidate was Ève-Mary Thaï Thi Lac, the first Canadian of Vietnamese origin to win office at the federal level. Conservative gains in the contest sunk the Liberals to fourth place, falling below the New Democrats.

As a result of the by-elections the distribution of seats was Conservatives 126, Liberals 96, Bloc Québécois 49, New Democratic Party 30. There were three independents and four vacancies in the House at year's end.

Liberal veterans depart

As if things were not bad enough for the Liberals, a number of senior MPs declared their intentions to leave during the year. On 22 February Bill Graham announced that he would not contest the next election. In the event he resigned Toronto Centre on 22 July, accelerating his timetable to become chancellor of Trinity College at the University of Toronto. A calm and studious type, Graham was the leader of the Opposition in the interregnum between Martin and Dion. Just possibly on the brighter side, Graham's departure set the stage for a return to the federal arena by Bob Rae, an MP for the New Democrats and one-time NDP premier of Ontario. Disenchanted with social democracy, Rae drifted steadily towards the Liberals (where his older brother had been a long-time adviser) until 2005, when he sought to replace Martin in the leadership contest that ended with Dion's installation in 2006. Rae was chafing at the bit, and many Liberals warmed to the thought of him taking on Harper (or, as some dared to dream, even replacing Dion).

Another Toronto-area seat became available when Jim Peterson vacated the riding of Willowdale. Peterson, brother of a premier of Ontario and himself Cabinet minister, saw his career rejuvenated with the advent of Martin, and he was named minister of international trade. Peterson, a lawyer who had gained fame by helping ballet star Mikhail Baryshnikov to defect, returned to private practice in Toronto. He was also asked to be Ontario's chief negotiator in trade talks with Quebec (20 Dec.).

On 27 July Stephen Owen vacated Vancouver-Quadra. An MP from 2000 to 2007, Owen moved up from secretary of state portfolios to the full Cabinet rank of minister of public works and government services. After leaving office, Owen became a vice president at the University of British Columbia. Also departing was Lucienne Robillard. A social worker by profession, and one-time provincial Cabinet minister, Robillard was tabbed as a star candidate by Prime Minister Chrétien when she opted for federal politics. After winning in the safe riding of Westmount–Ville-Marie in 1992, Robillard was the minister responsible for the federal campaign during the 1996 Quebec sovereignty referendum. She went on to hold a number of other high-level positions.

Novice MP Gary Merasty vacated the Saskatchewan riding of Desnethé–Missinippi–Churchill River on 31 August. A grand chief of the Prince Albert Grand Council before entering partisan politics, Merasty barely won his seat in 2006. During a brief stint in the House he earned a reputation for advancing Aboriginal causes. It was his motion, belatedly embraced by the Conservatives, that led to a formal apology to First Nations, Inuit, and Métis over the internment of children in notorious residential schools (1 May). In 2008 Merasty was appointed to the board of Enterprise Saskatchewan, a private-public provincial economic development agency.

House transitions

Given the thorny nature of the issues, it seemed prudent for the government to get all the advice it could on its Middle East and South Asian files. Oddly Harper asked a low-profile Liberal backbencher, Wajid Khan, to be his special adviser on these matters. It was Khan who made the overture. In August 2006 and after first checking with interim Liberal leader Bill Graham, he offered his services to the prime minister. The arrest of seventeen Toronto-area individuals charged with terrorism activated his patriotism. When this curious arrangement came to light, Dion expressed confidence that Khan would remain steadfast in his loyalties. He was wrong. Khan crossed the floor to the Conservatives on 5 January. Declaring that he was bound to put country ahead of party in perilous times, and forced to choose by his erstwhile leader, Khan made known his disdain for Dion. The former air force pilot and automobile dealer had strong ties with the Pakistani Canadian community, a bonus for the Conservatives as they sought to penetrate the Greater Toronto Area and expand their base.

At the outset, Khan relished the publicity surrounding his defection and post. He came to rue the media attention. First he was satirized over a six-nation fact-finding tour of the Middle East. His travelogue, he said, would be released to the public. The government did not issue any of Khan's reports or recommendations. To do so, it argued, would have made Khan more of a pundit than a confidential adviser. It was not clear, of course, if Khan's thinking had any impact on policy. The Liberals considered the junket a bribe rather than a commission.

Shortly thereafter Khan found himself in hot water after Elections Canada charged him with exceeding campaign expense limits by some $30,000 and putting up his own money for certain expenditures that could not be covered personally. His auto dealership was also alleged to have wrongly defrayed some costs, and charges were laid against Khan's then-Liberal riding president. NDP MP Pat Martin had been the first to raise concerns about possible financial improprieties in the riding, and Elections Canada took the unusual step of de-registering the riding association in 2006. The Conservatives blamed the Liberals for not revealing these details to Harper. With a court date in the offing, Khan withdrew from the Conservative caucus on 23 November.

Another Grit MP in trouble, British Columbia's Blair Wilson, also moved into the ranks of the unattached on 28 October. The member for West Vancouver–Sunshine Coast–Sea to Sky Country departed under a cloud after the launch of an investigation by Elections Canada. Wilson's troubles began with a citizen's complaint about alleged overspending in the 2006 campaign. He also had to endure public scoldings from his father-in-law for mishandling money (*Vancouver Province*, 28 Oct.). Wilson continued to sit as a self-styled "non-caucus Liberal" but, on 21 December, the Liberals disqualified him from running again under their banner.

In 2005 Thunder Bay MP Joe Comuzzi resigned from Cabinet rather than vote in favour of same-sex marriage. Re-elected as a Liberal in 2006 but still out of sync with his party, Comuzzi was expelled from caucus after voting in favour of the Conservative budget (20 March). His renegade support was motivated by provisions that would inject federal funding for a regional cancer centre in his hometown. Having already decided not to seek another term, Comuzzi sat as an independent. On 26 June he tossed in his lot with the Conservatives. Like Khan, Comuzzi made known his disdain for Dion.

Partially offsetting their losses, the Liberals added backbench strength when former Conservative MP Gather Turner crossed the floor to the Liberals. Banished from the Conservatives for alleged breaches of caucus confidentiality in October 2006, Turner appeared to be toying with the idea of joining the Greens. Appearances at the side of Green Party leader Elizabeth May reinforced this impression. In the end this denizen of the blogosphere switched to a party that, he said, was closer to Turner's progressive conservative roots while lacking the autocratic and right-wing rule of Harper (6 Feb.).

The Conservatives took action against one of their own when Bill Casey was turfed from caucus on 5 June. The sin perpetrated by the MP for Nova Scotia's Cumberland–Colchester–Musquodoboit Valley riding was to vote against the budget. At first Casey was dutifully adherent. The more he thought about it, however, the less he liked the government's apparent disregard for the terms of the Atlantic Accord, a pact between Ottawa, Nova Scotia, and Newfoundland and Labrador that kept offshore oil revenues out of the equalization calculus. Styling himself as an "Independent Progressive Conservative," Casey was renominated by the Conservative riding associate in October. Party headquarters refused to accept this decision and took over the nomination process (2 Sept.). Defiance by the association's board resulted in its suspension by the Conservatives in October.

The Bloc lost one of its members when Louise Thibault bolted on 12 April. The member for Rimouski–Neigette–Temiscouata–Les Basques left with her sovereignist convictions intact. The problem was that Bloc Québécois leader Gilles Duceppe was too closed and intransigent (*Montreal Gazette*, 13 April). Thibault was particular peeved by hostility and silencing following her decision to abstain on a vote upholding same-sex marriage in 2006 against the party line. Bloc members defended Duceppe, attributing the rupture to Thibault's inability to accept consensus.

Electoral law

Changes to Canadian election laws are often technical and inconspicuous. Such was not the case with several of the bills laid before Parliament in 2007.

Bill C-16, which fixed election dates in October every four years, passed the Commons in late 2006. Traditionalists decried this deviation from long-standing conventions that made ongoing confidence in the government a requisite for continuation in office. Senate Liberals did not pursue this line but did assay an amendment permitting the Chief Electoral Office to deviate from the appointed date if it conflicted with provincial or municipal elections or with a day of cultural or religious import by adding referendums. The Commons balked. After a brief stand-off, the Senate relented and added its endorsement on 2 May.

Before this the House passed C-31, which was intended, or so most everyone thought, to require voters to openly verify their identity. On the

Party Standings in the House of Commons
Election 2006 and 31 December 2007

Party	2006 Election	31 December 2007
Conservatives	124	125
Liberals	103	95
New Democrats	29	30
Bloc Québécois	51	49
Independent	1	3
Vacant		4

eve of three Quebec by-elections, chief electoral officer Marc Mayrand declared that visual identification of voters was not stipulated in the law. Voters were required to present one government-issued photo identification or two documents bearing their address. This meant there was nothing to force those wearing veils to lift them. This ruling bothered members of all parties, with secularists from Quebec, where the issue of face-obscuring religious garb was heated, among the most upset. When the second session began, the government swiftly introduced a new bill, C-18, to provide greater certainty (26 Oct.). Sped through both chambers, the bill was given royal assent on 14 December. Amidst the din it did not go unobserved that there were actually vanishingly few instances of women refusing to lift veils and that an increasing number of voters were submitting ballots by mail, obviously without showing their faces.

Bill C-55, An Act to Amend the Constitution Act, 1867 (Democratic representation), was introduced on 9 May 2007. It sought to take on more advance polling dates prior to an election such that the polls would be open on four consecutive dates in the prior week or the Sunday just before polling day. The bill expired with prorogation but resurfaced with the designation C-16 on 1 November.

The government introduced legislation to expand the House of Commons on 11 May. Bill C-56 would amend the constitution by revising the formula by which seats are allocated to the provinces. Alberta, British Columbia, and Ontario would have more seats when the formula was applied, and their total allocation would be closer to a pure representation-by-population formula. Even so, Ontario's government complained that ten new seats would still leave the province underrepresented. Quebec was even more concerned because the seats awarded that province would fall proportionately. The Assemblée National passed a resolution critical of the proposal (17 May). The bill returned as Bill C-22 after lapsing with prorogation.

"In and out" transactions in campaign 2006

A number of Conservative candidates were dumbfounded when Elections Canada declined to reimburse them for certain advertising expenses they incurred during the 2006 campaign. Citing a requirement that claims of up to 60 per cent could only be defrayed if media placements featured appeals for or criticisms against individual candidates, the agency turned down the requests on the grounds that the spots were essentially variations on national Conservative campaigns. By a technique that came to be known as "in-out" transactions, local candidates were given sums of money by national headquarters and then promptly asked to purchase televised spots packaged for them. Transfers totalled $1.2 million. According to Elections Canada, the national campaign would have exceeded its mandated expenditure ceiling had it not been for this accounting legerdemain. The Conservatives insisted that each advertisement included a tag line in favour of local candidates. However, some of the party's candidates were known to have rejected the arrangement.

With an investigation by Elections Canada pending, the agents for thirty-four candidates filed suit against the chief electoral officer in support of their expense claims. When court proceedings began, a filing by Elections Canada listed sixty-seven candidates among those who participated in the transactions. While most had little hope of winning, seventeen MPs, four of them ministers, were involved. As the legal proceedings evolved, the Commons Procedures and House Affairs Committee decided to have a look. The nature of its inquiry, which the Conservatives dismissed as mischievous, was to probe "allegations made against the Conservative Party of Canada's systematic attempt to defraud Elections Canada, as well as the Canadian taxpayer, in relation to the 2006 federal election." The committee majority framed the transactions as an illegitimate ploy. One member of the committee, Government Whip Jay Hill, was among those implicated, and Opposition members argued that he should recuse himself (*Ottawa Citizen*, 10 Sept.). He did not, and helped lead a procedural assault on the investigation. The House probe was curtailed by prorogation.

Senate

Just one Senate appointment was made during the year, but it was a significant one. Following the retirement of Dan Hays, appointed by Pierre Trudeau, Harper summoned Bert Brown to the upper chamber. Harper delighted in naming the winner in an Alberta "election" to fill the vacancy, for Brown emerged victorious from a campaign to designate the province's senators-in-waiting. The Conservatives had inherited from the old Reform Party a belief in an "equal, effective and elected" Senate. Alberta was alone in conducting the sorts of ballots, not sanctioned by the constitution, that Brown had won. Previous prime ministers had ignored results from Alberta's run-offs given their modest turnouts and absence of competitors from other national parties. No matter; the appointment was consistent with Conservative ideology and that was good enough for Harper.

Legislative efforts to widen and routinize senatorial elections had yet to bear fruit. On 13 November the government revived its efforts through Bill C-20. Designated as C-43 in the first session, but unresolved, it stipulated that consultations with electors would be tied to either general elections or provincial ones. It was proposed that eligibility be restricted to those thirty years of age and over, but candidates would no longer have to have a minimum wealth. Companion legislation to limit the terms of senators also came to naught. Bill S-4 was the mechanism by which senators would be held to eight-year, renewable terms. The matter was taken up by a Special Senate Committee on Senate Reform and received second reading in the Senate on 20 February. The Standing Senate Committee on Legal and Constitutional Affairs took up the matter but, on 19 June 2007, the Senate decided not to proceed with the third reading of Bill S-4 until the Supreme Court of Canada has ruled on its constitutionality. Bill S-4 made its return to the House of Commons as Bill C-19 in the second session in 13 November, the same date C-20 was introduced.

Only one appointment was made during the year, but there was a change in affiliation. Senator Anne Cools was excused from the Conservative caucus after she voted against the budget. Originally appointed to the Red Chamber as a Liberal, Cools had a reputation for independence. One senator's term was in jeopardy. On 15 August Liberal Raymond Lavigne was charged with fraud, breach of trust, and obstruction of justice as the result of an investigation by the Royal Canadian Mounted Police. The indictment focused on erroneous travel expense claims and work done on his rural estate, by salaried members of his staff, without proper authorization. The Senate had already demanded reimbursements from Lavigne for wrongly billing taxpayers for his legal fees.

Speech from the Throne

In a text the *Globe and Mail* described as "richer in policy content than expected" (17 Oct.), the government set out its plans for the second session of the thirty-ninth Parliament on 16 October. The core of the speech repackaged the government's pillar priorities: "strengthening Canada's sovereignty and place in the world; building a stronger federation; providing effective economic leadership; continuing to tackle crime; and improving our environment." Among the specific measures were another chop of the GST and a prolongation of the Afghanistan mission. Crime legislation halted in the previous session would be rolled together into an omnibus bill. The speech also heralded a new approach to federal-provincial relations, one that would entail Ottawa forever abandoning federal spending powers in return for a dismantling of internal trade barriers. In the eyes of opponents, working families were ignored, cities were brushed off, and the environment given short shrift.

The speech seemed to turn a truer face of conservatism towards the electorate while tweaking the noses of the Opposition. In the view of Chantal Hebert, Conservatives practically "begged for an election" by arrogantly dishing out such unpalatable fare (*Toronto Star*, 17 Oct.). Predictably, the NDP and Bloc slagged the speech. Jack Layton said it sent Canada hurtling off in a new and wrong direction while Gilles Duceppe decried desultory environmental initiatives he dismissed as appeasement of the United States (ibid.). Both parties signalled their intentions to vote against the ensuing resolution. That left things to the Liberals. Stéphane Dion was spoiling to take on the Conservatives. Desperate to prove his mettle and change his image of temporizing and timidity, the Liberal leader was reined in by sober advisers and uneasy caucus members wary of a premature contest. One option was to have the front bench rise against the speech, leaving backbenchers to sit on the fence. When the vote was called, the Liberals abstained, en masse, as taunts rang out around them.

Auditor general's reports

Busy as ever, Auditor General Sheila Fraser filed three substantial reports during the year. The first was a scorecard on progress made in addressing previously enunciated concerns. In this Status Report, issued in February, Fraser gave satisfactory marks to Public Services and Government Works Canada for instituting better control over advertising and public opinion polling contracts (this was especially noteworthy, for it was in this domain that the notorious sponsorship scandal had festered prior to 2003). Passing marks were also assigned to the government for fixing problems with passports, international taxation, preservation of national heritage sites, and management of the National Research Council. Unsatisfactory progress had been made by the Coast Guard and by Human Resources Canada with respect to the social insurance number.

In a special report on the Department of Foreign Affairs, Fraser concluded that a variety of administrative problems, some flagged decades in the past, had resulted in a depleted diplomatic workforce and badly lagging renewal of staff posted abroad. Relatively poor compensation was among the factors that had left the department unable to find qualified replacements in Canada and host nations. Slow hiring practices worsened the situation and, when the Department of Foreign Affairs tried to recruit from outside of the diplomatic corps, the union representing the department's overseas employees challenged the government in court. All in all, the department lacked the human resources to fully discharge its responsibilities (*Ottawa Citizen*, 2 May).

The office's annual report was released on 30 October. It was found that the Canada Border Services Agency's expensive tracking system was incapable of properly assessing and rectifying procedures that were permitting an inflow of dangerous goods and persons crossing into Canada. In a more general vein, Fraser's team faulted departments for not undertaking appropriate security clearances when awarding contracts for work in sensitive areas (*Toronto Star*, 31 Oct.).

Fraser found herself in a slightly awkward position when, in January, she fired Environment Commissioner Johanne Gélinas. The ousted commissioner was caught completely off guard. Fraser was asked to explain her actions before the Commons Environment Committee on 31 January. Leaks out of private meetings with MPs suggested that Fraser had nudged Gélinas on the grounds that she had become more of an advocate than an independent monitor. This was symbolized by the harsh language of a September 2006 report which criticized the Liberals and, to their astonishment, the Conservatives for their laxity on environmental matters (*Globe and Mail*, 31 Jan.).

Notes on partisan politics

Conservative Party

With the smallest minority in the history of Canada, yet flush with cash from the swelling ranks of eager supporters, Conservatives never had an election far from their minds. Just a year after the election of January 2006, the party was rumoured to be gearing up for a campaign.

The *Globe and Mail* confidentially relayed details of morale-boosting speeches given to organizers and prospective candidates in which senior officials revealed ambitious plans for a luxurious campaign expected following the spring budget (15 Feb.). According to the *Toronto Star*, serious preparations were also underway in the autumn prior to a provocative Speech from the Throne. There was a catch. While the party may have been spoiling for a chance to take on the impoverished Liberals and their neophyte leader, it would have to rely on a defeat in Parliament over the budget or a similar test of confidence. Simply seeking the governor general's assent for an election would fly in the face of legislation to fix election dates on a four-year cycle.

Try as it might, the government was unable to trap the Opposition parties. Warmed by the prospect of more money for Quebec, the Bloc voted in favour of the budget. Wary of an election it could ill afford to fight, the Liberals abstained en masse when the Speech from the Throne was debated. If the Conservatives could not goad their adversaries into recklessness, they at least were able to delight in their empty bravado and squirming.

Facing down fair-weather foes was the easy part. The difficulty the Conservatives confronted was inescapably debilitating: without a permanent partnership in the House they had limited opportunities to move legislation along. With the exception of provisions in the budget, it proved impossible to win approval of cherished policy initiatives. As in other representative democracies, delivering on campaign promises had become a litmus test for incumbents. It could be awkward to ask the electorate for a robust mandate on the basis of complaints that the Conservative agenda had stalled because of Opposition intransigence.

The Conservative effort to build a big electoral tent left many hardcore members embittered. Alienated by Harper's supposedly centrist politics, pandering to special interests, and placation of Quebec, several dozen party members even met in Kingston, Ontario, to plot the re-establishment of the old Reform Party (*Globe and Mail*, 12 May). The revolt never gained traction, and the Conservatives continued to busy themselves for a showdown that would, they hoped, result in a majority government.

Liberal Party

Stéphane Dion was a dark horse when he claimed the leadership of his party in 2006. Even after a full year in office, he was still isolated and doleful, not quite a tragic figure of Shakespearian proportions, but speculation about his future was not helped by a series of defections by chief Quebec strategists and a creeping sense that the political instincts of this academic-turned-politico were poorly honed. His own Quebec lieutenant, MP Marcel Proulx, left the fold. Two other MPs turned down the job. Into the breach stepped Senator Céline Hervieux-Payette. This was good news for Dion, but the Liberals also lost the director general for Quebec over disgruntlement. The party's showing in Quebec by-elections was downright dismal.

Dion tried to set things right in his party. He named leadership campaign rivals like Michael Ignatieff to prominent positions in the shadow Cabinet or asked them to take on special assignments. He embarked on a coast-to-coast tour obliging him to participate in the familiar sort of photo ops that leave most politicians looking a trifle silly in cowboy hats, aprons, and sundry accessories. Dion seemed especially ill at ease in these rituals. His command of English vocabulary was entirely proficient, but his vocalization was judged to be poor. These are mere mannerisms to be sure. For some detractors, the biggest liability for Dion was his one-note hammering on the environment. Worse, the youthful vanguard that propelled him into office went missing in polls and at the ballot box.

New Democratic Party

For Jack Layton and the NDP it was an auspicious or at least promising year. Liberal disarray opened a space for the NDP to position themselves as the rightful opposition to the government, and Layton made much of the fact that his party had been alone in voting against the government on the questions that matter most, throne speeches and budgets. The caucus welcomed a new member from Quebec, a place where it had failed to capitalize on that province's progressive bent. Moreover, Thomas Mulcair possessed sterling environmental credentials even as the NDP was battling to ward off inroads into its space by the Greens. Yet, for all this, there was as yet no definitive, widely distributed bump in the party's support. Public opinion polls showed the party holding onto its base but failing to supplant the Liberals. Layton was earning the kinds of opprobrium that predecessors had received, and the NDP enjoyed a certain clarity in the minds of voters.

Green Party

Elizabeth May was unsuccessful in her first attempt to win a House seat, a 2006 by-election. But a surprising pact between her and Dion may have increased her chances of victory the next time around. The two leaders agreed that they would not contest one another's ridings, leaving May to take on Conservative Cabinet minister Peter MacKay in Nova

Scotia's Central Nova without a Liberal in the mix. No Green would challenge Dion in Saint-Laurent–Cartierville, Quebec. Dion hoped to buff his green credentials in the process, but many Liberals were miffed by what they thought of as a stunt. If the Conservatives were bothered by the prospect of this tacit mini-alliance, they hid it well.

Bloc Québécois

Finally, Gilles Duceppe took the plunge. On 11 May he announced that he would contest the leadership of the Bloc Québécois's provincial cousins, the Parti Québécois (PQ). A perennial prospect whenever there was a vacancy at the helm of the PQ, Duceppe moved to fill the void left after André Boisclair stepped down following a disastrous third-place showing in March's provincial election. He tossed his hat into the ring prematurely it seemed. Scheduled to meet with the only other plausible aspirant, Pauline Marois, to sort out between themselves who should run, Duceppe decided to move precipitously. Stunned by this, but resolute, Marois instantaneously announced her candidacy as well.

Although a kindred soul, Duceppe was considered by Péquistes to be an outsider. Initial polls had Marois well in front. Just twenty-four hours after declaring, Duceppe backed away from the contest. Convinced he would have been a constructive leader, he reasoned that it was "time for a woman, and one of quality, to come in to lead the Parti Quebecois, then Quebec" (*Toronto Star*, 13 May). Chastened, Duceppe asked for, and received, an expression of confidence from his caucus almost immediately.

It was not an especially auspicious year for sovereignists in Quebec and Ottawa. Support for an independent Quebec certainly stalled and perhaps was on the wane. The Bloc was undeterred, having witnessed low ebbs in the cycle before. Although his quick turnabout was demeaning and temporarily divisive, Duceppe was becoming something of an elder statesperson in Ottawa. This may have been galling to some. To others it was a welcome sign of the core civility characterizing the contest over Quebec's future.

Party finances

Data compiled by Elections Canada showed that the Conservatives raised more money than all other major political parties combined in 2007. The number of individual donors to the party also surpassed the total for the Liberals, NDP, Bloc, and Greens. The Liberals barely

Contributions to Federal Political Parties in 2007 (Elections Canada, 2008)

	Conservative	Liberal	NDP	Green	Bloc
Total number of contributors	159,122	35,783	53,110	12,003	5,038
Total amount of contributions	$16,990,766	$4,537,966	$3,979,737	$984,605	$430,061
Transfers from registered associations	$16,000	$331,683	$352	$21,026	$33,379
Transfers from candidates	$5,282	$331,683	0	0	$1,855
Total transfers	$21,282	$368,249	$352	$21,026	$35,234
Grand total	$17,012,048	$4,906,215	$3,980,089	$1,005,631	$465,296
Per cent of total	62.2%	17.9%	14.5%	3.7%	1.7%

Political Party Preferences Among Canadian Voters (Environics Polling, 2007) by Month and (Rounded) Percentage

Party	January (December 2006 Sample)	April	June	October
Conservative	34	36	37	33
Liberal	32	28	28	29
New Democratic	14	16	17	19
Green	11	12	11	11
Bloc Québécois	8 (Quebec only 36)	8 (Quebec only 33)	7 (Quebec only 31)	7 (Quebec only 32)
Other	1	1	–	1

surpassed the NDP in contributions and, for the first time, trailed in the number of supporters who gave money. For the first time, more people donated money to the NDP than to the Liberal Party.

Budget and economics

Economic indicators

By the lights of conventional economic performance measures, the economy continued a longish run of vitality in 2007. The gross domestic product grew by 2.7 per cent. Although down from 2.8 per cent the previous year, this figure surpassed the United States (where downturns in the financial sector and housing market spelled trouble). It also exceeded the performance of many other comparable nations. Given economic turbulence south of the border, this relative vitality called into question that commonplace assumption that Canada's outlook was forever tied to American fortunes. Could the two economies actually be de-coupling? It was difficult to imagine the economy being wholly immunized, but there was a growing sense of independence among some analysts.

Soaring commodity prices lifted the currency. On 6 November the dollar hit a modern record of 108.52 US cents before edging just below parity as the year ended. This heady value sent shoppers on cross-border buying sprees and made seasonal citrus imports more affordable. Consumers spent 4.7 per cent more in 2007, the highest spurt since 1987. There was a catch, though: the loonie was fast becoming a petrodollar. As the price for oil and other commodities rose, the currency climbed. This was a boon to other sectors, and, with some exceptions such as aerospace and machinery, manufacturers continued to struggle. Exporters scurried to find alternative markets, but time was not on their side. With a vigilant Bank of Canada gripping tight, inflation was up by just 2.4 per cent. Tracking its American counterpart, the bank began to roll back interest rates in step as the year ended. Defaults on so-called sub-prime mortgages were weighing down the financial sector south of the border and stimulation was the new paradigm.

Unemployment fell to a thirty-year low in 2007. At 6 per cent, it was only fractionally above the OECD average of 5.7. Job creation was stronger in the western half of the country. Regional and demographic discrepancies persisted. Unemployment was highest in the Atlantic provinces, and job prospects were relatively grim for those aged 15–24 (11.6 per cent), recent immigrants (12.3 per cent), and Aboriginals (14.8 per cent). Although more people were working, poverty rates were stubbornly high. According to Statistics Canada, three million Canadians lived in low-income circumstances. This was down by 400,000 over the previous year, but it still represented 9.2 per cent of the population (3 June 2009). Campaign 2000 (so-named because Parliament had targeted that date for the eradication of child poverty in 1988), estimated that the poverty rate for children was at 9.5 per cent in 2007. Although lower than 1989, the sheer numbers of young people were shamefully high. It was almost universally understood that the gap between rich and poor had grown in Canada.

Budget 2007–8

For his second budget as minister of finance, Jim Flaherty served up a buffet of goodies (19 March). Taken together, new program spending amounted to $4.4 billion, an infusion that translated into a record high level of spending. Even so, total outlays as a percentage of gross domestic production were down at 13.7 per cent. Taxes were trimmed, by some $4 billion. There were few big-ticket items. Instead, the government widely distributed smaller packets.

Ordinary taxpayers were gifted with a $2,000 child tax credit of up to $310 per child (with amounts tied to family income), increased tax credits for low-income spouses and dependants of single individuals, and an extension of mass transportation tax credits. Non-refundable tax credits are not available to those without taxable income, and there were some worries that tax expenditures of this kind did nothing for those most in need. In what was billed as an incentive to find work, the government established a working income tax benefit of up to $500 for individuals and $1,000 for families on welfare.

Small business also reaped benefits. Lifetime capital gains exemptions for farmers, fishers, and small business owners grew from $500,000 to $750,000. Farmers were also eligible for a share of a one-time-only fund pegged at $400 million to help them cope with higher production costs. In addition a new savings account designed to simplify price stabilization regimes was opened, and the government chipped in the first $600 million of a system that would be sustained on a 60:40 basis with provinces and territories. Larger corporations were allowed to write off machinery and equipment acquisitions made in 2007 and 2008. Mineral exploration tax relief was extended, and capital cost allowances were increased for manufacturing. Promises were made to mitigate tax avoidance by corporations by eliminating the deductibility of interest from extraterritorial investments and to beef up the policing of tax haven operations.

Tourists and cross-border shoppers, already benefiting from a strengthening dollar, received a bonus in the form of an additional $200 in the value of personal use goods that could be imported free of duty and taxes. Seniors welcomed a rise in the age credit exemption from $1,000 to $5,066 for those aged 65 and over. More importantly, older couples would be allowed to split their pension incomes. The government also reworked registered annuity regulations in favour of seniors. A new Registered Disability Savings Plan was created to encourage savings that would improve the financial security of people with severe disabilities.

The post-secondary education sector got a series of boosts. Parents of prospective university students saw a $4,000 limit on tax-free contributions to annual registered education savings plans abolished while lifetime totals were capped at $50,000, up from $42,000. The Canada Graduate Scholarships program was bumped up by $35 million for two years (and $27 million per year in subsequent years) to fund an additional 1,000 students. A new round of Canada Foundation for Innovation competitions, funded at $510 million, would permit successful applicants from universities, colleges, and other non-profit research institutions to upgrade research infrastructure. New funding was also authorized – and targeted – for health, business, commercialization, and environmental projects. Modest emoluments were also made to the armed forces and to municipalities.

Although the business community applauded the thrust of the budget, there was distress in some quarters. Apoplectic petroleum producers denounced a "disastrous" decision to phase out special tax relief for oil sands exploration, while others, notably in the western part of the country, critiqued the rise in debt (*Calgary Herald*, 20 March). To John Ibbitson of the *Globe and Mail*, the Conservatives had poached so freely from Liberal recipes of the past that they had abandoned their own principles and, in the process, deprived Canadians of a conservative choice (20 March). His colleague Brian Laghi opined that the government used the budget to try and bolster their support by propitiating segments of the electorate left out of the 2006 budget – a "narrow-casting" gambit (20 March).

While the Liberals and NDP berated Flaherty and signalled their opposition, the Bloc Québécois tossed in its lot with the government. The reason was the sweetened equalization payments. Although Duceppe calculated that Quebec was still owed another billion and a half, the budget had gone far enough. Moreover, the provincial Parti Québécois, scuffling in a provincial election, would then have additional money to invest in the sovereignty project. The federalist premier, Jean Charest, boasted that the new framework was a vindication of federalism. Coincidentally or not, the PQ fell to third place in the Quebec election won by the Liberals. Bill C-52 passed in the House by a margin of 176–119 on 17 May.

Equalization

The centrepiece of the budget was Flaherty's equalization makeover. In 2006 an Expert Panel on Equalization and Territorial Formula

Financing, established by the previous Liberal government, submitted a series of recommendations aimed at modernizing the equalization program, which dated back to 1957, that enhances revenue for the less affluent provinces. Knowing that consensus would be difficult, the government did not tip its hand at the time as it worked through diverse interests. Ontario premier Dalton McGuinty favoured a cap on transfers to prevent "have-not" provinces from surpassing those deemed ineligible for equalization payments (*Toronto Star*, 7 June). Provinces relying on natural resource revenues wanted to exclude this stream from calculations, as was provided for in the Atlantic Accord of 2005.

Confident that the fiscal imbalance had been solved once and for all, Flaherty offered up a range of options from which the provinces could choose. Atlantic Accord signatories could opt into the new framework or stay with an agreement that excluded their resource revenues until 2012. A province like Saskatchewan, with abundant natural resources but nevertheless eligible for equalization, could remove half of their resource revenues if it was advantageous. British Columbia was able to exclude property taxes for a three-year period in view of dramatic rises in housing prices that had swollen property tax coffers. In all, the six provinces in line for equalization would realize an additional $1.5 billion in 2007–8. The three northern territories would also gain. With other transfers to the provinces added in, the net benefit amounted to $39 billion over five years.

It all sounded impressive, and some jurisdictions, such as Quebec, found the deal irresistible. Politicians farther east were not wholly persuaded, and Danny Williams, premier of Newfoundland and Labrador, was vociferous in his condemnation. Ontario continued to be troubled by the imbalance resulting from the emphasis on equalization as opposed to more equitable per capita transfers. Perhaps Flaherty was overly optimistic?

Autumn economic update

Finance minister Jim Flaherty was scheduled to deliver the traditional autumn economic update on 23 November. Well before then, however, the government announced that the budget surplus was running ahead of expectations. Outpacing the results for 2006–7, when it reached $13.2 billion, the surplus seemed bound to eclipse the forecast of $3.6 billion for the year. New estimates pegged it at just over $11 billion. Experts were certain that surpluses were sustainable for at least five years. Flaherty aimed to pocket some $10 billion to pay down accumulated debt but had enough left over to move forward with his idea of giving Canada the lowest business taxes in the world and reducing taxes for individuals.

Tax reductions were announced on 30 October, Flaherty getting ahead of himself in order to cocoon a populist message in case an election was called later in the autumn. Taken together, the reductions amounted to $60 billion over six years. Because of this, surpluses were almost completely wiped out in the next two fiscal years. So too was the wiggle room for any new government that might form from the ranks of the Opposition. Flaherty was confident that there was enough of a cushion to pay down the debt by a few billion dollars annually from 2008–9 to 2010–11.

The 23 November message, when it came, was not given to the House finance committee. Blocked by the NDP from reading his statement in the House, Flaherty ambled over to the National Press Theatre while his staff herded journalists and dispensed briefing books. The big news was a further reduction of 1 per cent in the Goods and Services Tax (GST) effective 1 January 2008. Having already lopped off 1 per cent in 2006, and on record as vowing to chop the unpopular GST again by 2011, the government chose to accelerate its own timetable while the coffers were full. At the same time, the basic amount exempted from taxation was hiked, retroactively, by $670 to $9,600. New Year's Day in 2009 would see a rise in this threshold to $10,100. The lowest personal tax bracket was shaved by 0.5 per cent. As a result, nearly 400,000 individuals would be removed from the tax rolls. The net gain for most individual taxpayers was modest – on the order of $150 a year – but the symbolism was crucial. On 31 December Harper returned to a Mississauga, Ontario, electronics store to recreate a 2006 photo opportunity involving him cutting cash register tape.

Approximately 25 per cent of the tax reductions went to businesses. The general corporate rate was reduced by 1 per cent, and planned decreases on small businesses were accelerated. A chuffed finance minister crowed that Canada was poised to have the lowest level of business taxation in the developed world. However, by foregoing the revenue from personal and corporate taxes ($9.4 million and $14 million respectively) he was skimping on social programs (Les Whittington, *Toronto Star*, 31 Oct.).

The Liberals panned the mini-budget's wholesale surrender of revenues, but a skittish and quite possibly envious Dion almost instantly confirmed they would not oppose any of the measures in the House and thereby impel an election. Tax-fighting lobby groups expressed rather more satisfaction, as did neoconservative commentators in the mass media. A chorus of economists argued that cutting the regressive GST was a mistake and that reducing individual income taxes would have had a bigger bang in terms of stimulus. In the opinion of *Toronto Star* columnist Thomas Walkom, the approach taken by the Conservatives was milder and more mainstream than their ideological convictions would have predicted with one exception: investing almost all of the surplus in debt payments seemed wanton at a time when there were crying needs for infrastructure, housing, public transit, poverty eradication, and environmental protection (31 Oct.).

The GST drop dashed the hopes of the Federation of Canadian Municipalities (FCM) and Toronto mayor David Miller, chief advocate for a campaign to shift some of the money it generated to cash-starved urban governments (Jeff Gray, *Globe and Mail*, 31 Oct.). Municipal leaders were even more downhearted by Ottawa's reaction to a 21 November study by the FCM predicting an infrastructure crisis caused by a shortfall of $123 billion for new and rejuvenated projects. Transport minister Lawrence Cannon, extolling his government's "Building Canada" program and other initiatives, insisted that a considerable investment had been made. Questioners in the House argued that cities were being forced to make up the funding gap at a time when the government was squandering its excess funding (*Toronto Star*, 21 Nov.).

Bank of Canada turnover

After steering the Bank of Canada for a full seven-year term, David Dodge announced a retirement date of early 2008. A search committee passed over the deputy governor, Paul Jenkins, in favour of Mark Carney. An investment banker by profession who had risen to the second slot at the Department of Finance following a career switch, Carney was slated to become the second-youngest governor in history. Profiled in a *Globe and Mail* article, the new governor was described as affable and intelligent. He was also well-rounded but at heart a "financial market guy" (5 Oct.). Controversy attached to Carney's championship of taxes on income trusts but, in general, new leadership was unlikely to have an impact on the bank's fixation on the containment of inflation.

Mergers and acquisitions

For better or worse (and opinion divided sharply), it was a banner year for mergers and acquisitions. A 7 January 2008 report released by KPMG put the 2007 tally at 2,098 deals, with a total value of $268 billion in US currency. Both were records. Many iconic Canadian enterprises fell on the auction block during the spree. The acquisition of domestic giant Alcan by the British-Australian mining concern Rio Tinto was the largest deal of the year. At $37.6 billion, it topped the purchase of Thomson Learning by a pair of private Canadian equity groups.

The action ran in both directions. Canadian companies acquired 527 foreign concerns with a value of US$72.4 billion. But this amount was dwarfed by the $132.6 billion spent on 485 takeovers of domestic companies by external entities. The significant increase in transactions was occasionally attributed to a stronger Canadian dollar with its concomitant reduction in competitiveness. Rising commodity prices also made the resource sector attractive to covetous dealers. Less charitable analysts cited slipshod management, relatively poor productivity, and a global pattern of convergence and consolidation.

Open market economists were generally phlegmatic about the trend lines, and the business-friendly government in Ottawa paid little heed. Canadian banks, brokers, and law firms stood to gain from the activity. CIBC World Markets reckoned that 44 per cent of the 2,000-point jump in the value of stocks listed on the Toronto Stock Exchange was attributable to combinations. There was, however, a growing unease in some quarters about the "hollowing out" of the economy. The sale of so many large enterprises was worrisome to nationalists and labour unions. Even members of the corporate elite chimed in with reservations. *Toronto Star* business columnist David Olive quoted Manulife CEO Dominic D'Allesandro's concern that the country may find one day that "we have lost control of our affairs" (8 May). Fears also percolated that there would be little left on the Toronto Stock Exchange worthy of long-term investment.

Intra-national takeovers had the potential for a different sort of political dynamic. Takeovers could lead to a high degree of concentration and higher costs for consumers. One example was the putative takeover of BCE, the parent company of Bell Canada, by upstart Telus. The hypothesized merger of two of the largest telephone interests in the country was bound to catch the eye of the Competition Bureau and the Canadian Radio-Television and Telecommunications Commission. The government was reluctant to interfere in the process by signalling their attitude, and in the end, BCE was taken over by a suitor without overlapping interests. Even so, it seemed likely that this sort of tricky political situation would arise again as Canadian corporations blended assets in order to compete with large competitors in a globalized world.

Omnibus tax reform and the hidden trapdoor

Bill C-33, with the unappealing title of "An Act to amend the Income Tax Act, including amendments in relation to foreign investment entities and non-resident trusts, and to provide for the bijural expression of the provisions of that Act," wrapped together a slew of changes to the taxation system in an omnibus form. Meandering through the approval process for the better part of a year, this seemingly innocuous initiative lapsed at the third stage with the prorogation of Parliament. It rebounded as C-10 in the second session (27 Oct.). Having invested so much time on the bill in the past, the House was receptive to allowing swift passage through every stage by the House in a single day.

MPs may have rued not looking more carefully. Deep within the voluminous text was a provision that would permit Cabinet to deny tax breaks on investments in films that were deemed, even retroactively, to be at odds with public policy. What the Conservatives meant to do, said opponents, was to create the conditions for family-friendly, decent films. As the year ended, the few that had eventually noticed this provision argued that they would take their fight against censorship to the Senate.

Afghanistan

Thirty Canadians lost their lives in Afghanistan during the year. This brought the number of military and civilian fatalities attributable to the conflict to seventy-four. Carnage abounded. Anti-occupation forces headed by a resurgent Taliban clawed back terrain from the feeble central government. Meanwhile NATO admitted that too many Afghan civilians had been killed by mistake in the conflict (3 Jan.). Prospects appeared grim for a full or quick resolution to a war that had involved Canadian forces for nearly six years.

As the toll mounted, Parliament was animated across several dimensions. The principal issue turned on how long the country should continue to provide NATO with front-line fighters. At the beginning of the year the Conservatives asserted that the aggressive posture would end in 2009, after which Canada would return to a role of supplying aid, materiel, and training. A document suggesting the contrary required the government to discredit the plan. Pressure to stay beyond this putative deadline was intense. NATO publicly asked Canada to extend its mission (20 June), as did Afghan president Hamid Karzai. Early in the year, Harper's stated intention was to keep to the original timelines unless there was "consensus" among parliamentary parties (22 June). Later he lowered the threshold, insisting that a majority was all that was needed to stay (3 Oct.). There was little doubt that the Conservatives regarded a 2009 pull-out as premature. Harper hinted as much during a quick visit to Afghanistan on 22 May when he spoke of the moral responsibility owed to the struggling Afghan people and of the pivotal role played by Canadian soldiers in protecting the fragile cradle of Afghani democracy.

The prime minister was rather more reticent about discussing options in places like Quebec, where opposition to involvement ran highest. He was also wary of a House vote on extension unless the government would prevail. A non-binding motion did come to the floor on 24 April. The text called for a withdrawal by 2009. It was defeated when the Liberals divided on the question. Despite further entreaties for a proper debate and formal decisions from the House defence committee and others, the matter was left unresolved. As an alternative, the government chose to undertake a review of Canada's options. The Independent Panel on Canada's Future Role in Afghanistan was headed by former Liberal Cabinet minister John Manley. He was joined by a quartet that included former television journalist Pamela Wallin, former ambassador to the United States and Conservative adviser Derek Burney, Paul Tellier (now in business), who was clerk of the Privy Council under Brian Mulroney, and Mulroney-era Cabinet minister Jake Epp. Collectively they were asked to weigh the merits of four primary options for future involvement:

- continue to train Afghan army and police;
- focus on reconstruction in Kandahar while another NATO country assumed responsibility for security;
- deploy to another region of Afghanistan; and
- withdraw troops in February 2009.

The group, expected to make its recommendations early in 2008, had no plans for public hearings but did open an interactive Web site to solicit opinion. Manley himself travelled to Afghanistan for a site visit.

The other aspect turned on the fate of individuals turned over to Afghan authorities by Canadian combatants – the "detainee" issue. A lawsuit filed by Amnesty International and the British Columbia Civil Liberties Association seeking to halt the transfers shone a spotlight on an issue that had been percolating for some time. The situation was highly confusing. For most of the year, senior Cabinet ministers denied knowing of any tortures. Yet on 23 April, the *Globe and Mail* published extensive evidence from victims refuting that stance. Defence minister Gordon O'Connor insisted that the International Committee of the Red Cross was monitoring the handovers. The Red Cross denied it. He and his government colleagues contended that binding agreements were in place to prevent the maltreatment of prisoners, only to be proven wrong or at least unaware. When Opposition members in the House tried to get at the truth in committee, they faced resistance and wrangling.

Justice

Crime rates continued to fall in 2007. Homicides were down overall, with only the number of murders committed by young offenders higher. Statistics Canada reported drops in burglaries, break-ins, homicides, and firearms offences (17 July 2008). This continued a three-year trend. Even so, the government was active in pursuing its tough-against-criminals agenda. The budget included funding for a national anti-drug regime, protection of minors against sexual exploitation and trafficking, extra white-collar crime investigation, screening of first-time firearms licence applicants, and upgrades for the Correctional Services. The Speech from the Throne reiterated the government's intentions, and Conservatives insisted that Canadians themselves had deemed this one of their top priorities. Befittingly a significant proportion of the bills introduced between in 2006 and 2007 featured anti-crime measures.

Criminal Code amendments

Miffed by the snail's pace of key bills introduced in 2006, the government produced an omnibus bill right out of the blocks when Parliament resumed in October. Bill C-2 stitched together mandatory minimum sentences for firearms offences (Bill C-10 in the first session), reverse onus on bail for firearms offences (formerly Bill C-35), longer sentences for presumptively dangerous offenders convicted of violent crimes or sexual offences (C-27), raising the age of consensual sex from 14 to 16 years (C-22), and new powers to take and verify roadside tests of sobriety and drug use (C-32). Entitled the Tackling Violent Crime Act, the legislation troubled civil libertarians on account of its scope and detail. There was every good reason to ponder carefully before enacting laws that invest such sweeping powers in the police and limit the discretion of judges. There were also questions about efficacy. As MPs were deliberating, a new study released in the United States argued that an approach similar to that of the Conservatives had been discredited south of the border. In *Unlocking America: Why and How to Reduce America's Prison Population*, a group of criminologists warned that harsh sentencing and criminalization of minor offences amounted to a prohibitively costly failure. Sympathetic Canadian academics expressed concern that the importation of American tactics would be ineffective and might even exacerbate rates of crime by inserting individuals into a hostile culture (Don Butler, *Ottawa Citizen*, 24 Nov.).

The government had an easier time with amendments that attracted a majoritarian consensus, including the following:

- a prohibition on conditional sentencing (i.e., serving some time in the community) for persons convicted of causing serious personal injury, terrorism, or participation in a criminal organization offence (Bill C-9);
- creation of a new category of offence when individuals failed to appear for a DNA sample as part of a criminal investigation, together with an expansion of the offences for which the police could demand a sample and the retroactive application of the law (C-18);
- removal of some usurious loans from the Criminal Code in order to facilitate the provincial regulation of payday loan companies (C-26);
- technical adjustments facilitate implementation of the United Nations Convention against Corruption of 2005 (C-48); and
- new offences and sentencing guidelines for the crime of recording films shown in theatres (C-59).

Cannabis laws and anti-drug strategies

In a ruling that struck at the heart of the government's intolerance for recreational drug use, Ontario judge Howard Borenstein declared, in *R. v. Long*, that a defendant was not guilty of cannabis possession on constitutional grounds (13 June). On 19 October, following this precedent, a pair of individuals in Oshawa were exonerated for similar reasons. At issue was the fact that the government had failed to adequately provide access to medicinal marijuana even when it was necessary. Availability was not mandatory in the applicable legislation, the Controlled Drugs and Substance Act. Rather it was regulated by programs. Since recreational and medicinal usage were addressed in the same law, Borenstein ruled that the entire legal framework was negated. Crown prosecutors appealed. They also averred that the law remained intact and that these lower court actions did not amount to precedents. Police forces also ignored the ruling.

The government forged ahead with ambitious plans to curtail and punish illegal drug use. Harper announced a new initiative at a Salvation Army function in Winnipeg on 4 October. Pledging to crack down on drug producers and traffickers, Harper argued that it was time to confront a rampant drug culture having its roots in the 1960s when the Beatles, among others, made drug abuse casual and cool. Funding of $63.8 million was invested. Of this amount, approximately one-third went into enhanced capacities to finding grow-ops and laboratories and to curtail cross-border shipments. The rest was slotted for prevention and treatment. A posted transcript of the prime minister's speech identified these components:

- a promotional campaign aimed at deterring use by young people;
- funding for upgrading treatment services;
- developing and widening access to new, more effective treatment options;
- financial assistance for provinces and territories to expand treatment of addicted youth and;
- a new National Youth Intervention Program whereby police could shorten detention periods and accelerate the entry of youth into assessment and treatment programs.

Critics were unimpressed. The Americans had embarked on a long, costly, and largely futile war against drugs, and there was no reason to believe that a Canadian version would meet with success. Making criminals out of recreational users of soft drugs seemed unduly harsh, and the sheer cost of policing, prosecution, and incarceration would far outstrip any benefits. Moreover, the government seemed antithetical to so-called harm reduction approaches, such as the establishment of safe-injection sites available to heroin addicts, designed to curb the incidence of HIV/AIDS and promote detoxification. Sceptics also pointed to evidence that previous advertising and educational campaigns had done little to reduce drug use.

Gun registry

It was no surprise that the Conservatives bid once again to end the long gun registry, their bête noire, on 19 June. If approved, the changes in Bill C-21would have amended the Criminal Code and the Firearms Act by ending the requirement that owners of rifles and shotguns register their weapons. Ownership would still require a police check, documentation of appropriate training, and a licence. Conservatives had vowed to abolish the registry altogether but focused, for the time being, on the long gun inventory. Registration of restricted firearms would remain in place.

The registry was vigorously opposed by the Conservatives when it was introduced in 1995. It gained notoriety thanks to wildly excessive costs and mismanagement. Although expensive and discredited, the registry was supported by the Opposition parties (with some dissent on the backbenches), many senior law enforcement officials in the country, and women's organizations from coast to coast. Hunters, rural residents, and libertarians tended to despise it on principle.

Having disappeared with the prorogation of Parliament, the amendments quickly resurfaced as Bill C-24 on 16 November. Public safety minister Stockwell Day took the opportunity to confirm that an amnesty for non-compliance with the law would be extended to 2009 (*Calgary Herald*, 17 Nov.). In Quebec, Premier Jean Charest made a pitch for the status quo; and, if the Conservatives dissolved the national registry, he wanted the power and the funding to establish a provincial version (*Globe and Mail*, 14 Dec.). Support for gun control was strong and deep in Quebec society and the National Assembly, for it was the slaughter of female engineering students at the Ẽcole Polytechnique in 1992 that had inspired the registry. The provincial legislature had more recently approved a law, known as the Anastasia Bill, in honour of Anastasia De Sousa, a student murdered at Montreal's Dawson College in 2006.

Security certificates

Following the events of September 2001, the Immigration and Refugee Protection Act (IRPA) was amended to permit the government to detain non-citizens suspected of terrorist activity by means of a so-called security certificate. Once applied, a certificate enabled prosecutors to present information in court without having to reveal details to accused persons or their counsel. Lawyers for Adil Charkaoui and other individuals held on suspicion of terrorist-related activities challenged the process. They won. In a unanimous decision released on 23 February, the Supreme Court declared that the certificate framework violated rights in the constitutionally embedded Charter of Rights and Freedoms by denying access to particulars. The court acknowledged that national security concerns were germane and that some information could be concealed. Their order was suspended pending the development of appropriate remedies. The government responded with Bill C-3, which was given first reading on 22 October. The bill amended the IRPA by creating a special advocate with responsibilities for protecting the interests of persons named in certificates and ensuring that foreign nationals had the same review rights as permanent residents.

The environment

Greenhouse emissions: turning the corner, or stepping back?

With polling data reflecting heightened concern about environmental degradation among Canadians, the Conservatives offered up a series of measures wrapped together as the ecoEnergy Renewable Initiative in January. Rolled out in a wave of the three announcements, the framework had these elements:

- ecoEnergy for Renewable Power, budgeted at $1.48 billion over ten years, bundling numerous incentives for the production of renewable energy;
- ecoENERGY Efficiency, with $300 million invested in new technologies;
- ecoENERGY Efficiency program consisting of ecoENERGY Retrofit, which made $220 million available to homeowners, businesses, and organizations seeking to modernize facilities;
- ecoENERGY for Buildings and Houses, featuring $60 million in incentives for the construction and renovation of energy-efficient buildings and houses; and
- ecoENERGY for Industry program ($20 million), a database of best practices.

Critics charged that ecoEnergy merely and cynically repackaged programs terminated when the Conservatives succeeded the Liberals.

As the debate intensified, the Conservatives ran a series of attack ads against Stéphane Dion. This involved blaming the Liberals for allowing emissions to rise during their tenure as part of a charmless offensive led by John Baird. For their part, the Liberals unearthed an old fundraising letter from Harper wherein he mocked the science behind global warming, claimed the impetus for Kyoto was to punish oil companies and wealthy nations, and extolled carbon dioxide as essential to life (30 Jan.). Meanwhile, Bill C-30, the Clean Air Act introduced in

October 2006, had been tied up in a special committee created at the insistence of the NDP. The Legislative Committee on Bill C-30 produced its report on 30 March. The Opposition parties loaded the bill with myriad amendments aimed at toughening the regulatory regime. The government considered most of them anathema and kept the bill off the legislative calendar until it finally lapsed.

The budget contained measures addressing the environment, including the following:

- consumer incentives of up to $2,000 for the purchase of a new fuel-efficient or alternative-fuel vehicle;
- a tax, starting at $1,000 and levied on manufacturers, for gas-guzzling vehicles, replacing an excise tax based on fuel efficiency ratings;
- $36 million over two years to help rid the road of older, fuel-needy cars;
- approximately $2 million annually for seven years in lieu of tax exemptions on ethanol and biodiesel and for renewable fuel development;
- a doubling of environmental enforcement officers to total nearly 200; and
- $110 million over two years to implement the Species at Risk Act and $10 million to create or expand protected areas in the Far North over two years.

The budget was also the occasion to unveil a national water policy, with allocations to the removal of contaminated sediments in the Great Lakes, a study on the outflow of water from Lake Superior, and clean-up of Ontario's Lake Simcoe and Lake Winnipeg in Manitoba.

On 14 February the House passed a private member's bill, crafted by Liberal backbencher Pablo Rodriguez, calling on the government to live up to its obligations under Kyoto. Bill C-288, the Kyoto Protocol Implementation Act, gave the government sixty days to table a climate change plan to meet emissions targets. The Conservatives attacked the bill's legality, and three times the Speaker ruled that it was valid. Grudgingly, the government filed its report on 26 April. Entitled "Turning the Corner," it had targets that were far less ambitious than those assumed under Kyoto. As summarized by the *Globe and Mail* the next day, the main components were:

- a reduction of 18 per cent per unit of production from 2006 levels for existing industry by 2010, with a mid-term goal of a 26 per cent reduction by 2015;

- a drop in total emissions from all sources of 20 per cent by 2020;
- achievement of the Kyoto-backed cuts of 6 per cent below 1990 levels by 2025 – thirteen years behind schedule;
- options for industry of cutting emissions outright, contributing to a technology fund, an internal trading system, or a one-time credit for reductions achieved between 1992 and 2006;
- manageable price increases for cars, home appliances, electricity, and fuel;
- emission caps for air pollutants including nitrogen oxides, sulphur oxides, volatile organic compounds, and particulate matter by 2010; and
- mandatory but unspecified fuel efficiency standards for automobiles beginning with the 2011 model year.

The government foresaw savings of $6.4 billion in annual health costs by 2015 owing to decreased illness. At worst, the cost to the economy would be in the range of $7 to $8 billion annually (rather than the Conservatives' estimate of $51 billion if the country kept pace with Kyoto). John Baird was publicly challenged by renowned environmentalist David Suzuki at the podium on which the minister of the environment laid out the plan. Opposition parties were also hostile, with Dion calling it a sham (*Globe and Mail*, 27 April). He and others were appalled that large corporate polluters would be responsible for less than their fair share of toxic emission reductions.

Shunning Kyoto did not exempt Canada from engaging with other countries on environmental issues. At the conclusion of the annual meeting of the Asia-Pacific Economic Cooperation, Harper joined the leaders of the twenty-nation group in signing a Declaration on Climate Change, Energy Security and Clean Development (8 Sept.). Although it called for reforestation efforts and a reduction of energy intensity by 25 per cent by 2030, the goals were voluntary and aspirational. They were also widely dismissed by environmentalists. The government remained as implacably opposed to fixed targets as it was comfortable with volunteerism. In a *Toronto Star* article captioned "Canada isolated on climate," officials inside the Commonwealth of Nations alleged that a "disingenuous" and "cynical" Canada had teamed with Australia at a Heads of Government conference to thwart binding reduction targets (24 Nov.). Meanwhile, the acting commissioner of the environment and sustainable development chimed in with a damming critique of the government's strategies, calling them vague and absent of appropriate accountability mechanisms (Mike de Souza, *Ottawa Citizen*, 31 Oct.).

Aboriginal affairs

In 2006 the Commons approved a private member's bill, brought forward by former prime minister Paul Martin, requiring the government to implement the Kelowna Accord, a 2005 agreement between Ottawa, the provinces, and First Nations and Aboriginal groups. Conservative MPs voted against, and the government was quick to emphasize that private bills cannot oblige the expenditure of money. The budget contained little for Aboriginal peoples: $300 million over two years to encourage private home ownership on reserves, $105 million over five years for job training, $20 million for Aboriginal fisheries, and $15 million over two years for an Aboriginal justice strategy. As the *Globe and Mail* pointed out, the private dwelling incentives were at odds with Aboriginal concepts of collective ownership (20 March). Aboriginal leaders, such as Phil Fontaine of the Assembly of First Nations, were extremely disappointed. They were also troubled when Canada voted against the United Nations Declaration on the Rights of Indigenous Peoples in the company of Australia, New Zealand, and the United States. Fontaine called it "a stain on Canada's international reputation" and a "slap in the face for all indigenous peoples" (*Toronto Star*, 14 Sept.). Canadian negativity, said UN ambassador John McNee, was based on language on the rights to traditional lands that was "overly broad, unclear and capable of a wide variety of interpretations" (Canadian Broadcasting Corporation Web site, 13 Sept.).

A motion tabled by Saskatchewan MP Gary Merasty apologizing for injustices arising from Indian residential schools passed unanimously on 1 May. The text of the resolution read "that this House apologize to the survivors of Indian Residential Schools for the trauma they suffered as a result of policies intended to assimilate First Nations, Inuit and Métis children, causing the loss of aboriginal culture, heritage and language, while also leaving a sad legacy of emotional, physical and sexual abuse." Initially the Conservatives discounted the need for the apology, not least in the context of the pending establishment of a truth and reconciliation commission to take up the matter. Sensing isolation and possible ignominy, they executed a turnabout in the days prior to the House vote (*Ottawa Citizen*, 2 May).

Creation of the Truth and Reconciliation Commission of Canada culminated lengthy and delicate negotiations between the government and Aboriginal groups resulting from a class-action suit. It was given effect by a formal settlement agreement, approved by the courts, on

19 September. The commission was one aspect of the settlement, and its mandate, as described on its Web site, was to:

- create an accurate and public historical record of the past regarding the policies and operations of the former residential schools, what happened to the children who attended them, and what former employees recall from their experiences;
- complete a public report that will include recommendations to all parties of the settlement agreement concerning the Residential Schools System;
- host seven national gatherings in regions across Canada to promote awareness and public education about the Residential Schools System legacy and its impacts;
- support a Commemoration Initiative that will fund initiatives that pay tribute to survivors;
- support community events designed by communities to meet their unique needs;
- establish a national research centre that will be a permanent resource for all Canadians; and
- guide and inspire Aboriginal peoples and Canadians in a process of truth and healing on a path leading towards reconciliation and renewed relationships based on mutual understanding and respect.

Controversies

The Mulroney-Schreiber hearings

German authorities wanted to repatriate Karlheinz Schreiber, a German-born, Canadian-based facilitator of business dealings (but more frequently and rightly referred to as an arms dealer). He was wanted on charges of evading taxes in the 1980s. If the name sounded familiar to Canadians it was because Schreiber had been linked to former prime minister Brian Mulroney during the Airbus scandal. In 1988 Air Canada purchased A-320 passenger planes from Airbus after a fierce competition. It was alleged that the deal was greased by payoffs to and from Schreiber. Mulroney was identified as a suspect in the case but vehemently denied any wrongdoing. Insisting that he barely knew Schreiber, Mulroney sued the federal government for libel after it became known that the Royal Canadian Mounted Police (RCMP) had asked Swiss authorities to allow them access to bank accounts that were supposedly set up for the ex–prime minister and cronies. Mulroney's denials of any involvement were given under oath. In 1997, the government of Jean Chrétien apologized to Mulroney and gave him a settlement of $2.1 million.

The Airbus trail never grew cold thanks to dogged investigative reporting by the CBC and the *Globe and Mail*. New information about the case came to light in January. Then, on 1 February, the Supreme Court cleared the way for Schreiber's extradition. Even so, Schreiber was released from jail until he had exhausted the dwindling number of legal manoeuvres available to him. While at large, he filed a lawsuit charging that Mulroney failed to deliver on a $300,000 retainer to lobby on behalf of Thyssen AG, which wanted to build a plant in Nova Scotia to manufacture light-armoured vehicles (24 March). Mulroney countersued and continued to deny dealings with Schreiber.

On 31 October the CBC broadcast "Brian Mulroney: The Unauthorized Chapter," a documentary with new, unsavoury revelations about Mulroney's relationship with Schreiber. Opposition MPs demanded answers to the question of how Mulroney was able to wring huge sums of money from Ottawa given the mounting and increasingly credible evidence of a relationship. In a fresh affidavit, Schreiber acknowledged that he and Mulroney did have dealings over Airbus and reported that he had corresponded with Prime Minister Harper in July 2006 to confirm that he and Mulroney remained on good terms. This letter also complained of a monstrously unjust scandal buffeting him (8 Nov.).

The front page of the 9 November edition of the *Globe and Mail* featured a photograph of Mulroney and Schreiber in the Prime Minister's Office. Their easy poses seemed to belie the assertion that they were barely acquaintances. Worse for Mulroney, Schreiber asserted that he made arrangements for the $300,000 at Harrington Lake, the prime ministerial retreat. That would mean that the transaction took place while Mulroney was still in office. Under growing pressure from a growling House and a howling press gallery, Harper announced that he would appoint a third party to advise him on how to respond to Schreiber's bombshells (9 Nov.). In doing so he stressed that he had not consulted with Mulroney about this step. He also distanced himself by declaring Mulroney persona non grata to members of his government. Bidding to staunch the flow of harmful revelations, Mulroney called for a public inquiry (12 Nov.). The very next day, Harper switched gears, too. The third party (who was University of Waterloo president David Johnston) was given an expanded mandate to recommend the terms of a public inquiry along with any other appropriate measures. The House was stunned when Harper sprang this news during Question Period. Mulroney said he was grateful.

Impatient parliamentarians took matters into their own hands. With Schreiber's departure in the offing as the result of losing a final appeal on 15 November, the House Ethics Committee launched their own probe over the objections of its Conservative members. There was a catch. Schreiber insisted he would only cooperate with a domestic investigation if his expulsion was delayed. Yet he was now incarcerated and due to be sent packing by 1 December. At first the government refused to release Schreiber. Then they protested that they did not have the jurisdiction to free him from provincial custody (an opinion that scoffing legal analysts rejected). On 26 November the committee issued its summons. Still the government would not budge. The NDP's Pat Martin had a solution. The committee passed his motion asking for a Speaker's Warrant, a device that had not been used since 1913, to compel Schreiber's appearance. On 27 November, the House granted Speaker Peter Milliken his warrant. Transported from Ottawa to Toronto on 28 November, Schreiber was given access to documentation retrieved from his home and made his first appearance before the committee on 29 November.

Committee chair Paul Szabo opened the "Study of the Mulroney Airbus Settlement" in an electric atmosphere. Schreiber titillated listeners on the first round of questions, begging off answering key questions until he had a chance to review his files. Over the span of four days, Schreiber made numerous claims:

- Mulroney confidants, including one-time Cabinet minister Elmer McKay, had assisted him in a variety of ways or had received his benefaction in return;
- Jean Charest received a donation of $30,000 from Schreiber for his unsuccessful run at the Progressive Conservative Party in 1993, far more than had previously been speculated;
- money paid to Mulroney had come from a Swiss account where Schreiber held his fees from past deals and may have come from Airbus;
- a campaign to oust Tory leader Joe Clark (in favour, as it turned out, of Mulroney) received funding from German individuals and, perhaps, the Dutch Christian Union party; and
- some of the payments were arranged while Mulroney was still prime minister.

Schreiber was granted bail on 4 December, but he had little hope of staying in Canada.

Mulroney had much to answer for. In his only appearance before the committee, he combined regret with defiance (12 Dec.). A Mulroney spokesperson, Luc Lavoie, had indicated that his boss was virtually broke when he received the first cash instalment from Schreiber in 1993 (1 Dec.). Mulroney disputed that but did admit to having entered into a deal with Schreiber. A discomfited witness fleshed out the tale, and by the time he had finished he had stated the following:

- the amount received from Schreiber was $225,000, not $300,000, and it was kept in safe deposit boxes at his Montreal and New York City residences;
- the transaction occurred after he left public office;
- he had not paid taxes on the cash until 1999, and then only after Schreiber had been charged with bribery;
- he felt under no obligation to amplify on his relationship in the 1997 deposition, only to answer questions that were put to him by government lawyers;
- none of the money doled out by Schreiber was related to the Airbus transaction.

Blaming the CBC and the *Globe and Mail* for his troubles, Mulroney rued the day he met Schreiber and the act of accepting his benefaction. Others would be left to sort out this murky affair.

Chalk River shutdown

Few Canadians were aware that Atomic Energy of Canada's Chalk River facility in Ontario was responsible for two-thirds of the world's radioisotopes, the short-lived nuclear material necessary for medical imaging. Production at the facility was halted for maintenance on 18 November. Responding to concerns expressed by the Canadian Nuclear Safety Commission, AECL extended the shutdown of the National Research Universal Reactor until it was upgraded to prevent overheating in a major seismic event. It had discovered that orders made by CNSC in the past had not been fulfilled. The cessation precipitated a very public, partisan imbroglio.

With supplies running low around the world, and over the dissent of the head of the CNSC, Linda Keen, the government demanded that production be resumed even if the mandated upgrades had not been completed (8 Dec.). Harper gambled that siding with AECL over the regulatory agency was the superior alternative. When Keen resisted, the government introduced emergency legislation, C-38, to restart the reactor and keep it humming for at least four months. The legislation also suspended the CNSC's regulatory authority, an exigency that worried environmentalists. Under an expedited and unorthodox procedure, witnesses were invited to testify on the floor of the House in a Committee of the Whole setting as legislators sifted the pros and cons of ordering a restart. Bill C-38 was passed by the House on 11 December and was then rushed through the Senate to the desk of the governor general the next day.

Swift passage did not end the matter. Despite accommodating the government, Opposition parties queried why Keen had been left without counsel from the Justice Department in an appearance for a committee hearing (the government responding that independent counsel avoided a conflict of interest). They also wondered why one of the "independent" experts who advised the House on the safety matter happened also to be on the executive board of the Conservative Association in the riding of Durham. Then there was the matter of when Health Canada was informed that supplies were threatened. Health minister Tony Clement was shocked that his officials were not notified immediately of the shutdown, while his boss warned that heads would roll (*Globe and Mail*, 13 Dec.). Opposition parties thought they had the answer. To them, the minister of natural resources, Gary Lunn, had sat on the story. To the Conservatives, it was the "Liberal-appointed" members of CNSC who had behaved irresponsibly.

Peter Calamari of the *Toronto Star* added context to issue in an article published on 13 December. He noted that AECL was slated for privatization and that bad publicity was harming sales prospects. Calamari also pointed to a history of friction over the operations at Chalk River between CNSC and the regulator. He argued that Canada had become, apart from Iran and if only for a spell, the only jurisdiction without an independent regulator.

CHRISTOPHER SPEARIN[1]

Foreign affairs and defence

To help frame a consideration of Canadian foreign and defence affairs in 2007, one should note that Prime Minister Stephen Harper shuffled his Cabinet on 14 August and, in so doing, replaced both his foreign affairs and defence ministers. The prime minister moved Gordon O'Connor from the defence portfolio and made him minister of national revenue. Minister O'Connor's seeming demotion was likely based on four factors: (1) his difficulty in selling the Afghan mission to Canadians; (2) controversy surrounding his handling of soldiers' funeral expenses; (3) the Afghan detainee issue; and (4) his fraying relationship with the popular chief of defence staff (CDS), General Rick Hillier (see these issues later). Nevertheless, the prime minister contended that Minister O'Connor merited a new challenge and that he had served the defence portfolio well: "I think Mr. O'Connor has accomplished a great deal" (Canadian Broadcasting Corporation, 14 Aug.).

Peter MacKay, who was in the foreign affairs portfolio, replaced O'Connor in defence. Minister MacKay was not only a more prominent member in the Conservative Party, he was also more popular and a better communicator than Minister O'Connor. Because of MacKay's status and understanding of the foreign affairs portfolio, Opposition parties noted that the prime minister was likely embracing the status quo. Jack Layton, the leader of the New Democratic Party, said this of MacKay's appointment: "What we see with Mr. MacKay, the foreign minister moving into defence, is someone who has defended Mr. Harper's policies in Afghanistan." He continued, "Where we wanted to see a change in direction, all we get really is a continuation of the same old policies" (ibid.).

Maxime Bernier, the industry minister and a relative newcomer to politics, received the high-profile position of foreign affairs minister

1 The author would like to thank Donald Spearin for his assistance in the preparation of this chapter.

after only two years in federal politics. In part because Bernier was not a strong English-language speaker, it was clear that his role was twofold: (1) to improve the Conservative Party's electoral fortunes in Quebec; and (2) to sell the Afghan mission specifically to Quebecers, the element of Canada's population least supportive of the military's efforts in Afghanistan. Nevertheless, the prime minister stressed that Minister Bernier would be competent on the international stage: "Mr. Bernier is a young minister who has a very strong perspective on economic affairs, but in terms of the development of this government, and his own development, I think he deserves a new challenge." He continued, "I hope and I believe that he will be a very effective representative of Canada at the world level" (ibid.).

Foreign affairs

Summitry

G8 Summit: Three issues framed Prime Minister Harper's participation in the annual G8 leaders summit, hosted in 2007 by Germany in Heiligendamm from 6 to 8 June. One issue concerned how fellow G8 leaders would receive the Harper government's "Made in Canada" solution on climate change. This solution called for Canada to reduce its greenhouse gas emissions by 20 per cent by 2020 compared to 2006 levels.[2] This goal, however, effectively meant that Canada was jettisoning its Kyoto Protocol commitments, a fact hosting German chancellor Angela Merkel criticized on the eve of the summit: "Of course, we are not happy at this point that Canada has abandoned Kyoto's goals" (*Calgary Herald*, 5 June). Yet Prime Minister Harper argued during a pre-summit meeting in Berlin on 4 June that with his government's plan, at least Canada was doing something: "Normally, Canada is a country that prides itself on living up to its international obligations and commitments. But frankly, up to now, our country has been engaged in a lot of 'talking the talk' but very little 'walking the walk' when it has come to greenhouse gases" (ibid.).

In the end the prime minister defended his government's climate change plan during the summit and was able to contend that Canada was much more active on this file than other states. With France and Germany agreeing to Canada's long-term commitment to counter greenhouse gas

2 The Kyoto Protocol required the cutting of emissions by 6 per cent of 1990 levels by 2012.

emissions, the prime minister proudly contended that "I am particularly pleased to see that the other G8 Leaders recognized Canada's plan to reduce emissions by 60 to 70% by 2050 over 2006 levels, as set out in our new domestic plan of action on climate change" (Prime Minister's Office [PMO] News Release, 8 June). In fact the United States was the only country not to endorse the goal of halving emissions by the middle of the twenty-first century and, as such, the G8 leaders could not declare an agreement on exact timelines and targets. This division was a point the prime minister wished to stress for international and domestic audiences alike: "One of the things about climate change and emissions control is that they're a lot simpler if everyone does them." He argued, "If everyone does them, there's nobody gaining competitive advantage over the others as a consequence. Then I think the real benefits of technological change and adaptation can come to the fore – changes by which I think Canada can be a huge beneficiary" (*Edmonton Journal*, 9 June). Nevertheless back in Canada, Liberal leader Stéphane Dion argued that the prime minister could have done more to ensure a more substantive G8 initiative on climate change: "When the prime minister said that he wanted to be a bridge at the G8, he did not say that it was a bridge to nowhere" (ibid., 8 June).

The second issue concerned Canada's aid contributions and the potential impact of celebrity diplomacy. Going into the summit, Bob Geldof, the Irish rock musician responsible for the LiveAid phenomenon, felt that Canada was slowing G8 initiatives to counter poverty in Africa: "Canada is the worst culprit in blocking a significant communique ... All our information says they are refusing point blank to allow concrete figures" (*Calgary Herald*, 5 June). NDP leader Jack Layton picked up on Geldof's assessment: "Instead of adopting the firm targets and goals that are needed to reduce suffering in Africa, our government is trying to come up with ... general language, no longer committing us to getting the job done" (*Toronto Star*, 8 June).

During the summit the prime minister had to continually defend his government's aid policy. The G8 leaders reiterated their 2005 commitment to double aid to Africa by 2010, and they made an additional promise to spend US$60 billion to fight infectious disease. However, aid activists said this was not enough, and Bono, the lead singer of the rock band U2, contended that Canada was in fact blocking further initiatives: "I said some years ago that the world needs more 'Canadas' ... I can't believe that this Canada has become a laggard" (*Edmonton Journal*, 9 June). DATA, an aid agency co-founded by Bono, estimated that the Canadian government was CDN$479 million short in meeting its commitments. The prime minister, however, felt that Canada was doing more than its share: "I can say with absolute certainty that Canada was not blocking anything on this … Canada's on target to meet those obligations … I think we're the only country on target to meet them, and to meet them early, in fact" (ibid.). This debate, however, did not come to a finer point as Prime Minister Harper refused to meet with Bob Geldof and Bono during the summit, although the leaders of the United States, Germany, France, and Italy all did.

The third issue concerned Canada's relations with Russia. Before the summit's start, Russian president Vladimir Putin had strongly criticized the US decision, supported by NATO, to develop a missile defence system to be based in the Czech Republic and Poland. Although the Bush administration claimed the system was meant to counter missiles coming from rogue states such as Iran, President Putin nevertheless felt that his country's nuclear arsenal was the impetus for the decision. Prime Minister Harper, however, was keen to support the decision and assuage Russian fears: "We are convinced that NATO's actions are totally clear … There is no reason to interpret this act as a threat against Russia" (*Toronto Star*, 6 June).

Contentious issues remained evident during a bilateral meeting Prime Minister Harper held with President Putin on 7 June. Both leaders challenged each other on their commitment to human rights. The prime minister emphasized that as a G8 member, Russia had to do more to embrace democratic reform and to promote human rights. President Putin said that Canada's human rights record was not perfect, likely a veiled reference to the treatment of Canada's Aboriginal communities. For the prime minister, engaging in this sort of discussion was the exact thing Russia should be doing more of: "[M]y reply to that general line of discussion is that that's fine, as long as we all accept the legitimacy of that criticism, we're all prepared to listen to it and be open to it and allow that kind of debate to occur in our societies. That's the real test, not whether we're perfect, but whether criticism can happen, and is tolerated and is part of the political process" (*Calgary Herald*, 8 June).

North American Leaders' Summit: On 20–21 August Prime Minister Harper hosted a summit with North America's two other leaders, US president George W. Bush and Mexican president Felipe Calderón, at Montebello, Quebec. This was the third meeting of the so-called "Three Amigos," the previous two occurring in Waco, Texas, in 2005 and in Cancun, Mexico, in 2006. The focal point of the past meetings had been the Security and Prosperity Partnership, a trilateral initiative meant to bring about substantial security and economic integration in the face of economic competition from the European Union, China, India, and elsewhere.

On the one hand many legislative, social, and economic groups feared that the partnership would bring about reduced social benefits and environmental standards and lead to the erosion of national sovereignty. Other concerns related to the meetings occurring behind closed doors and to the fact that the leaders were predominantly hearing from business voices. Of particular concern was the influence of the North American Competitiveness Council, which consisted of thirty corporate chairmen and CEOs, ten from each of the three countries. This council had a direct input on the summit's agenda whereas the roles of others, elected legislators included, were negligible.

On the other hand, even as the summit approached, US and Canadian officials were at pains to suggest that achievements at Montebello would likely be limited. White House officials announced that they did not expect there to be major commitments to be made and Prime Minister Harper noted limitations too: "Canada, the United States and Mexico are good neighbours and also good friends. As sovereign countries in the modern world we are both independent and interdependent" (PMO News Release, 21 Aug.).

In the end the summit's results were indeed modest. The leaders agreed to cooperate on fuel efficiency standards. They also agreed to develop policy concerning the movement of cross-border traffic in the midst of a crisis and to block the importation of unsafe products and food (e.g., from China). The summit, however, yielded no significant steps forward in terms of ensuring the efficient flow of people and goods across North American borders, a point criticized by Liberal leader Stéphane Dion: "If the prime minister needs an international summit to conclude that he needs to ban dangerous products coming into Canada, well Canadians expect more from him" (*Calgary Herald*, 22 Aug.). In fact, the summit came to an early close because President Calderón had to return to Mexico in order to manage his country's response to Hurricane Dean, the strongest hurricane of the 2007 Atlantic season.

A few sensitive matters did come to the fore during the summit. First, following a separate ninety-minute bilateral meeting between President Bush and Prime Minister Harper, the president keenly acknowledged Canada's contributions in Afghanistan: "I believe Canada's done a fabulous job in Afghanistan and I'd like to thank the people of Canada … The Canadian people have sent some of your finest into harm's way to enable a young democracy to be able to survive and thrive" (ibid.). The prime minister, however, made it clear that his government would not extend Canada's commitment in Afghanistan without first obtaining a parliamentary consensus (see later). On another matter President Bush felt the need to respond to comments made earlier in the week by Paul Cellucci, the former US ambassador to Canada, that Canada possessed sovereignty over the Northwest Passage. The president said, "We believe it's an international passage ... Having said that, the United States does not question Canada's sovereignty over its Arctic islands. We'll manage the differences, because there are differences on the Northwest Passage" (ibid.). Finally, despite the summit's theme about openness and competitiveness and Prime Minister Harper's urging, President Bush remained committed to his administration's Western Hemisphere Travel Initiative. This initiative imposed a passport requirement on all travel between Canada and the United States.

Second, the response of the Sûreté du Quebec to the several hundred protestors that came to Montebello came under severe criticism. Officers had infiltrated the mostly peaceful protest, perhaps with the intent to instigate violence. On 20 August protest organizers accused three individuals, who had covered faces and were holding rocks, of being members of the police. The three were let through police lines, after which they were promptly "arrested." Video footage of the incident, soon available on the Internet, revealed that the three individuals and the uniformed police members wore the same boots. The Sûreté du Quebec subsequently issued a statement which acknowledged the officers' presence but asserted that it was not their intention to commit violent acts: "They had the mandate to spot and identify violent demonstrators to avoid the situation from getting out of hand ... The police officers were identified by demonstrators when they refused to throw projectiles. At no time did the Sûreté du Quebec police officers act as agents provocateurs or committed [*sic*] criminal acts" (*National Post*, 24 Aug.).

As the Royal Canadian Mounted Police was ultimately responsible for event security, Opposition members criticized the federal Conservatives. Liberal justice critic Marlene Jennings suggested that "[t]he RCMP has some explaining to do ... If the RCMP was responsible for all security at this summit like [public safety minister Stockwell] Day says it was, the RCMP should have known that the Sûreté du Quebec was using undercover officers to infiltrate the demonstrators" (*Globe and Mail*, 24 Aug.). The NDP's Peter Julian raised similar concerns: "Now that we have this revelation that police forces were under federal supervision, it raises a whole series of questions. Did they send agents into the crowd dressed as demonstrators, aggressive demonstrators at that? What was the mandate? Why were they carrying rocks?" (ibid.). Minister Day, in response, indicated that should demonstrators feel aggrieved, then they should utilize the formal complaints processes of the RCMP and of the Sûreté du Quebec. He turned down Opposition calls for a public inquiry. Similarly, during the summit, the prime minister discounted the protestors' overall impact: "I've heard it's nothing … A couple of hundred? It's sad" (*Leader-Post*, 21 Aug.).

APEC summit: Prime Minister Harper travelled to Australia in order to participate in the Asia-Pacific Economic Cooperation (APEC) Leaders' Meeting and the associated APEC Business Summit on 8–9 September.[3] Climate change was again the focus of this international gathering and again the prime minister asserted that a new way was required other than the path laid out in the 1997 Kyoto Protocol: "Kyoto divided the world into two groups – those that have no targets and those that would reach no targets" (*Globe and Mail*, 10 Sept.). Instead the prime minister argued that in seeking a balance between economic growth and environmental stewardship, all states needed to be on board and the cuts required had to be reasonable.

The resulting "Sydney Declaration," therefore, was somewhat of a victory for the prime minister. From one standpoint, the declaration made no mention of the Kyoto Protocol. Major emitters such as the United States, Russia, and China also signed on to the declaration's "aspirational goal" of achieving a common long-term global objective to make cuts in emissions. This was a major accomplishment according to Prime Minister Harper: "I think this is as much as we were going to achieve at this summit and frankly it was unthinkable even six months ago that you would have major emitters agreeing to these very goals" (*Toronto Star*, 10 Sept.).

From another standpoint, the declaration was criticized for two main reasons. First it included no mention of targets. The declaration's only specific numbers concerned energy efficiency and reforestation. Second, by ignoring Kyoto, the Sydney Declaration did not include measures for technology transfer to the developing world. Chinese president Hu Jintao criticized APEC's developed-world members on both accounts: "Developed countries should face their historical responsibility and their current high per capita emissions, [and] strictly abide by their emission reduction targets set forth in the Kyoto Protocol … [They should]

3 Following the APEC meetings Prime Minister Harper travelled to Canberra for meetings with Australian prime minister John Howard. While in Canberra, Harper became the first Canadian prime minister ever to address a joint session of Australia's Parliament.

honour their commitment on making technology transfer and providing financial support to developing countries, and continue to take the lead in reducing emissions after 2012" (*Edmonton Journal*, 9 Sept.).

Commonwealth summit: During his first trip to Africa as prime minister, Harper confronted two vexing issues while attending the Commonwealth Summit in Kampala, Uganda, from 23 to 25 November.[4] One was the decision to suspend Pakistan's membership in the fifty-three-country grouping for the second time in eight years. Although Pakistan was an important actor in regard to the security situation in Afghanistan, recent political events in the country had negatively affected its democratic credentials. On 3 November President Pervez Musharraf, who was not at the summit, had declared a state of emergency. This decision saw the arrest of the chief justice and the detention of opposition members and human rights activists. For the prime minister Musharraf's actions could not be ignored, but a conciliatory approach was still necessary: "[It was] a difficult decision, but one which we have done while emphasizing our desire to help Pakistan back to the path of democracy" (*Montreal Gazette*, 26 Nov.).

The second issue concerned the wish of most Commonwealth countries to develop a strong declaration on climate change, one that would give impetus to the United Nations Framework Convention on Climate Change conference to occur in Bali in December. Although the prime minister was under considerable diplomatic pressure, he nevertheless balked at endorsing a common position that stressed that only developed-world countries should commit themselves to binding targets.[5] Instead the prime minister wanted the Commonwealth's action plan to include the body's developing-world members, an approach that forced the removal of timelines and targets.

This approach raised the ire of politicians both at the summit and back in Canada. For instance on the Canadian stance, Malaysian prime minister Abdullah Ahmad Badawi said that "[i]n some way, I do feel a little bit disappointed … We would like the [*sic*] see the developed countries taking a lead role. Some of the developed countries present at the (meeting) recognized that" (*Calgary Herald*, 26 Nov.). Liberal leader Stéphane Dion went a step further by contending that the prime

4 Following the conference the prime minister visited Tanzania on 26 November. In 2007 Tanzania was Africa's largest recipient of Canadian foreign assistance.

5 The pressure was amplified by the fact that although Australia also followed a similar position to the Canadian one, Australian prime minister John Howard was not at the conference. At the time he was preparing for the upcoming Australian federal election, one which he ultimately lost.

minister had embarrassed the country: "The prime minister does not believe in climate change – does not believe that it's so dangerous for the future of humanity … And so when you don't have the motivation, you come with the weak arguments, saying, 'I will not move unless the other moves; I will not take the lead'" (ibid., 25 Nov.). Prime Minister Harper, however, remained adamant that an all-inclusive approach was required to tackle the climate change problem. In reference to the Kyoto Protocol, the prime minister said that "[w]e already did the 'One-third of the countries will take binding targets and let's hope the rest fall into line' … We're already there. That hasn't worked" (*New Brunswick Telegraph-Journal*, 26 Nov.).

United Nations Framework Convention on Climate Change – Bali: This conference was to set the way for the international fight against climate change after 2012 – the year when the Kyoto Protocol was to expire. The protocol required its thirty-eight ratifying states to cut emissions by 6 per cent of 1990 levels by 2012. Going into the conference, the Harper government's position, as mentioned earlier, was that binding targets should be for all states. Moreover, this position stressed that the 1990 baseline was too aggressive for the Canadian economy to handle, especially if the United States was not participating. Instead, the Harper government employed the 2006 baseline in its desire to see a 20 per cent cut by 2020.[6]

Two position reversals were evident in the dual outcomes of the two-week-long conference. One pertained to the overall agreement applicable to the 190 participating states. US negotiators had successfully worked to remove any mention of binding targets or timelines from this overarching document. These were to be the subjects for two more years of talks. The US negotiators, however, initially balked at language calling for greater transfers of green technologies going to the developing world. It was only after substantial international pressure that the US negotiators agreed to accept the language. For environment minister John Baird, who led Canada's negotiating team, this shift represented a small victory for Canada: "I think the exciting part is that America is on board, which is a good thing … We've said we need to get all the big emitters on board – the United States, China and India. The good news is that we came out with one of the three. We've got two years to negotiate and maybe we'll get the other two on board" (*Globe and Mail*, 15 Dec.).

6 As of 2005, Canada was producing 25 per cent more emissions than it did in 1990. As such, Canada's 2020 target with a 2006 baseline would have Canada producing 2 per cent more emissions than it did in 1990.

The second reversal pertained to Canada and concerned the conference's second outcome that dealt only with the thirty-eight states that had ratified Kyoto. With US negotiators not present because of US non-ratification, Minister Baird attempted to prevent the inclusion of language that called for wealthy states to strive to reduce their emissions by 25–40 per cent by 2020 based on 1990 levels. Indeed the minister may have intentionally skipped some sensitive meetings in order to slow the process, a decision that earned him the moniker of "fossil of the day" by environmentalist groups (ibid.). In the end Minister Baird announced to the delegates that he would "stand down" after representatives from seventeen countries publicly pleaded with him (*National Post*, 17 Dec.). But despite the seeming reversal of Canadian policy espoused by the Harper government throughout 2007, Minister Baird indicated that Canada's work would go on: "There are 190 countries represented here in Bali, and 38 of them agreed to take on national binding targets today … We've just got to work on some of the other 150" (*Globe and Mail*, 17 Dec.).

Prime ministerial trip to Latin America and the Caribbean: Prime Minister Harper made good on his promise to renew Canada's economic and political ties with Latin America and the Caribbean by launching a six-day, four-country tour on 15 July. The trip, which was his first to the region as prime minister, was to reverse Canada's neglect of the region as a whole: "We are a country of the Americas … Re-engagement in our hemisphere is a critical international priority for our Government. Canada is committed to playing a bigger role in the Americas and to doing so for the long term" (PMO News Release, 17 July).

Harper's first stop, Colombia, marked the first official trip to the country by a Canadian prime minister since diplomatic relations were established in 1953. Prime Minister Harper held talks with President Álvaro Uribe and then announced the launch of free trade talks with both Colombia and Peru. This announcement faced some criticism given recently exposed linkages between Uribe's government and paramilitary death squads. Indeed at the time, the US Congress was holding up the passage of a free trade deal the Bush administration had negotiated earlier with Colombia. Nevertheless Prime Minister Harper contended that economic linkages, human rights promotion, and deepening political ties worked hand in hand: "I don't think you say to a country, 'Well, you still have problems, therefore we'll back off and we won't have anything to do with your economy' … Quite the contrary" (*Calgary Herald*, 17 July).

After Colombia the prime minister travelled to Chile to commemorate the tenth anniversary of the Canada-Chile Free Trade Agreement and to sign the Canada-Chile Partnership Framework marking expanded relations between the two countries. Following talks with Chilean president Michelle Bachelet, Prime Minister Harper, in a speech to business leaders, espoused the Canadian way of governance and international relations by criticizing both the Hugo Chavez regime in Venezuela and the United States. Regarding Venezuela, the prime minister said that "in certain countries … we are witnessing regressive economic policy, dangerous political conflict and persistent poverty, social inequality and insecurity" (ibid., 18 July). As for the United States, Prime Minister Harper said that Canada's international approach was different because "[i]t is not in our past, nor within our power, to conquer or dominate" (*Toronto Star*, 18 July).

A small number of protestors greeted the prime minister when he visited the Chilean headquarters of Barrick Gold. The Canadian company had proposed the creation of an open-pit gold and silver mine, the Pascua-Lama project, to be located near the Argentinean border. At the time of the prime minister's visit, Chilean officials were investigating whether Barrick's initial work on the site had contributed to the 70 per cent shrinkage of three nearby glaciers. Rodrigo Jimenez, Barrick's Chilean director of corporate affairs, linked the melting instead to global warming. As for the protestors, he said "[t]hat's just part of today's society … There's a small, very vocal minority, a lot of it promoted by anti-globalization NGOs" (ibid., 19 July).

The trip's third stop was Bridgetown, Barbados, and there the prime minister focused specifically on the fifteen-member Caribbean Community (CARICOM) by announcing the launch of free trade talks with the organization.[7] Again the prime minister stressed that these talks were part of a larger Canadian engagement strategy: "Canada's relationships with the countries of this region matter greatly to us … Canada is committed to playing a bigger role in the Americas … we're all in this together as members of the western hemisphere" (*Calgary Herald*, 20 July). In this vein, with Canadian investment valued at more than CDN$60 billion, Canada was one of the largest investors in CARICOM member nations. Given fears, however, that a deepening of economic relations through free trade might swamp CARICOM's weaker national economies, the prime minister also indicated that Canada would provide a CDN$600 million incentive package that dealt particularly with education and disaster-support.

7 At the time Barbadian prime minister Arthur Own was CARICOM's chairman.

The final stop, Haiti, was instrumental for both domestic and international reasons. Domestically the prime minister's visit recognized the important and influential place Haitian Canadians have in Quebec. Internationally, Canada was Haiti's second-largest donor of assistance and, after Afghanistan, Haiti was the second-largest recipient of Canadian aid. Between 2005 and 2011, the Canadian government had earmarked CDN$520 million worth of assistance to go to Haiti. Prime Minister Harper stressed that Haiti was a "test case for the Americas" meant to reveal Canada's growing involvement in the region: "Our success in Haiti will depend on the extent to which we stay committed, to show the people of Haiti that we mean what we say when we speak of working toward the achievement of real and lasting improvement in their lives" (*Toronto Star*, 20 July).

To underscore Canada's particular commitment to Haiti, the prime minister became the first foreign leader ever to visit Cite Soleil, a crime-ridden slum in Port-au-Prince. Indeed this particular visit itself was possible because of the international community's efforts to promote better policing, an endeavour involving one hundred Canadian military and police personnel at the time: "You go into a neighbourhood like Cite Soleil, where there has been considerable improvement in security and life, and yet you see how difficult that life is obviously for most people" (*Leader-Post*, 21 July). While in Cite Soleil, the prime minister visited the Sainte Catherine Laboure Hospital, a facility funded by both Canada and the United States.

Human rights

Maher Arar: On 26 January the prime minister offered Maher Arar and his family an official apology covering the role any Canadian government official might have played in his rendition to Syria from the United States and in his subsequent imprisonment and torture. This apology followed the release of Justice Dennis O'Connor's two reports in 2006, which stemmed from his two-year inquiry pertaining to Arar's detention and the challenges that Arar encountered after his release.[8] The prime minister wished to convince Arar that his government was

8 US authorities at New York City's Kennedy Airport had detained Arar on his way home to Canada after a vacation in Tunisia. Rather than return Arar to Canada or inform Canadian consular officials of his detention, US authorities sent Arar to Syria under the US extraordinary rendition policy. These US officials may have been relying upon inaccurate information provided to them by the RCMP. Arar was detained from 26 September 2002 until 5 October 2003.

doing all that was possible to right past wrongs: "Although these events occurred under the last government, please rest assured that this government will do everything in its power to ensure that the issues raised by Commissioner O'Connor are addressed" (PMO News Release, 26 Jan.).

Coupled with the prime minister's apology was a compensation agreement with Arar for CDN$10.5 million. This amount was the largest compensation package ever awarded by the Canadian government, and it was the first pertaining to the torture of a Canadian citizen abroad. The agreement also included an additional CDN$1 million for Arar's legal fees. This compensation terminated Arar's lawsuit launched against the federal government in 2004 for CDN$400 million. In December 2006 Arar's legal team had reduced the lawsuit's amount to CDN$37 million and mediation then ensued.

Given the still substantial monetary figure agreed upon, one of Arar's lawyers, Julian Falconer, warned that "[t]o those few who may regard the compensation directed to Mr. Arar as some kind of windfall, I ask you to consider this: no amount of money would cause a rational person to choose what Maher Arar and his family have been through" (*New Brunswick Telegraph-Journal*, 27 Jan.). While some members of the Canadian public were supportive of the government's stance and sympathetic towards Arar's ordeal, others suggested the amount was too much for taxpayers to swallow and some contended that compensation should have instead been forthcoming from the US and Syrian governments.

Although the Canadian government removed Arar from Canada's no-fly list, he remained on the US list despite the attempts of Canadian officials. In particular, the US ambassador to Canada, David Wilkins, took Public Safety Minister Day to task in January for suggesting that US information did not justify Arar's continued presence on the US list: "It's a little presumptuous of him to say who the United States can and cannot allow into our country … Canadian officials would rightly never tolerate any American official dictating to them who they may or may not allow into their country" (*Winnipeg Free Press*, 25 Jan.).

Omar Khadr: Canadian Omar Khadr's imprisonment at the US military jail at Guantánamo Bay, Cuba, continued throughout 2007. US authorities had held Khadr at the prison since the fall of 2002, after he was captured by US forces following a battle at an al-Qaeda compound near Khost, Afghanistan, on 27 July 2002. Amongst the approximately 380 prisoners held at Guantánamo Bay, Khadr stood out for two reasons: (1) he was the only remaining Westerner in the jail and; (2) US forces might have considered him as a child soldier given that he was captured at the age of 15.

The year 2007 featured several legal machinations and a great deal of political wrangling regarding the Khadr case. The charges against Khadr had initially been thrown out by the US Supreme Court in 2006 because it disagreed with the legal process developed by the Bush administration to bring "enemy combatants" to justice. Charges were, however, laid against Khadr again on 24 April. They were the following: murder in violation of the law of war, attempted murder in violation of the law of war, conspiracy, spying, and providing material support to terrorism. And yet, on 4 June, a US military judge, Colonel Peter Brownback, dismissed these charges "without prejudice" because he argued that Khadr's case was out of his jurisdiction. Under the Military Commissions Act of 2006, the Bush administration's response to the Supreme Court's decision, only unlawful enemy combatants were to face trial. Because US officials had earlier labelled Khadr simply as an enemy combatant, Colonel Brownback felt he had to dismiss the charges. Nevertheless, in September a three-member military appeal panel, a US Court of Military Commission Review, decided that Brownback had erred and it reinstated the charges. Although Khadr's legal team filed an appeal, Khadr's trial was to proceed nonetheless.

As Khadr's fate remained in the balance, Canadian Opposition parties argued that unlike the British and Australian governments, which had secured the release of their citizens being held in Cuba, the Canadian government had not done enough to help Khadr. For Liberal deputy leader Michael Ignatieff, "[w]hatever we may think about Mr. Khadr and his past, he is a Canadian citizen with the rights of a Canadian citizen – and the government should take up his case actively with U.S. authorities" (CTV.ca, 4 June). In September Liberal leader Stéphane Dion met with the US military lawyers defending Khadr and he pointed out the Canadian government's lack of activism on the Khadr file: "Canada is alone among Western nations in not having secured the release from Guantanamo of one of its nationals. Prime Minister Harper must finally ensure Mr. Khadr receives the same consular support that any other Canadian – detainee or not – would receive" (ibid., 20 Sept.). Lieutenant Commander William Kuebler, a member of Khadr's legal team, hoped that Opposition party pressure would eventually lead to Khadr's transfer out of Cuba and, in particular, his removal from the US Military Commission system: "All we're asking for is a fair trial in a legitimate system … The U.S. federal courts could provide that.

Certainly, the Canadian courts could provide that … Guantanamo Bay and the military commissions will not provide that" (ibid.).

Iran: The case of Canadian Iranian photojournalist Zahra Kazemi returned to the news in November 2007, in large part because of the Iranian Supreme Court's decision to open a new investigation into Kazemi's death in 2003. Although a 2004 judicial finding contended that Kazemi had died after an accidental fall caused by a hunger strike, earlier conclusions were that she died as the result of severe beatings following her arrest in July 2003. She had been photographing protestors outside of Evin Prison in Tehran at the time of her detention by Iranian security officials. A spokesperson for the Supreme Court, Ali Reza Jamshidi, argued that the "[j]udges at the Supreme Court have objected to the court investigating the case, saying it was not competent to investigate the case" (*Toronto Star*, 27 Nov.).

The response to the Iranian Supreme Court's decision was mixed. John Terry, a lawyer representing Kazemi's son, Stephan Hachemi, was uncertain about the decision given the opacity of the Iranian judicial system: "You could say we're approaching this in a pessimistic way, but I would say a realistic way – our perspective is that it's a highly politicized judiciary … Iran has a very complex judicial and political system, and there are various factions at work within it. Sitting here in Canada, I can't claim to know what it is that's caused the court to do this" (CTV. ca, 27 Nov.). For a legal scholar at McGill University, Payam Akhavan, international politics were at the root of the court's decision: "I think this is an attempt by the Iranian government to pre-empt the international community, and in particular the Canadian judiciary, by saying, 'We're investigating the matter, there is no need for international intervention'" (ibid.). As for Hachemi himself, he had little hope that anything good would come from the new investigation: "Skepticism really means doubt. I have no doubts about the government of Iran … They are criminal from A to Z, and there is no hope whatsoever" (Canadian Broadcasting Corporation, 27 Nov.).

In fact because Hachemi felt that the Canadian government had been lax in its response to his mother's death, he launched a civil suit in Quebec court against the Iranian government in 2007: "I have no help from the Canadian government. They're not willing to do any concrete measures to to [*sic*] take any serious action" (ibid.). His suit specifically targeted three individuals: Ayatollah Ali Khamenei, the Supreme Leader of the Islamic Republic of Iran; Saeed Mortazavi, the chief public prosecutor for Tehran; and Mohammad Bakhshi, the former Iranian deputy chief of intelligence for Evin Prison. Hachemi's case was to begin in 2008.

In December 2007 the diplomatic spat between Iran and Canada heated up again because the Iranian government ordered Canada's ambassador to leave the country. This was likely a response to two Canadian provocations. First, in November Canada had sponsored a resolution at the United Nations General Assembly which condemned Iran for systematic human rights violations. Second, the Canadian government had rejected two Iranian candidates to serve as ambassador to Canada, in part because of their possible linkages to the taking of US hostages in Tehran in 1980.

Dalai Lama: The Dalai Lama concluded his 2007 tour of Western countries with a visit to Canada in late October (earlier destinations included Australia, Europe, and the United States). In particular his Canadian visit came on the heels of a visit to Washington a week earlier during which he met with President Bush and received the Congressional Gold Medal, the highest civilian honour bestowed by the US Congress. While in Canada, the exiled Tibetan leader addressed public assemblies at the Ottawa Civic Centre and the Rogers Centre in Toronto. He also met with Prime Minister Harper, Governor General Michaëlle Jean, members of Parliament, and senators.

The Dalai Lama's meetings with Canadian politicians marked Canada's increasing promotion of human rights in Tibet specifically and in China generally. In 2004 Prime Minister Paul Martin was the first Canadian prime minister to meet the Dalai Lama, although he did so in the private residence of Ottawa's Roman Catholic archbishop. In this sense the Dalai Lama was viewed as a religious leader rather than as a political leader. In 2006 the Canadian Parliament granted the Dalai Lama honorary Canadian citizenship. In the 2007 visit Prime Minister Harper formally received the Dalai Lama at his office on Parliament Hill and held a forty-five-minute meeting with him.

Chinese authorities denounced the Dalai Lama's meetings with Canadian officials. Sun Lushan, a political councillor at China's embassy in Ottawa, warned the visit would undermine Canada-China relations: "The China side urges Canada to take immediate and effective measures to remove the serious impact of its erroneous act … Stop supporting and conniving at the separatist activities of the Tibet independence forces, stop interfering with China's internal affairs and take concrete steps to safeguard the China-Canada relationship" (*Toronto Star*, 30 Oct.). Liu Janchao, a Chinese foreign ministry spokesman, took a step further by asserting that "[t]his kind of disgusting conduct from Canada has seriously hurt Chinese people's feelings and seriously undermined Sino-Canadian relations" (*Leader-Post*, 31 Oct.).

Although Prime Minister Harper did not directly comment on China's criticism, Jason Kenney, the secretary of state for multiculturalism, defended the government's interactions with the Dalai Lama: "It was just a natural and right thing to do. And I hope that the entire world gets the message that attacking a pacifist Buddhist monk who advocates nothing more than cultural autonomy for his people is counterproductive" (*Toronto Star*, 30 Oct.). What is more, Kenney appeared to brush off Chinese threats by suggesting that Canada-China trade had actually increased substantially since the Dalai Lama received honorary Canadian citizenship in 2006. Exports to China were up 27 per cent and imports were up approximately 15 per cent.

Amidst all the controversy, the Dalai Lama had words both for China and Canada. For China he emphasized that his political goal was simply Tibetan autonomy under Chinese sovereignty. So long as Chinese authorities respected Tibetan language, culture, and religion, "[t]hen we are very much willing [*sic*] remain in People's Republic of China. So that means we are not seeking separation" (ibid.). As for Canada, the Dalai Lama worried about the amount of money Ottawa was spending on military conflict. As well, in his assessment of Canada's military engagement in Afghanistan, the Dalai Lama was concerned about the utility of violence: "Using violence to counter violence, sometimes it creates more complicated [situations] ... Violence, you see, controls your physical, not control your mind [*sic*]. Mind can change through reason, through affection" (*New Brunswick Telegraph-Journal*, 30 Oct.).

Defence policy

Afghanistan

Afghan detainees: In 2007 controversy continued to dog the Canadian government in its handling of Afghan detainees transferred from the Canadian Forces to Afghan authorities. First in early March, Defence Minister O'Connor travelled to Afghanistan in part to meet with Abdul Noorzai, the director of the Afghanistan Independent Human Rights Commission (AIHRC) for the Kandahar region. Earlier in February the government had signed a deal with Afghanistan so that Noorzai's organization was to monitor and report back to Canadian officials on the well-being of transferred prisoners. This arrangement was an expansion on an earlier agreement made in December 2005. It was also a deal criticized by human rights groups because, unlike plans made by the United Kingdom and the Netherlands, Canada did not possess the right to monitor the treatment of transferred prisoners. As such Minister O'Connor expressed during his trip that he wanted to ensure that the AIHRC was up to the task: "I want to look the man in the eyes and I want to confirm that they are going to do what they say they're going to do ... I just want assurance from him that he will monitor and he will inform us of any abuses" (*Edmonton Journal*, 12 March).

Shortly after returning from his trip to Afghanistan, Minister O'Connor was forced to make an apology in the House of Commons. The minister had earlier indicated that the International Committee of the Red Cross (ICRC) would monitor detainees and report back to Canada if abuses were discovered. ICRC policy, however, was not to disclose information to third parties; it only reported to the government holding prisoners. Regarding Minister O'Connor's conduct, Liberal defence critic Denis Coderre assessed that "[h]e has to come clean ... Either he's incompetent or he's hiding something" (*Globe and Mail*, 12 March). Thus on 19 March, Minister O'Connor apologized for his misleading remarks: "I fully and without reservation apologize to the House for providing inaccurate information for members ... I take full responsibility and do so without hesitations ... The International Red Cross Committee is under no obligation to share information with Canada on the treatment of detainees transferred by Canada to Afghan authorities" (ibid., 19 March).

The AIHRC's monitoring capacity came into doubt later in April, which in turn catalysed another political controversy. Media reports published on 23 April indicated that torture of detainees had occurred and that the AIHRC had been prevented from visiting detainees. Liberal leader Stéphane Dion was quick to pounce on the seeming inadequacy of the government's policy: "We should seek to find other solutions. We may bring them to Canada, we may keep them under our control in Afghanistan ... We cannot send human beings to torture even though they are the enemy. We cannot" (*Toronto Star*, 24 April). Similarly, for the NDP's Jack Layton, "[t]he organization that's supposed to supervise detainees, make sure there isn't mistreatment, hasn't got the resources to do the job" (ibid.).

Subsequently Minister O'Connor made a surprise announcement during a 25 April session of the Foreign Affairs Committee that a new deal had been reached with Afghan authorities. Under this new arrangement, Canadian officials would be able to access Afghan prisons directly. However on 26 April Prime Minister Harper contradicted Minister O'Connor by saying that an agreement was still under negotiation. Public Safety Minister Day muddied the waters further by contending that Canadian corrections personnel had been in Afghan prisons "for a considerable period of time" (ibid., 27 April). In light of the government's disarray and amidst calls for Minister O'Connor's resignation, Layton commented that "[w]e are seeing day-by-day a patchwork quilt of inventions and fabrication" (ibid.). Canada eventually signed the new deal with Afghanistan on 3 May.

Funeral benefits: In the House of Commons on 28 May, Defence Minister O'Connor sparked a controversy when he responded to a question concerning whether his department was covering the complete costs of funerals for deceased military personnel. He answered that families were properly compensated and that "[w]e have been doing it since I have been in office. If any family had to bury one of their loved ones, they are entitled to full recompense for the funeral" (ibid., 31 May). Contradicting Minister O'Connor, however, were the parents of Corporal Matthew Dinning, a military policeman who died in a roadside bombing in Afghanistan on 22 April 2006. Although the Dinnings had received CDN$6,400 from the department, the total bill was CDN$12,000. To make their point, the Dinnings travelled from their home in Wingham, Ontario, to participate in a news conference on Parliament Hill: 'We stand here today telling you that we have not been fully reimbursed for Matthew's funeral costs despite that Mr. O'Connor stood up in the House of Commons and told the Canadian people the exact opposite ... We could no longer stay silent" (ibid.).

The government's response to the Dinnings' case was multifold. First Prime Minister Harper indicated that discussions had occurred between the Dinnings and the department. The Dinnings responded that the discussions constituted one email. Second Minister O'Connor fended off calls for his resignation, but he did indicate that, because of negligent military bureaucracy, "for some reason, a few families may not have received their proper compensation" (ibid.). On the military side, General Hillier said that "the responsibility to support the families begins and ends with me" (ibid.). Rear Admiral Tyrone Pile, the chief of military personnel, eventually contacted the Dinnings and indicated that additional funeral costs would be covered, as would Mrs Dinning's ongoing grief counselling.

In June the Defence Department increased its burial stipend for military personnel killed in the line of duty. The new amount, CDN$12,000, was made effective 1 June but was to be applied retroactively to 7 October 2001 – the start of operations in Afghanistan. This amount put the Canadian Forces on par with the stipend offered by the RCMP. The change was the first revision of the military's policy on funeral benefits in over decade. The previous claimable baseline was CDN$4,675 and the policy was focused on fewer claimable expenses.

Manley panel: With Canada's commitment in Afghanistan scheduled to end in February 2009, Opposition parties pressed the Conservative government about what Canada's future would be in the country. While the NDP demanded an immediate end to Canada's combat operations and a withdrawal of the 2,500 military personnel, the Liberals called for at least a termination of Canada's combat role in 2009. As expressed by NDP leader Jack Layton, the government was not being clear in its intentions: "We think Canadians are owed answers to a whole series of questions about how deep and how long this engagement is going to be, about the nature of the mission and to face directly the fact that it's not working the way it's being conducted at the moment" (*Toronto Star*, 17 April). Similarly Liberal deputy leader Michael Ignatieff argued that the Canadian population was left wondering: "There are too many different answers to the same basic question, which is how long are we going to be there? When will the government begin to level with the Canadian people about its intentions in Afghanistan?" (ibid.).

The prime minister indicated in June that Canada's military mission would only continue after February 2009 with the consensus of Parliament. He echoed this point in September: "I want to finish the mission. At the same time, I want to ensure that when we have men and women in uniform in the field in a dangerous position, that they have the support of their Parliament" (*New Brunswick Telegraph-Journal*, 10 Sept.). In short, given the need to assess the international and domestic political impact and the long-term requirements for any shift in military mission, 2007 was to be a "crunch" year regarding Canada's controversial presence in Afghanistan.

On 12 October to handle the issue and temporarily dilute its political impact, Prime Minister Harper announced the creation of a five-person advisory panel. At the panel's head was a former Liberal deputy prime minister and foreign affairs minister, John Manley.[9] Although the panel was not limited in its approach, the prime minister suggested that it examine four main options: "1) Continue training the Afghan army and

9 The panel's other members were Jake Epp, a former Cabinet minister from the Mulroney era and the head of the NGO Health Partners International; Paul Tellier, a former clerk of the Privy Council and top executive at CNR and Bombardier; Derek Burne, a former Canadian ambassador to the United States; and Pamela Wallin, a former Liberal-appointed Canadian consul general in New York City. At the time of the panel's appointment, John Manley was serving as a director of CARE Canada.

police so Canada can begin withdrawing its forces in February 2009; 2) Focus on reconstruction and have forces from another country take over security in Kandahar; 3) Shift Canadian security and reconstruction effort to another region in Afghanistan; 4) Withdraw all Canadian military except a minimal force to protect aid workers and diplomats" (PMO News Release, 12 Oct.). As well the prime minister charged the panel to consider implications along a number of fronts: "[T]he sacrifices Canadians have made to date in Afghanistan, the potential for deterioration in security and development, Canada's obligations to NATO and the United Nations, and the implications for Canada's international reputation" (ibid.). The panel was to report back by the end of January 2008.

The panel's membership was designed to provide impartial advice. Prime Minister Harper was keen, for instance, to reiterate the panel's credentials: "I am pleased to announce the formation of an independent panel of eminent Canadians who will consider our options and provide expert non-partisan advice that will help parliamentarians make our decision" (ibid.). For Manley Canada's involvement in Afghanistan was too important to allow for partisanship to intrude: "I'm a Liberal; I'ma [*sic*] supporter of the Liberal party … But I have some history in Afghanistan in my two visits that have touched me very deeply in terms of the humanitarian needs that I've seen there, and I'm very conscious of the responsibility that Canada has as a member of the global community" (*National Post*, 13 Oct.). In this vein, although Manley had told Liberal leader Stéphane Dion of his appointment in advance, he did not seek his permission.

The Opposition parties' response to the panel's appointment was mixed. For Gilles Duceppe, the Bloc Québécois leader, the panel's appointment was a political diversionary tactic: "I've been around Ottawa long enough to know that when there's an important issue and a party wants to get around it, they create a committee" (*Toronto Star*, 13 Oct.). Layton was upset that that the prime minister had not chosen the right forum: "It's a delay tactic with a partisan edge … The House of Commons should be the place where these discussions happen" (*National Post*, 13 Oct.). As for Dion, although he publicly supported Manley's appointment, he asserted that the panel should not become "a pretext to postpone the clarity we need on the combat mission" (*Vancouver Sun*, 13 Oct.).

For the Liberals, on the one hand, the panel's creation and subsequent removal of the Afghan issue from the immediate political agenda brought some relief. It reduced by one the number of potential confidence-related measures that could bring down the minority Conservatives and trigger an unwanted federal election. In this sense the announcement of the panel was timely as the Conservatives presented their throne speech on 16 October. On the other hand, Manley was a well-known supporter of the Afghan mission and a prominent member of the Liberal government led by Prime Minister Jean Chrétien that made Canada's initial military commitment to Afghanistan. At the very least Manley's involvement on the panel exposed divides within the Liberal Party and potentially pointed towards a longer-term Canadian presence in Afghanistan, something many Liberals opposed.

General Hillier: The year 2007 was marked by episodes of tension in the relationship between the CDS, General Hillier, and his political masters. In July for instance, General Hillier said, in reference to a 2006 Conservative election promise to create fourteen territorial defence battalions to respond to urban emergencies, that "we don't need new units" (*Globe and Mail*, 27 Oct.). Later, on July 22, Defence Minister O'Connor appeared on CTV's *Question Period* and said that the Canadian Forces would be shifting to a monitoring role in Afghanistan within six months and that they would "basically be in reserve" (ibid.). However, a week later on the same television program, General Hillier said, in regard to training Afghan forces, that "[i]t's going to take a long while ... We've just started the process" (ibid., 31 July).

In late October General Hillier again seemingly contradicted the government's message about the appropriate timelines to stand up the Afghan National Army. In its 16 October throne speech, the government indicated that "Canada should build on its accomplishments and shift to accelerate the training of the Afghan army and police so that the Afghan government can defend its own sovereignty. This will not be completed by February 2009, but our Government believes this objective should be achievable by 2011" (ibid., 27 Oct.). A few days later, however, the CDS offered a different time frame: "It's going to take 10 years or so just to work through and build an army to whatever the final number that Afghanistan will have, and make them professional and let them meet their security demands here" (ibid.). Opposition politicians such as Liberal deputy leader Michael Ignatieff noted the discrepancy: "You can't go out in a Throne Speech and say 2011 and then have your Chief of the Defence Staff saying well, actually, it's 2017" (ibid.). Later the CDS contended that he was not contradicting the government; the Afghan military would be able to lead military efforts in Kandahar Province specifically by 2011. The throne speech, however, made no mention of political geography. A senior Conservative official later said that the CDS would be wise in the future to tread carefully to avoid political intrusions: "He got his marching orders … He was reminded what his role is. His role is not to be the chief spokesperson for the mission" (ibid., 1 Nov.).

Amidst these issues a rumour arose that the Conservative government was going to replace General Hillier as CDS at the start of 2008. A generally negative media and public response to this rumour led the prime minister on 3 October to praise General Hiller as an "outstanding soldier" and to deny the rumour: "There has been no discussion in my office, or with me or any senior officials, about the possibility of changing the chief of defence staff … As a matter of fact, I think I just approved a pretty good rating for the chief of the defence staff" (*Ottawa Citizen*, 4 Oct.). The CDS presented a similarly positive front: "My prime minister has not told me he that is unhappy with my performance … The government is happy. As far as I know, the prime minister is still pleased" (ibid.). At the very least General Hillier remained as CDS until the end of 2007.

Prime Minister Stephen Harper's travels: In 2007 Prime Minister Harper made his second trip to Afghanistan. This trip, lasting two days, started on 22 October in Kabul where he met with Afghan president Hamid Karzai. During this meeting the prime minister implied that despite the debate back in Ottawa, his government would continue Canada's commitment: "We are not daunted by shadows because we carry the light that defines them – the light of freedom and democracy, of human rights and the rule of law. The light of this country's tangible progress to date, and its determination and hope for the future" (*Leader-Post*, 23 May). President Karzai also indicated that it was certainly in Canada's security interests to remain engaged because otherwise terrorists "will re-emerge and haunt you back home whenever they want to" (ibid.). On a lighter note the prime minister presented the president with a small Ottawa Senators jersey for his new son born four months earlier.

On the trip's second day, the prime minister visited Kandahar Airfield and, in his address to Canadian troops, reiterated that Canada's work in Afghanistan was to be ongoing: "You know that your work is not complete … You know that we can't just put down our weapons and hope for peace. You know that we can't set arbitrary deadlines and simply wish for the best" (*Vancouver Sun*, 24 May). But back in Canada Liberal defence critic Denis Coderre asserted that the prime minister was being two-faced: "[He was] deeply troubled that Mr. Harper continues to support an open-ended counter-insurgency mission in Kandahar … [in the House of Commons he keeps] repeating the stock line that Canada is only committed until 2009 … Outside of the House, Mr. Harper keep[s] hinting that our soldiers will stay longer" (*Toronto Star*, 24 May).

The prime minister did leave the relative security of Kandahar Airfield to make a two-hour visit to the forward operating base at Ma'sum Ghar, located twenty-five kilometres to the southwest. Just a week earlier a rocket attack on the base had killed an Afghan interpreter and wounded another. For the deputy Canadian commander, Colonel Mike Cessford, the prime minister's decision to visit the outpost was historic: "No serving prime minister has been closer to combat … It's a happening place. It's a forward operating base in every sense of the word" (ibid.). Only photographers captured this special trip for posterity; the night earlier plans to have reporters meet the prime minister at the base were cancelled without explanation.

Defence Minister Peter MacKay's travels: For his first time as Canada's defence minister, MacKay conducted a four-day visit to Afghanistan in early November in order to meet Canadian military personnel and Afghan government officials. During his visit to Forward Operating Base Wilson in the Zhari district on 6 November, two rockets landed at the base within fifteen minutes of each other, one detonating close to fifty metres from the minister. Although Minister MacKay was unhurt in the attack, four Canadian soldiers were slightly wounded. Back in Ottawa General Hillier contended that the minister had not been specifically targeted: "The minister was not subjected to an attack, what was subjected to an attack was one of our forward operating bases and that has been consistent because the Taliban have been driven back so that they have to resort to long-distance attacks in most cases" (*Ottawa Citizen*, 7 Nov.). While the attack did halt the minister's visit of Canadian forward installations and he was airlifted back to the safety of Kandahar Airbase, the minister indicated that he would not be deterred: "The visit will continue. We're going to continue on with our schedule … We're going to see the things that we came here to see. In fact, I would suggest that I've already seen more than I expected" (ibid.).

Minister MacKay's trip coincided with the worst suicide bombing to occur in Afghanistan since the launch of the international military intervention in 2001. On 6 November seventy-five people died in an explosion that happened outside of a sugar factory in Baghlan. The bombing occurred at a ceremony marking the factory's reopening; schoolchildren and parliamentarians were in the crowd as part of the celebration. During his meeting with Minister MacKay, President Hamid Karzai condemned the attack: "In the very miserable incident … six of Afghanistan's hard-working, honest members of parliament were martyred, and Afghan people including school teachers, students and children were also martyred, and many were wounded" (*Montreal Gazette*, 8 Nov.). Minister MacKay indicated that although this was a setback in a relatively quiet part of the country, the overall effort to make Afghanistan secure would certainly go on: "While this explosion was a terrible tragedy, particularly for the families and the victims, this is sadly not unique to this country … I expressed of course, on behalf of Canadians our condolences, our commitment to work with them, to combat the scourge of terrorism that is so plaguing this country" (*New Brunswick Telegraph-Journal*, 8 Nov.).

Later in December Minister MacKay, along with General Hillier and the US ambassador to Canada, David Wilkins, visited Afghanistan over Christmas in order to spend some of the holidays with the troops based at Kandahar Airfield and at forward operating bases. During a Christmas dinner with 1,000 military personnel, MacKay described Canada's contributions in Afghanistan as part of Christmas giving: "What greater gift could we ever bring to a people, to a country, than peace and security and a quality of life, and a beautiful expectation that families, children can grow up and achieve their dreams" (CTV.ca, 25 Dec.). During his two-day visit, he singled out Iran as being complicit in the shipment of weaponry and bomb-making equipment that ultimately ended up on the Afghan battlefield: "We're very concerned that these weapons are going to the insurgents and are keeping this issue alive. We've certainly made our views to the Iranian government about this known … It's so difficult to cut these supply lines when you have people from other countries giving out weapons that are being used against Canadian Forces and troops from other countries" (*National Post*, 25 Dec.). MacKay also emphasized the contributions made by Quebec's Royal 22nd Regiment, which had been in the theatre since the summer: "The 22nd Regiment has distinguished itself again … and we in Canada are so very grateful" (ibid.).

The minister's latter remarks reflected two facts: (1) almost 70 per cent of Quebecers opposed Canada's military mission in Afghanistan and; (2) 2007 was the bloodiest year for Canadian soldiers in Afghanistan since the launch of operations shortly after the terrorist attacks of 11 September 2001. Thirty Canadian soldiers lost their lives in Afghanistan in 2007.

Vimy Ridge anniversary

The year 2007 marked the ninetieth anniversary of the Battle of Vimy Ridge, the famous First World War battle initiated by Canadian soldiers on 9 April 1917. To mark the occasion, the prime minister and his family travelled to France for a series of events over the Easter weekend. As expressed by the prime minister before the trip, "[t]he Battle of Vimy Ridge was a critical victory for the Allies in the First World War and it was an important milestone for Canada … Our young country came of age as an independent nation that day and I am extremely proud to represent Canada at the 90th anniversary" (PMO News Release, 3 April).

The trip culminated in a ceremony rededicating the recently restored Canadian National Vimy Memorial. Since 2001 the memorial, along with twelve other Canadian First World War monuments, had been the focus of a CDN$30 million refurbishment program. Over 25,000 people attended the rededication ceremony, including Queen Elizabeth II and France's prime minister, Dominique de Villepin. The Queen's presence was particularly symbolic as her uncle, King Edward VIII, unveiled the monument back in 1936.

Controversy, however, intruded before the official Canadian delegation left for France. When the Liberals were in power, invitations had been extended to the leaders of Opposition parties, Harper included, to attend past war-related ceremonies in Europe. For the Vimy events, however, although certain Opposition politicians were part of the official delegation as a result of their parliamentary roles, the governing Conservatives did not initially offer invitations to Opposition party leaders. The government did eventually extend invitations to the leaders on 30 March, although not with any official duties attached. For Elizabeth Whiting, the spokesperson for Liberal leader Stéphane Dion, more involvement was desirable: "At this stage, we're pushing for a broader role and are hopeful the government will put politics aside and allow representatives of all parties to participate in the ceremony" (*StarPhoenix*, 2 April). In the end no official roles were given to the Opposition leaders, and amongst the Opposition leaders, only the NDP's Jack Layton attended. The Bloc Québécois sent Roger Gaudet and Michael Ignatieff represented Dion.

The trip's political sensitivity heightened considerably when, on 8 April, a roadside bomb in Afghanistan killed six Canadian soldiers and wounded two more. During a dinner speech to veterans on 8 April, the prime minister did attempt, in a general way, to link Canada's past sacrifices in Europe with its ongoing presence in Afghanistan: "For these men and women, the terrain of Kandahar province looks as desolate and dangerous as Flanders Field did 90 years ago … But those who wear the Maple Leaf on their uniform move forward against tyranny and fear with the same courage and determination that you did in your time and that the heroes of Vimy Ridge did before you" (*Globe and Mail*, 9 April). While the prime minister did not make explicit linkages with recent events in Afghanistan during the rededication ceremony on the following day, others present did, the Queen and the French prime minister included. Ignatieff warned, however, that making the linkage was somewhat of an overreach: "I think we have to be careful … [Vimy] was a hard-fought victory and we're in the middle of something in Afghanistan. I think it's right to take pride in our military traditions but we ought to be very, very careful about using them to justify current conflicts. Let's keep them separate" (ibid., 10 April).

Major military equipment decisions

Naval ships: Within a week, and on two coasts, the prime minister announced two major investments in Canada's naval capacity. First in Halifax on 5 July, he indicated that a CDN$3.1 billion modernization process would commence for the country's twelve Halifax-Class frigates. The prime minister contended that the modernization efforts would make the frigates, the Canadian navy's workhorses, even more capable in the contemporary security environment: "New updated equipment will make these ships stronger, safer and better able to do all the work we ask of them … The result is that more than ever, our Halifax-Class frigates will be giant floating command posts – standing up for Canada at home and abroad" (PMO News Release, 5 July). What is more, the refits, which were to start in 2010 and end in 2017, would be a boost to Canada's shipbuilding industry: "All of the work done on the ships will be done in Canada, by Canadian companies, and this is great news for Canadian shipyards, their employees and their suppliers" (ibid.). Dockyards in Halifax were to work on seven frigates and the remaining vessels were to be refitted in Victoria.

Second in Victoria on 9 July, the prime minister announced another multi-billion-dollar investment, this one to help protect Canadian sovereignty, particularly in the Arctic. Approximately CDN$7.4 billion was to be spent on the procurement of six to eight Canadian-made patrol ships that could operate in ice up to a metre thick. This price tag had two components: CDN$3.1 billion for the vessels and CDN$4.3 billion for the operations, repair, and refit of these vessels over their projected twenty-five-year lifespan. In addition to their ice-related attributes, the ships were to have several characteristics: (1) a helicopter pad capable of accommodating the Cyclone helicopter ordered by Prime Minister Paul Martin's government; (2) a 6,000-nautical-mile range with a top cruising speed of 20 knots; (3) an ability to operate out of port, particularly the not yet designated deepwater port in the Arctic, for four months;[10] (4) a displacement of 3,000 metric tonnes and a length of approximately 100 metres. Although the prime minister offered no timelines for the ships' delivery, he did indicate that eighteen to twenty-four months would be required to finalize the ships' design.

Conservative politicians argued that these ships would help to assert Canada's sovereignty in the Far North. For the prime minister, "Canada has a choice when it comes to defending our sovereignty over the Arctic ... We either use it or lose it. And make no mistake, this government intends to use it" (*National Post*, 10 July). Similarly Defence Minister O'Connor contended that these vessels would "stand among the world's heaviest armed naval vessels capable of sustained operations in ice" (*Globe and Mail*, 10 July). Indeed these vessels would be the first ice-capable ships in the Canadian navy's inventory for more than fifty years.

The ships' proposed capabilities did differ somewhat from the procurement promise made by the Conservatives in the 2006 federal election. During that campaign, the Conservatives asserted that they would purchase three armed icebreakers. The vessels announced in 2007, instead, were to be ice-strengthened vessels. They would be able to operate year-round in the approaches of the Northwest Passage, but they would be unable to enter the passage during heavy ice periods. Michael Byers, an Arctic expert at the University of British Columbia, suggested that this Canadian procurement decision was not enough: "That capability to operate anywhere in Canadian waters at any time of the year will not be answered with this announcement ... It's not what we really need for the decade or two ahead and it's not what [the prime minister] promised" (*National Post*, 10 July).

Nevertheless the prime minister and defence officials rationalized the switch as getting greater bang for the buck. With this announcement, more vessels could be purchased, they would be more flexible and could operate on Canada's other two coasts, and they could relieve some of the domestic security duties performed by the aforementioned Halifax-Class frigates. The prime minister defended his announcement, saying that "[i]n the campaign, we talked about three heavy icebreakers. Upon reflection and having the Department of National Defence and our office take the past year to look at various options,

10 On 10 August Prime Minister Harper announced that the port would be located at Nanisivik in Nunavut.

we concluded that we wanted a more versatile fleet, so went with more of the medium icebreakers that frankly allow us to patrol the Arctic waters and the Northwest Passage when it matters" (*Globe and Mail*, 10 July). Similarly Vice Admiral Drew Robertson, the chief of maritime staff, contended that "[t]hese ships will significantly enhance the navy's ability to provide armed support to other government departments for enforcing sovereignty and security in all three of Canada's ocean approaches (ibid.). Overall for the vice admiral, the procurement would allow for the Canadian navy's diversification such that the navy would develop "a fleet that can both control our maritime backyard and also influence events in far distant waters long before potential threats arrive off our shores" (ibid.).

Tanks: Back in 2006 the Canadian Forces sent seventeen tanks to Afghanistan. These tanks, thirty-year-old C2 Leopards, were designed for Cold War operations in central Europe against conventionally armed adversaries. What is more, four years previously, the then Liberal government had announced the tanks' retirement. Defence officials were increasingly concerned that the C2 crews would not be able to operate in the 60 degree Celsius heat, likely because of the tanks' hydraulic systems and the hot Afghan summer. There were additional concerns that as insurgent bomb-making techniques became more potent, the C2s would be at risk. The Canadian Forces, however, were stuck as investing in the retrofit of the C2s with air conditioning was not an option because spare parts for the old tanks would no longer be available as of 2012. Similarly the outfitting of tank crews with cooling vests was thought to hamper the vehicle's operation. Thus, Lieutenant General Andrew Leslie, the head of the Canadian army, asserted in early April that he would have to curtail the tanks' operations: "We will have to restrict their operations because we are not going to lose soldiers because they overheat" (*Toronto Star*, 4 April).

Hence on 12 April Defence Minister O'Connor announced a multifaceted deal to replace Canada's C2s. For a combined sum of CDN$650 million, Canada was to lease from Germany twenty operationally ready 2A6 Leopard tanks and purchase, second-hand from the Netherlands, one hundred additional Leopards (twenty 2A6s and eighty of the slightly older 2A4 variant). These tanks were better armoured, more advanced, and less heat-emitting than their C2 predecessors and could be upgraded for Afghan operations. The German tanks were to be ready for operations right away, and some of the Dutch tanks, after upgrades to be performed in Canada, were to be sent to Afghanistan to replace them. Minister O'Connor placed this procurement decision in the larger context of the government's activism on defence-related matters: "Equipping Canada's soldiers with the best protection is my top priority. By immediately acquiring stronger and more heavily protected tanks, our soldiers in Afghanistan have the best equipment possible to offer them protection during this mission … This government is committed to providing our Canadian Forces with the equipment they need to do the very demanding jobs we have asked of them" (DND News Release 07.022, 12 April). In addition the combined lease/used purchase arrangement was to save the taxpayer money because new tanks were likely to be three times more expensive. Buying new tanks would also have likely led to a multi-year delay in delivery.

A few "hiccups" did arise in the procurement process for the "new" Leopard tanks. First Minister O'Connor made the announcement in April before the government finalized the long-term support contract for the tanks. This broke with the usual policy of announcing procurement and operations and maintenance policies simultaneously. The following month Minister O'Connor announced in the House of Commons that the support contract over twenty years would be an additional CDN$650 million. Second concerns were raised that the 2A4s, unlike the 2A6s, might not be able to handle the air conditioning upgrades. Third, despite Minister O'Connor's promise that "[a]ll the work will be done in Canada," the government was having a hard time finding a Canadian firm able to complete the upgrades, thus making foreign involvement more likely (*StarPhoenix*, 13 April). For Chris Corrigan of the Royal Canadian Military Institute, this problem was symptomatic of the larger lack of defence industrial capabilities in Canada: "This isn't rocket science, but given that we haven't done it in a while it's like ramping up anything … Once you lose a capability, it's tough to get it back … This is [*sic*] example of the argument people will give your for maintaining a defence industrial base. A nation like Canada needs to be able to service its own armoured vehicles" (*New Brunswick Telegraph-Journal*, 26 July).

Strategic airlift: The Conservative government fulfilled another election promise through its announced purchase of four strategic lift aircraft, Boeing's C-17 Globemaster III, on 2 February. The total cost was CDN$1.8 billion for the aircraft acquisition and an additional CDN$1.6 billion for in-service support to be conducted by the US Air Force and Boeing. Canada received the first C-17 in August and a second arrived near the end of 2007. The remaining two aircraft were to come to Canada in 2008.

These four aircraft were to fulfil a number of requirements: (1) they would allow for a timely response to disasters within Canada; (2) they would be an asset in the NATO context; (3) they would reduce the need to contract with commercial carriers or to rely upon allies; (4) they could be used in humanitarian missions and disaster relief operations the world over; (5) they would support Canada's commitment to Afghanistan; (6) they would relieve Canada's overtaxed tactical aircraft fleet.

Several government ministers echoed these issues. For Defence Minister O'Connor, "Canada's New Government has long recognized the importance of acquiring our own strategic airlift aircrafts to allow us to quickly deploy equipment, supplies or passengers when and where needed around world, and without having to rely on our allies or contractors" (DND News Release 07.074, 11 Aug.). Public Safety Minister Day emphasized the aircraft's domestic importance: "Here in Canada, this aircraft can help to bring stability to communities which have been struck by crisis situations ... Like never before we'll be able to quickly provide relief to crises that hit our own communities, such as floods, ice storms and forest fires" (ibid.). Similarly Josée Verner, the minister of international cooperation, identified Canada's enhanced ability to respond to those in need outside of Canada: "Canadians have always responded generously to international appeals for assistance in times of emergency and disaster ... we will be able to quickly answer a variety of humanitarian needs around the world – contributing to a more secure, equitable, and prosperous world" (ibid.). Indeed shortly after Canada received its first C-17 in August, the government sent it to Jamaica as part of its response to Hurricane Dean.

At the time of the February announcement government ministers stressed the procurement's urgency but also its long-term value for money. The C-17 procurement was made under the Advance Contract Award Notice process, which sees the government identifying a contractor based on capabilities required, in this case Boeing, but also provides other producers the opportunity to submit a statement of capabilities within thirty days. This approach of purchasing "off the shelf equipment" also sped up the procurement process and in fact, according to Minister O'Connor, saw Canada jumping into the line-up for faster delivery: "The United States air force ... has allowed us to step into the assembly line so we will get the aircraft quickly" (*Calgary Herald*, 3 Feb.). Nevertheless ministers asserted that even with the increased speed in procurement, Canadian industry would benefit as usual through the requirement that for every dollar spent, the manufacturer had to invest an equivalent amount in Canadian industry. For Maxime Bernier, then serving as minister of industry, the government struck the right balance: "We have worked hard to deliver real benefits to Canadian industry as a result of our defence procurements … This agreement represents tremendous opportunity for Canadian companies to compete and stay at the forefront of the global industry" (Government of Canada News Release, 2 Feb.).

It did become clear, however, that only a portion of the CDN$3.4 billion, perhaps CDN$1.1 billion, would see reinvestment in Canadian industry. Canadian policy related specifically to the airframes and the engines, not to the training and the ongoing maintenance to be performed by Boeing and the US Air Force. Nonetheless Minister Bernier's spokesperson, Isabelle Fontaine, defended the deal: "The policy of $1 for $1 applies for foreign manufacturers. We have always been clear on that … The U.S. air force is not a foreign manufacturer" (*Ottawa Citizen*, 3 Feb.).

EMMANUEL BRUNET-JAILLY, SERENA KATAOKA, AND WARREN MAGNUSSON

Municipal affairs

In January the municipal council in Hérouxville, Quebec, attracted worldwide attention when it released a *Publication of Standards* for potential immigrants. It seemed an odd thing to do, because Hérouxville – a small rural community northeast of Montreal – is not the sort of place that attracts immigrants. On the surface the standards were a simple affirmation of liberal values ("men and women are of the same value"; "parents can be of the same race or not, be from the same country or not, have the same religion or not, even be of the same sex or not") and local customs ("We listen to music, we drink alcoholic beverages in public or private places, we dance and at the end of every year we decorate a tree with balls and tinsel and some lights"), but they were obviously framed in response to certain stereotypes: potential immigrants were told that in Hérouxville there could be no stoning of women in public, no hurling of acid in their faces, and no female circumcision. There was a storm of protest, not least from Muslim groups who were offended by the implicit stereotyping, but the Hérouxville council just responded by making their standards more general – "we consider that killing women in public beatings, or burning them alive are not part of our standards of life" – and reaffirming its opposition to wearing veils or *kirpan*. Most of the neighbouring municipalities supported Hérouxville. The controversy prompted the Quebec government to appoint the Bouchard-Taylor Commission to investigate ways and means for "reasonable accommodation" of immigrants and cultural and religious minorities. The commission's hearings highlighted social and cultural tensions that many municipalities across the country confront.

Otherwise municipal issues in 2007 were the old familiars: decaying infrastructure, inadequate public transit, the lack of affordable housing, ongoing deterioration of the natural environment, and the persistent fiscal crisis of the local governments that have to deal with these issues. Interest groups and local leaders concerned about the fate of Canadian cities tried to maintain pressure on the new federal government, which they feared would not be as sympathetic as its predecessor to demands for assistance. Provincial governments were under similar pressure. There were municipal elections in Alberta, which led to no great change politically. Elsewhere, established municipal leaders pursued familiar agendas.

Cities in the marketplace

The Conference Board of Canada issued its four-volume "Canada Project" report in January, the third volume of which was entitled *Mission Possible: Successful Canadian Cities*. It identified seven challenges: the fiscal squeeze, growth management, the infrastructure gap, governance weaknesses, deepening social divides, environmental degradation, and competition from cities in North America and beyond. On the last count, it noted,

> From Tokyo and Barcelona to Glasgow and New York City, there is a heated race to develop industry clusters; to form networks among researchers, business and policy-makers; to revitalize historic downtowns, waterfronts and decaying neighbourhoods; to diversify the industrial base; to educate highly skilled workers; to develop affordable housing in urban cores in order to attract middle-class workers; and to build integrated mass transit systems (11).

It noted that municipal governments collected just 12 per cent of total government revenue and that their share was declining in relative terms. Whereas population was falling in some places, most of the big cities were expanding rapidly, with all the consequent challenges and stresses, not least the ongoing pressure on municipal infrastructure. The fact that "Canadian municipalities live in a condition of political tutelage with respect to the provinces," without "the authority to levy income or consumption taxes, or to make decisions on many of the matters that affect them most," meant they could not easily respond to the challenges (9). Among the latter were the growing concentration of poverty among urban immigrants and Aboriginals and the evident environmental degradation associated with "low-density, car-dependent development" (7). The Conference Board concluded that all levels of government (and potential partners) must find ways to work together in order to make Canadian cities more competitive in the global rankings. "At the very least, Canadian public policy should focus on ensuring that Toronto has the resources to maintain its singular status among global cities" (11). The Conference Board might be accused of Toronto-centrism, but in fact it advocated "national strategic investment and focus" on nine "hub" cities: Halifax, Montreal, Toronto, Winnipeg, Regina, Saskatoon, Calgary, Edmonton, and Vancouver. The suggestion was that "the best policy course might be to devote a greater share of national resources to the economic powerhouses and to let their success leverage the catch-up of others" (16). To say that this would be difficult to achieve politically is to put it mildly. Interestingly, the Conference Board also advocated a broader approach to business promotion.

> Recent research indicates that cities' economic performance depends not just on business activity per se, but also on the quality-of-life assets that attract mobile workers and affect corporate decisions on business location and expansion. Cities' success and prosperity also depend on the availability of affordable housing and the existence of infrastructure adequate to support modern communications, transportation and utilities. The backlog in maintenance of existing infrastructure, as well as the need for new infrastructure to accommodate growth, currently imposes a huge burden on Canada's major cities, where infrastructure needs are the most extensive and costly (19).

In another report in December, *City Magnets: Benchmarking the Attractiveness of Canada's CMAs*, the Conference Board for the first time attempted to rank the twenty-seven Census Metropolitan Areas identified in 2001 in terms of their attractiveness to skilled workers. It chose indicators related to the economy (where Calgary shone), health (where Toronto came out on top), society (with Toronto again number one), housing (Sherbrooke best, because housing is relatively cheap, and Vancouver worst), environment (Abbotsford, Victoria, and Vancouver on top), innovation (Ottawa-Gatineau best: take that, Ottawa-haters), and education (Ottawa-Gatineau again). Overall, the Conference Board gave A grades to Calgary, Toronto, Vancouver, Edmonton, Victoria, and Ottawa-Gatineau, ranking the six in that order. Saguenay, Saint John, and Thunder Bay ranked at the bottom, with D grades.

A November report commissioned by the FCM was entitled *Danger Ahead: The Coming Collapse of Canada's Municipal Infrastructure*. The author, McGill engineering professor Saeed Mirza, revised previous estimates of the "infrastructure deficit" from $60 billion to $123 billion, including $31 billion for water and wastewater, $21.7 billion for transportation, $22.8 billion for transit, $40.2 billion for cultural, social, community, and recreational infrastructure, and $7.7 billion for waste management. Mirza suggested that all those figures could grow exponentially if the necessary investments – including investments in routine maintenance – were postponed. Relative to the needs, recent federal and provincial contributions to municipal revenue had been minor, certainly not sufficient to reverse the long-term trend:

> Since the late 1970s, as the responsibility for infrastructure investment shifted to municipalities and the municipal property tax, there was a precipitous decline in capital stock. As a result, the average age of municipal infrastructure increased significantly over this period. In short, a vicious cycle was created that led to a critical backlog of investment in municipal infrastructure, now known as the municipal infrastructure deficit (6).

An earlier FCM report by Pierre J. Hamel, *Public-Private Partnerships [P3s] and Municipalities*, dumped cold water on the idea that public-private partnerships could be a sort of "magic solution" to the problem of funding infrastructure: "the funds paid out each year to a P3 partner are more or less the same amount as the annual payments on a municipal loan taken out for a traditional project" (5). Clearly, there would be no easy fix.

The political complexities of attracting both public and private capital for the development or renovation of municipal infrastructure were especially evident in Vancouver, where preparations to host the 2010 Olympics were underway. Although the event was also supposed to rebrand the city for competitive purposes, controversies had arisen over the displacement effects of Olympic-related construction and the viability, location, and P3 financing arrangements for the new rapid transit line to the airport. In July, the Vancouver City Council, led by the new mayor, Sam Sullivan, became embroiled in a bitter labour dispute with civic workers, related partly to its demand for a contract extension that would provide for "labour peace" during the Olympics. The result was a three-month strike, finally resolved with the help of an outside mediator. The often bitter Left-Right divisions in Vancouver city politics were highly visible in this context.

The culture of cities

At the third "Toronto Summit" in February, one of the subjects was the city's "Cultural Renaissance," exemplified by a recent building boom including the Ghery facelift of the Art Gallery of Ontario, the new opera and ballet house, the redevelopment of the National Ballet of Canada School, the modernist Gardiner Museum, the Royal Conservatory of Music's new Centre for Performance and Learning, acoustic enhancements of Roy Thompson Hall, and the Toronto International Film Festival's new tower (replete with exhibition space, offices, a library and archives, theatres, and above [not to mention underwriting] all that, many storeys of condos). This is to say nothing of the many other arts-related developments that had been undertaken in the city over the previous couple of years,

But, as the summit report suggests, other things are required if there is to be real artistic flourishing in Toronto or elsewhere:

> A full cultural renaissance also faces other challenges including: limited and unbalanced funding, particularly for operations; little access to cultural and creative activity in low-income neighbourhoods and new immigrant communities; a limited supply of affordable, accessible space for artists and cultural enterprises; and weak legislation, planning tools and resources to develop and protect creative space (Toronto City Summit 2007, *Making Big Things Happen*, 7).

There was much talk about the "creative city," blurring the lines between economic innovation, artistic expression, and cultural diversity. Could there be a symbiosis?

To talk of culture is to raise questions of cultural difference. While the Bouchard-Taylor Commission in Quebec was hearing much about people's resentments about "accommodation," most of Canada's major cities were responding positively to the challenge of including newcomers. Edmonton, for instance, joined the Canadian Coalition of Municipalities Against Racism and Discrimination, adopted a new policy on immigration and settlement, and set up an Aboriginal Relations Office within its already established Office of Diversity and Inclusion. Whether such gestures were more than symbolic is difficult to judge. With respect to Aboriginal relations, the FCM completed an important project described in a report entitled *Building Capacity Through Communication: Municipal-Aboriginal Partnerships in Land Management*. The aim had been to develop a "toolkit" for municipalities and First Nations governments concerned about managing adjacent lands. A number of relatively successful "partnerships" were highlighted, between the Regional Municipality of Wood Buffalo and Athabasca Tribal Council (Alberta), Regional District of Central Okanagan and Westbank First Nation (British Columbia), the Town of The Pas and Opaskwayak Cree Nation (Manitoba), City of Fredericton and Saint Mary's First Nation (New Brunswick), Municipality of Temagami, Temagami First Nation and Teme Augama Anishnabai (Ontario), and City of Regina and Nekaneet First Nation (Saskatchewan).

In Vancouver, the city's Chinese Canadian police chief made a strong plea for increased funding in response to a rise in gang-related violence and violent crime in general (up 17 per cent since 2003). Western Canadian cities were, as usual, the ones with the highest crime rates: Regina, Saskatoon, Abbotsford, Winnipeg, Edmonton, Victoria, and Vancouver being the worst, in that order, but Saint John, Thunder Bay, and Halifax also had high incident rates. Nationally, the downward trend in the crime rate continued, despite public perceptions to the contrary. Toronto was among the CMAs with a relatively low rate, in per capita terms.

Social problems, such as the lack of affordable housing, obviously contribute to the conditions that lead people to turn to crime. The Toronto City Summit's summary of the situation in that city was sobering:

> Between 2000 and 2006, only 1,465 new affordable units were finished in Toronto while one-quarter of the affordable private rental stock, or 33,000 units, became unaffordable to the average tenant household. Social housing continues to deteriorate with a repair backlog that is reportedly in the $300 million range. As a result, there are currently 67,000 households on waiting lists for social housing in Toronto and almost 200,000 low-income households spending in excess of the recommended 30% of earnings on rent (23).

The Calgary Chamber of Commerce estimated that most of the homeless people in that city were making over $40,000 a year, an indicator of how difficult the situation was even in places where jobs were plentiful. Although there was more talk of the infrastructure deficit than the affordable housing deficit, it was obvious to most municipal leaders that the latter was a huge problem but not one to which they could respond effectively without support from the senior governments.

Toronto, Montreal, and Vancouver continued to attract a disproportionate share of international immigrants in 2007, although the data suggest that some of these people will move on to Calgary or Edmonton, as do many native-born Canadians. Altogether 28,000 people moved to Calgary in 2007. Although that city is not yet as diverse as Toronto or Vancouver, one in five Calgarians speak a language other than French or English, and 23 per cent of them are immigrants from other countries. Cultural diversity is clearly becoming the norm in much of urban Canada, especially in places that are booming economically, which includes edge cities like Mississauga and Vaughan in Ontario or Richmond and Surrey in BC.

An important issue identified at the Toronto City Summit was the poor representation of minority communities in major NGOs, businesses, and governments at all levels. Although 43 per cent of the people in Toronto are identified as "visible minorities," only 11 per cent of the members of city council are. One suggestion, promoted by many in Toronto including Mayor David Miller himself, is that all residents be allowed to vote in municipal elections, regardless of citizenship status. The campaigners claimed that measures of this sort (with precedents in Europe) were particularly important in Toronto where about 15 per cent residents are not eligible to vote, and turnout for municipal elections is relatively low in neighbourhoods with high concentrations of recent immigrants and visible minorities. Ontario premier Dalton McGuinty was not supportive, however, so there seemed to be little immediate prospect for change in this regard. Certainly, the lack of affordable housing makes things difficult for recent immigrants and refugees, as do the constrained economic opportunities for those with limited education or foreign credentials. Diversity without inclusivity is evidently a danger.

Regional governance

Calgary exemplifies some of the issues that booming cities are facing. In most metropolitan areas the growth pressure is most intense in the outer municipalities, but Calgary had been able to move its boundaries outward as the suburbs expanded, annexing yet more territory to the north and east in 2007. Thus, it is close to the "unicity" model traditionally favoured by municipal reformers. Nevertheless there is not much evidence that this expansion has allowed for more effective urban containment. Urban sprawl and related issues – such as public transit, the need for "vibrant, mixed communities," and "proper stewardship of the air, land, and water" – dominated the top six issues identified by the Better Calgary Campaign in the run-up to the fall municipal elections.[11] Of the remaining two issues, "[m]aking the political system work for people" spoke about the Campaign itself – as a non-partisan group that had "long advocated the need to bring better people into municipal politics, and to give those who choose to serve the tools they need to do a good job" (Naheed Nemshi, op-ed, *Calgary Herald*, 14 Mar.). Finally, "urban poverty and homelessness" gestured to the fact that as fast and

11 See op-ed by Naheed Nemshi, *Calgary Herald*, 14 Mar. 2007.

far as the city was spreading, housing construction was not keeping pace with population growth. More than half of absolutely homeless people were employed, but they could either not find housing, given the extremely low apartment vacancy rate (of 0.5 per cent), or afford the skyrocketing housing costs, which were rising by $500 per day (Poverty Reduction Coalition, *2007 Calgary Housing Facts*).

In January, the city had joined with various other organizations to establish the Calgary Committee to End Homelessness, based on an American model for interagency cooperation. The committee engaged in community consultations, held a city summit, and commissioned research over the course of the year in an effort to develop an effective ten-year plan for the period 2000–18.

Progress had already been achieved on another front. In April the Mercer 2007 Worldwide Health and Sanitation Survey rated Calgary as the cleanest city on the planet. In a close vote that month, the city council approved a new curbside recycling program, similar to the blue box programs in other Canadian cities. The city claimed in its annual report that public satisfaction with services was generally high, although not quite as high as it had been in the past.

For many municipal leaders, the key issue in regional governance is public finance. In September Calgary's mayor, Dave Bronconnier, hailed an agreement with the Alberta government under its Municipal Sustainability Initiative that would provide $3.3 billion in new grants to the city over the next decade. What he liked is that it would provide long-term, stable funding for infrastructure, with no strings attached. The city council almost immediately agreed on measures to double the capacity of Calgary's C Train (LRT) system and invest $300 million in new sports and recreation facilities. Soon after, it also established an Enterprise Housing Program to create 2,000 units of affordable housing over five years, in cooperation with private developers and non-profit agencies. As well, work began on the Rivers inner-city redevelopment project, which had been planned for over thirty years: "Within a decade, The Rivers will be home to 20,000 people. It will be an area of waterfront parks, community squares and markets, pedestrian bridges, and some of the most inviting streets in the entire city" (City of Calgary Annual Report 2007, *New Times, New Ways*, 39). Measures of this sort can bolster political support; the tax increases required to finance them are a different matter.

Mayor Bronconnier was one of the signatories of the 5 March report of the Minister's Council on Municipal Sustainability in Alberta, along with Mayor Stephen Mandell of Edmonton and the leaders of Alberta's two municipal associations. Recommendations included various proposals to facilitate and if necessary require inter-municipal cooperation on regional planning, as well as to allow municipalities to levy new kinds of taxes, at their own discretion. The latter would include amusement, tourism, property transfer, and vehicle registration taxes, along with new powers for development levies and special mill rates for non-residential properties. In response, the province promised modest steps to encourage regional planning and arbitrate inter-municipal disputes, but it put off the proposals for increased municipal taxing powers for further consultation. Bronconnier focused his attention on getting more in the way of grant funding from the province, rather than on new taxation powers; after all, he was facing re-election in the fall in a notoriously tax-averse city.

By contrast Toronto's Mayor Miller pressed his fellow councillors to take advantage of the new powers of taxation that the Ontario government had just granted to the city under the new City of Toronto Act. After lengthy disputes that forced Miller to modify his original proposals, council agreed in October to introduce new taxes on land transfers and personal vehicles. The land transfer tax gained the support of major developers and the Toronto Board of Trade, once it had been modified to meet their objections. The modifications reduced the expected revenue to such an extent that substantial property tax increases were forecast for 2008.

In Quebec the provincial government introduced legislation that would give Montreal the right to levy taxes similar to the ones being introduced in Toronto. Whether they would offer more of a revenue fix remained to be seen.

The Ontario government announced its Move Ontario 2020 plan in June, which was a promise to spend \$17.5 billion over twelve years to improve public transit in the Greater Toronto Area (GTA). No less than fifty-two rapid transit projects were mentioned, and a new regional body was tasked with developing the plans (i.e., the Greater Toronto Transit Authority). The catch was that the province was promising to provide only 65 per cent of the funding for these projects and was hoping or expecting that the federal government would provide the rest. Earlier in the year, the Big City Mayors' Caucus of the FCM had published a report recommending a National Transit Strategy, under which the federal government would commit \$2 billion a year – half of what the mayors said was needed – to fund transit maintenance and improvement. In their view this funding would get Canada "closer to meeting its objectives for competitiveness, quality of life, air quality and greenhouse gas emission reductions" (FCM Big City Mayors' Caucus, *National Transit Strategy*, 5 March, p. 15). Be that as it may, the pressure was on municipalities to take appropriate initiative themselves.

Local democracy

Relatively few of Canada's municipal leaders faced re-election in 2007. The main exception was in Alberta. There, Dave Bronconnier was returned for a third term as mayor of Calgary and Stephen Mandel for a second term as mayor of Edmonton. In neither case was there a stiff contest. In Edmonton, turnout declined from 42 per cent in 2004, when there was a tight three-way race for the mayoralty, to just 27 per cent. Although the latter figure is not impressive, it seems large compared to what Quebec saw in its elections for the school boards, held separately from municipal elections. Turnout on the English side was actually better than it had been – up to 16.9 per cent from 14.6 per cent previously, and at 17.6 per cent in Montreal – but for the French school board elections it was down from 8.4 per cent to 7.9 per cent, with just 3.9 per cent of those eligible showing up at the polls in Montreal. This turnout could well be described as a crisis in democratic representation.

Cynicism about politicians obviously did not help. In Ottawa the mayor, Larry O'Brien, was actually indicted on two counts in connection with the 2006 municipal election there. He was accused of having offered a bribe to another mayoral candidate to withdraw from the race. He denied the charges, of course, but the allegations obviously damaged him and soured an already difficult political situation, marked by acrid disputes about an abortive light rail scheme.

In spite of such cynicism, significant advocacy for civic participation was undertaken. In addition to the Toronto-based campaign to extend the municipal franchise to non-citizen residents in the city noted previously, the FCM launched a cross-country campaign to increase the percentage of women in municipal government. The goal was 30 per cent. A key initiative was to identify "regional champions" who could "develop networks whose members will encourage, support or mentor women who are interested in entering local politics" (FCM Annual Report, *Working Together for Change*, 10).

A shining example of women's civic empowerment, perhaps, was in Mississauga. Two-thirds of council members in 2007 were women, and one of them, Carolyn Parrish (a former Liberal MP), launched a series of challenges against Mayor "Hurricane" Hazel McCallion's "iron grip" on the council she has run for almost thirty years. At stake in this "opening salvo in the 2010 mayoralty campaign" were different approaches to local democracy. Councillor Parrish argued that council's proceedings should be open and transparent, whereas McCallion insisted on running council efficiently (and so privately) according to residents' interests – especially in terms of the bottom line. According to an Environics poll, "Hazel" (as she was referred to by residents) remained the darling of Mississaugans, with 95 per cent of those surveyed very or somewhat satisfied with her. Serious jockeying for the mayor's seat would likely have to wait until after Hazel's retirement.

For the time being, Mayor McCallion continued to reap the harvests of having grown an agricultural community into Canada's largest suburban municipality and sixth-largest city (with roughly 700,000 people), while providing community services and safety without going into debt. Awards continued to be showered on her, and for the tenth year in a row, building construction in the municipality exceeded $1 billion. Although less celebrated, other suburban municipalities were also booming. Neighbouring Brampton, for instance, had been outbuilding Mississauga for seven years, this year by $450 million. Despite being the kinds of places where most Canadians were living, suburbs continued to be overlooked by academic, journalistic, and policy-oriented reports alike. Absent the kind of public scrutiny that is provided in big cities (e.g., by dedicated local affairs reporters), and through the grapevine in small towns, suburbs can sometimes provide places where politicians can exercise authority relatively unchecked. Had it not been for Councillor Parrish grilling McCallion for double-dipping in the hydro utility board, and journalists in Toronto trying to figure out how widespread this problem was, it may have been many more years before it became known that council members were doing the same in the likes of Vaughan, Markham, Pickering, and Ajax. Troubling as such double-dipping was, suburban municipalities faced much bigger financial issues.

A report released by Pricewaterhouse Coopers tracking social service and hospital dollars flowing into the suburban regions around Toronto identified a deteriorating situation. With population growth in the area continuing to outstrip provincial funding reallocation, the average GTA resident was found to receive around $220 less than other Ontario residents for both hospital care and social services, and these gaps were expected to continue to grow. In media coverage of the short-changing of suburbs, fingers were often pointed at the central city. Its left-wing councillors were said to be especially adept at lobbying the provincial government for social service support (e.g., James, R. "It's time for suburbs to speak up," *Toronto Star*, 19 Sept., A6). Then there was the roughly $200 million Toronto took from the suburban municipalities for the GTA's social infrastructure hub. Although the provincial Liberals agreed this year to phase out the so-called "Toronto tax," it was over a longer period of time than the suburban governments would have liked.

Suburban governments might have taken cues from Surrey, BC (a suburb of Vancouver), which released an *Action Plan for the Social Well-Being of Surrey Residents* in 2007 that outlined how the city could develop and foster "understanding" in social issues and, in turn, play an "advocating" and "supporting" role in resolving those issues in collaboration with other stakeholders. It may have been the case, however, that what was working in Surrey rested more on Mayor Dianne Watts herself than on any particular action plan. Word on the street was that she was a powerhouse like Mayor McCallion – with the ear of upper levels of government and popularity with constituents.

Cities in the confederation

Municipalities across Canada continued to press for more federal support, especially for infrastructure. Although the federal Conservative government was cautious about making large new commitments, it was anxious to shore up its image in the Toronto region and other areas where the Conservatives had not done well in the 2006 election. Thus, it offered modest increases to previous Liberal commitments. Amongst the new measures was a two-year $500 million contribution to a Public Transit Capital Trust fund. The government also promised $962 million as its share of the costs of rapid transit improvement in Toronto, including the proposed subway north to Vaughan, as well as $225 million in new money for ecologically sensitive lands, such as the Oak Ridges Moraine. The Big City Mayors' Caucus was by no means satisfied, however. While acknowledging the relief afforded by previous investments in transit (e.g., the federal gas tax, the Canadian Strategic Infrastructure Fund, and the Public Transit Capital Trust), the mayors expressed concern that these funds are neither "sufficient" nor "scheduled to continue" and so called for "a long-term national transit strategy" (FCM Big City Mayors' Caucus, *National Transit Strategy*, 5 March 5, p. 15).

The projected federal surplus of $11.6 billion was seen as an opportunity to support infrastructure renewal projects in cities. Ontario's Premier McGuinty spoke directly with the prime minister about doing just that, but apparently Stephen Harper was not interested. For his part, the premier finally agreed to begin uploading social services that had been downloaded to municipalities by the former provincial

Conservative government of Mike Harris. Responsibility for lobbying the feds, however, fell back on mayors.

Toronto's Mayor Miller took the lead in a "One Cent Now" campaign to give the municipalities a one-percentage-point share of the GST. Weary of tying demands to the GST, Mayor McCallion initiated the "Cities NOW!" campaign to raise awareness about the need for federal funding for infrastructure by taking the bold step of implementing a 5 per cent infrastructure levy on Mississauga properties and pointing the finger at the federal government. Debates ensued about which campaign to move forward with, and in the end both the Large Urban Mayors' Caucus of Ontario and the FCM Big City Mayors' Caucus endorsed "One Cent Now" as the national campaign. The prime minister was not sympathetic, pointing out that the government had just cut the GST by 1 per cent and passed the savings on to Canadian consumers.

The municipalities were more successful with respect to the Gas Tax Fund, which the government agreed to extend until 2014. The FCM continued to lobby to make the fund permanent. The municipalities continued to get the GST rebates that they had been granted. Otherwise, there were relatively few changes in policy: not surprising, in view of the Conservatives' precarious position in the minority Parliament. A couple of measures that indicated the leanings of the new government were the merger of the transport, infrastructure, and communities portfolios, through which cities as such seemed to drop out of the federal policy picture; and a national fund to support Private-Public-Partnership Initiatives. Most municipalities could claim that, in spirit, they had long been believers in such partnerships. Absent sufficient and sustainable funding as and from governments, municipalities had long been in competition with one another to attract investment by modulating their "standards" – of building, zoning, behaviour, and so on.

KRISTIN BURNETT

First Nations

Federal

2007 federal budget

In mid-March the Conservative government under Stephen Harper released its budget. Harper used the budget to announce his "new approach" to Aboriginal spending. The federal government's new spending initiatives were to focus on "incentives to get individuals out of poverty through job training and home ownership." Over the next two years Ottawa announced it would make $300 million available to Aboriginal people to encourage private home ownership on reserves. Critics suggested that this approach overlooked the fact that housing on reserves is generally held as collective band property. Other areas of spending include $20 million towards helping Aboriginal fishers and $15 million more over two years to continue the Aboriginal justice strategy (*Globe and Mail*, 20 March).[12]

Indian and Northern Affairs Canada's budget

In 1996 the federal government placed a 2 per cent cap on funding increases to Indian and Northern Affairs Canada (INAC). In real terms the 2 per cent cap means a $50 million shortfall every year and a cumulative shortfall over ten years of $300 million. This cap has had a long-term impact on funding for schools, housing, and welfare in First Nations communities. Considering inflation levels over the last ten years in relation to the growing Aboriginal population, funding for basic services in real terms has declined 6 per cent. This year's federal

12 The Aboriginal Justice Strategy (AJS) was created in 1991 as part of a comprehensive federal Aboriginal crime strategy. This was the third time the strategy had been renewed.

budget will see a 0.6 per cent increase in spending on First Nations people (*National Post*, 9 April).

Canada was ranked in 2006 as one of the top five countries in the world to live in on the United Nations' human development index. However, if considered alone, Canada's Aboriginal population would rank seventy-eighth (ibid., 27 April).

Aboriginal children

In early February Phil Fontaine, national chief of the Assembly of First Nations (AFN), announced the AFN's intention to lodge a complaint against INAC with the Canadian Human Rights Commission alleging discriminatory treatment of Aboriginal children. The AFN maintains that the decision to remove Aboriginal children from their families and place them in care is prejudiced (ibid., 24 Feb.). As evidence the AFN pointed out that Aboriginal children, particularly those who live on reserves, are disproportionately removed from their homes and placed in care. As of February there were 27,000 Aboriginal children across Canada in the child-welfare system – 9,000 of those children were apprehended from reserves (ibid., 6 Feb.). One in 10 Aboriginal children were in foster care in comparison to one in 200 non-Aboriginal children (*Globe and Mail*, 5 Feb.). Half of the 22,000 children in Canada who were waiting to be adopted were Aboriginal. By comparison Aboriginal people composed only 3 per cent of Canada's population in the 2001 census (*National Post*, 27 April). These problematical statistics, in fact, had recently prompted international aid workers from the Save the Children organization to visit two First Nations in Ontario to investigate child poverty (*Globe and Mail*, 5 Feb.).

In part, the problem lay in the fact that First Nations child-welfare agencies received 22 per cent less funding than did those agencies that dealt with non-Aboriginal children (*National Post*, 24 Feb.). Nor did First Nations' Children's Aid Societies on reserves have access to the same kinds of respite and support services that families elsewhere do.

Fontaine said the complaint was part of a broader effort to pressure the federal government to provide First Nations groups and communities with more funding to "help them alleviate the suffering of their children" (ibid.). This was part of a broader campaign by the AFN to bring national attention to the extent of Aboriginal poverty. Unfortunately, the 2007 budget did not allocate additional resources towards alleviating child poverty in First Nations communities. Indian affairs minister Jim Prentice noted in late February, in response to the lobbying efforts of

Aboriginal organizations calling for action on Aboriginal poverty, that "Ottawa already spends an awful lot of money on Natives" (*Globe and Mail*, 23 Feb.).

No apology for residential schools

On 27 March Jim Prentice announced that the federal government would not apologize for subjecting thousands of Aboriginal children to the residential school system. Prentice explained that since "the underlying objective of the schools was to try to provide an education to the aboriginal children," an apology was unnecessary (*National Post*, 3 April). Canada has issued apologies for its treatment of other groups (for instance for imposing a heat tax on the Chinese and interning the Japanese during the Second World War), but Prentice noted, that circumstances in this situation were sufficiently different that an apology was unwarranted. "An apology is more important than compensation," said Gary Merasty, an Aboriginal MP from Saskatchewan, whose mother attended a residential school. As he opined, the "Conservatives need to show decency and live up to the promises made to Canada's Aboriginal peoples" (ibid., 2 May).

Prentice's announcement followed the Supreme Court's approval of a $1.9 billion settlement negotiated between the federal government, churches, and residential school survivors (ibid.).

Métis National Council (MNC)

Clem Chartier, president of the MNC, was removed from his position in August following a vote by the Board of Governors. Chartier had been elected in October 2003 and his term had expired in October 2006. However, the Board of Governors had voted to extend his term until problems with the MNC local in Saskatchewan were resolved. Following Chartier's removal, Bruce Dumont was appointed as interim leader. The MNC and several provincial locals have experienced funding freezes as a result of electoral discrepancies (*Windspeaker*, Nov.).

In early September Ontario Superior Court justice P. Cosgrove ruled that "since an agreement couldn't be reached as to who should be president of the MNC, no one would serve in that role until an election could be held." As a result, an annual general meeting (AGM) was scheduled for 13 and 14 October in order to hold an election. However, further disagreement over the composition of the delegation from the Métis Nation of Alberta (MNA) dominated the AGM and the election was not held. According to MNA vice president Trevor Gladue, "I'll be quite blunt. I think there was a move to try to manipulate the outcome of the election" (*Windspeaker*, Nov.).

Mortgages

Under Section 86 of the Indian Act Aboriginal people living on reserves are protected from the seizure of assets when they default on a loan. Initially this section was enacted in order to prevent reserve land from being alienated. In practical terms it has prevented Aboriginal people from being able to borrow money to purchase or build their own homes. On 20 April Prentice announced that the federal government would create a "default fund" out of the $300 million earmarked in March's budget for Aboriginal housing. The "default fund" would provide insurance for Aboriginal people seeking to take out mortgages with banks. The fund was to be administered by an independent body. Prentice considered this to be "one of the most important structural changes in a generation" (*National Post*, 20 April).

Land claims

Since 1970 some 1,300 land claims[13] had been submitted. Of those, 900 remained unresolved. Only ten land claims were being settled on average each year. At this rate, according to a report released by the Senate Committee on Aboriginal Peoples, it would take ninety years to resolve all land claims (ibid., 17 May).

The land claims process current in 2007 was established as an alternative to the judicial system. Unfortunately for everyone involved, the land claims process has become mired in bureaucracy and complicated by legal decisions. Lawyers examining the process have concluded that INAC is "organizationally and functionally incapable of processing claims more efficiently" (ibid.).

On 12 June Prime Minister Harper announced his government's intention to renovate the land claims process (*Globe and Mail*, 12 July). Beginning in January 2008, the federal government would allocate $250 million a year towards resolving land claims and create an "independent,

13 "A land claim is a formal statement made by an Aboriginal community that it is legally entitled to land and/or financial compensation. A claim may be submitted to the federal government and/or the provincial government." http://www.aboriginalaffairs.gov.on.ca/english/negotiate/aboutclaims/faq.asp#gen_land (accessed 29 June 2011). Archive of web page can be found at https://ospace.scholarsportal.info/bitstream/1873/14285/2/288771.pdf.

quasi-judicial tribunal to impose settlements on claims in which the government and native bands cannot agree" (*National Post*, 23 June).

Bill C-44

Bill C-44 was intended to repeal Section 67 of the Canadian Human Rights Act, which exempts the Act from being applied on reserves. Bill C-44 was introduced in 2006 but was met with a great deal of opposition from Aboriginal organizations because it proposed an unrealistic time frame of six months for First Nations communities to comply with the Act (*Windspeaker*, Dec.). According to AFN grand chief Phil Fontaine, "people in First Nations communities need time to prepare for this legislation, particularly because it will add new costs for First Nations governments, many of which are already under-resourced" (*National Post*, 25 July).

A new version of the bill, Bill C-21, was reintroduced to the House of Commons on 13 November by Chuck Strahl, minister of INAC (*Windspeaker*, Dec.). The House of Commons' Standing Committee on Aboriginal Affairs is currently considering how long bands and councils will have to meet the terms of the Canadian Human Rights Act (*National Post*, 25 July). The Act prohibits discrimination in employment and services on the grounds of sex, race, ethnic origin, and marital status.

Rising incidents of tuberculosis

A recent report by the Canadian Tuberculosis Committee entitled "Housing Conditions which Serve as Risk Factors for Tuberculosis Infection and Disease" revealed that TB rates were rising among Aboriginal people. The report found that the TB epidemic was fuelled by poor and overcrowded housing. According to Dr Patricia Larcombe, professor of internal medicine at the University of Manitoba and co-author of the report, "housing is a 'critical' factor in the airborne spread of the infectious disease and the likelihood of someone getting sick after being infected." This was exacerbated by the dangerous levels of mould that many First Nations' housing has: "It's not a little bit of mould we're talking about," said Larcombe. "[W]e're talking about whole walls that are covered in mould in crawl spaces and foundations of homes" (*National Post*, 5 Nov.).

In 2005 among the non-Aboriginal population born in Canada, TB rates over the previous decade were 0.9 new cases per 100,000. This is in comparison to the Aboriginal population, which had a rate of 27 new cases per 100,000 (ibid.).

United Nations Declaration on the Rights of Indigenous Peoples

On 13 September Canada voted against the United Nations Declaration on the Rights of Indigenous Peoples. The Declaration is a non-binding document that establishes basic human rights standards for Indigenous populations around the world. The General Assembly passed the Declaration almost unanimously. Only four countries voted against the Declaration – Canada, New Zealand, Australia, and the United States. Joseph Ole Simel, the coordinator for the African Indigenous Caucus, accused Canada of "trying to use aid as a tool" to convince African countries to vote against the Declaration (*Ottawa Citizen*, 13 Sept.).

According to Phil Fontaine, grand chief of the AFN, "this is a stain on the country's international reputation. It is disappointing to see this government vote against recognizing the basic rights of Canada's first peoples" (*Globe and Mail*, 14 Sept.).

National Day of Action

Aboriginal groups and activists held a peaceful day of protest on 29 June. The Day of Action was intended to raise awareness of Aboriginal issues (ibid., 24 May). Events were held across Canada. For example, in Edmonton, Alberta, the Friends of the Lubicon held a mock land grab at the provincial legislature (*Edmonton Journal*, 29 June).

British Columbia

New port in Prince Rupert

The Lax Kw'alaams and Matlakatla First Nations opposed the establishment of a new container terminal at Prince Rupert before the federal and provincial governments have resolved outstanding land rights claims. Prince Rupert is located closer to Asian markets and offers greater opportunity and quicker access to global markets. As of June, the project was under four judicial reviews (*National Post*, 1 June).

Treaty process

Jim Prentice, Indian affairs minister, announced that he has plans to restart British Columbia's stalled treaty process (ibid., 25 June).

In March members of the Lheidli T'enneh First Nation voted not to accept a treaty. The treaty in question was the result of thirteen years of negotiations between the province, the First Nation, and the federal government and cost more than $1 billion. The rejection of the treaty will stall the province's efforts to open up large portions of eastern British Columbia for the forestry and energy sectors. Mike de Jong, Aboriginal relations and reconciliation minister, acknowledged that the treaty process was "intended in part to provide greater investment certainty for business" (*Globe and Mail*, 2 April).

The Musqueam First Nation and the BC government have reached an agreement-in-principle (AIP) that, if finalized, will resolve three outstanding court cases. The dispute dates back to the 2003 sale of golf course land to the University of British Columbia, the relocation and expansion of the River Casino to Richmond's Bridgepoint lands by the BC Lottery Corporation in 2005, and the costs of environmental clean-up for the Musqueam-owned site at the Celtic shipyards land in Vancouver (*Windspeaker*, Dec.).

On 25 July the Tsawwassen First Nation voted to accept the terms of a proposed treaty (*Globe and Mail*, 26 July). The treaty will be British Columbia's first negotiated treaty under the current land claims process, and it took fifteen years to complete. The treaty will also be BC's first urban treaty. The treaty will double the size of the Tsawwassen's existing reserve, provide $16 million to the community, give them a guaranteed share of the Fraser River salmon run, and make $36.6 million available in funding for various other programs (ibid.).

Mining

The decision of a federal-provincial government review panel on a proposed project by Northgate Minerals Corporation was released on 17 September. Northgate had proposed to establish a second mine (Kemess North) located about 450 kilometres northwest of Prince George. The $190 million project has the potential to preserve 500 jobs over the next eleven years; however, the project also includes the use of Duncan Lake in which to dump tailings. Tailings are small sand-like materials that are left when ore is processed. The panel's report concluded that "the economic and social benefits provided by the project, on balance, are outweighed by the risks of adverse environment, social, and cultural effects" (ibid., 18 Sept.).

Fish stocks

In June a gathering was held by ten BC First Nations to discuss the dramatic decline in the numbers of eulachon, a small herring-like fish. Over the last decade there has been a coast-wide collapse of the eulachon.

According to hereditary chief of the Kitasoo band, Percy Starr, the decline has had an enormous impact on his community because it is "very painful when you lose something that has been the backbone of your people. It's about the loss of a culture. The loss of eulachon is spiritual … This is the foundation of a people" (ibid., 20 June).

Firsts

Steven Point, former chief of the Skowkale First Nations and provincial court judge, was appointed British Columbia's first Aboriginal lieutenant governor on 1 October (ibid., 1 Oct.).

Sharon McIvor v. The Registrar, Indian and Northern Affairs Canada

On 8 June BC's Supreme Court released its decision in *McIvor v. The Registrar*. The decision stated that Section 6 of the 1985 amendment to the Indian Act, Bill C-31, violates the equality rights guaranteed under Section 15 of Canada's Charter of Rights and Freedoms (*Wawatay News*, 15 Nov.). Bill C-31 was passed following decades of Aboriginal women struggling to rectify blatantly discriminatory sections of the Indian Act. According to Bill C-31 no longer would an Aboriginal woman who married a non-Aboriginal man lose her "Indian" status; a woman who married a member of another band no longer automatically became a member of her husband's band; and bands could now define their own membership rules. However, Bill C-31 did not entirely rectify the problem, and in fact it created further issues. The Indian Act continues to privilege male descent and the amendment merely created multiple classes of Indian status. For example, there are those women who have been able to regain status under the Indian Act but not membership in their natal communities.

Sharon McIvor and her son challenged Bill C-31 under the charter. While McIvor had regained her status after 1985 she could only transmit "partial status" to her children, who in turn could not pass status to their children. In contrast, McIvor's brother, his wife, his children and grandchildren, who all share the same lineage as Sharon McIvor, have full Indian status. According to Gwen Brodsky, McIvor's lawyer, the "1985 act established a hierarchy for status registration that perpetuates sex discrimination" (ibid.).

The prairies

Métis Nation Saskatchewan (MNS)

Funding for the MNS has been restored as of 4 October. Operating funds for the organization had been suspended in June 2004 after Maynard Sonntag, Saskatchewan's minister of First Nations and Métis relations, had received a number of complaints regarding the MNS's May 2004 election. The federal government followed Sonntag's example and suspended its funding as well. Funding was reinstated after a new election was held on 27 June 2007 (*Windspeaker*, Nov.).

Oil and gas revenue

On 30 August the Supreme Court of Canada overruled the decision of a lower court that disallowed the Samson Cree and Ermineskin First Nations of Alberta from appealing a 2005 decision made by Justice Max Teitelbaum. The Samson Cree First Nation filed the original court case in 1989 with the Ermineskin First Nation, launching a separate but related suit in 1992. Both First Nations contended that the federal government's policy of paying interest on oil and gas royalties rather than investing it had cost the First Nations hundreds of millions of dollars. In December 2005 Teitelbaum ruled that the First Nations had treaty rights but not Aboriginal rights to the areas in question. Therefore, since Treaty 6 made no mention of mineral rights, a trust-like obligation that required the government to do its best with the monies did not exist.[14] However, Teitelbaum did order the transfer of the oil and gas revenues held in trust to be placed under the control of the bands (*First Nations Drum*, March 2009).

An AIP has been negotiated between the Stoney-Nakoda Nation and the federal government. The Stoney-Nakoda Nation allege that INAC mismanaged its natural resources, particularly from the Jumping Pound Gas Field, between 1978 and 1992 (*Windspeaker*, Dec.). It has taken fourteen years to arrive at the AIP, which cannot be finalized until the deal is approved through referendum by the Stoney-Nakoda people.

14 Fred R. Fenwick, "Samson Cree Trial Decision: 365 Days of Trial End in Disappointment for Samson Cree." *LawNow* 30, no. 5 (2006).

Bill C-31

The Sawridge and Tsuu T'ina bands are launching court challenges against Bill C-31, an amendment to the Indian Act. Bill C-35 was passed in 1985 to address long-standing gender discrimination in the Indian Act. The First Nations are challenging the legislation on the grounds that the "laws, customs and practices which governed the plaintiff's institution of marriage resulted in a tradition of post-marital residence which was patrilocal, or woman-follows-man" (*National Post*, 25 Jan.).

Beverly Jacobs, president of the Native Women's Association of Canada, said that the bands' claims are being driven by "faulty logic. Essentially they are seeking to maintain the terms of the Indian Act; one of the most racist pieces of legislation that exists in the world. Not only are they not even following their own customary traditional laws, they're using colonial law to justify their own decisions" (ibid.).

Interim Métis Harvesting Agreement (IMHA)

The IMHA is an agreement signed in 2003 between the government of Alberta and the Métis Nation of Alberta in response to the Supreme Court's Powley decision. Powley recognized the Aboriginal rights of historic Métis communities and established a legal test to determine those rights. The IMHA recognized that members of the MNA have the right to harvest for food by hunting, trapping, and fishing. The IMHA faces a great deal of opposition in Alberta from non-Aboriginal groups.

In 2005 Kipp Kelley, an Alberta Métis, was arrested for hunting without a licence. While Kelley claimed that according to the IMHA he did not need a licence, he was convicted on the basis that he was ineligible because he had not established his constitutional right under Powley. Kelley appealed his conviction. Court of Queen's Bench justice Gerald Verville set aside Kelley's conviction on the grounds that the trial judge had erred. Although the IMHA was not legally enforceable, the province had signed it in order to meet its obligations under the Powley ruling; therefore, it was reasonable for Métis people to believe that they were covered by the IMHA (ibid., 31 Jan.).

The Mackenzie Gas Project (MGP)

The Dene Tha' First Nation (DTFN) of northwestern Alberta reached a settlement agreement with the federal government regarding the Mackenzie Gas Project (MGP) in mid-July. The agreement will provide the DTFN with $25 million to address the social, economic, and cultural impact of the MGP on the DTFN. The agreement also provides the DTFN with greater input into the MGP (*Turtle Island News*, 23 July).

In November 2007 a Supreme Court ruling stated that the federal government did not meet "even the most minimal threshold of consultation" in its dealings with the Dene Tha' First Nation during environmental and regulatory discussion (*Globe and Mail*, 26 July).

Manitoba Human Rights Commission (MHRC)

The MHRC released a report in early December which found that Winnipeg's police force is racist and abusive and that "there is profound distrust of police among the city's black and Aboriginal communities" (ibid., 7 Dec.). Jerry Woods, chairman of the MHRC, said that they uncovered evidence of extremely disturbing crimes being carried out by the police, ranging from "starlight tours" (when individuals are driven to the outskirts of the city in the dead of winter and left to walk home without adequate clothing, sometimes freezing to death) to accounts of rape and other forms of brutality and violence. One anonymous witness recounted an incident where the police drove her to an isolated location where they took turns raping her (ibid.).

Ontario

Mining

In June Frontenac Ventures, a uranium-prospecting company, began drilling for uranium core samples on 5,000 hectares of land near Sharbot Lake, 50 kilometres north of Kingston (*National Post*, 1 Sept.). The land in question is currently under dispute by the Ardoch Algonquian First Nation and the Shabot Obaadjiwan First Nation, two Anishinaabe communities, located north of Kingston. The Ardoch and Shabot Obaadjiwan First Nations did not sign treaties with the federal government and therefore have not extinguished their Aboriginal rights to the area.

The Ontario Ministry of Northern Development and Mines granted Frontenac Ventures the right to mine in the region. Protestors then occupied the site beginning in June. In response Frontenac Ventures is suing the protestors for $77 million (ibid.). In late August Justice Gordon Thompson of the Ontario Superior Court issued an injunction calling for the arrest and removal of the protestors (*Globe and Mail*, 20 Aug.).

Compensation over Caledonia

The Indian affairs minister, Jim Prentice, announced on 29 March that the federal government will be giving Ontario $26.4 million to help offset the "extraordinary costs" the province has accrued during the occupation of the Douglass Creek Estates properties by the Six Nations of the Grand River since February 2006 (*National Post*, 20 March). Douglass Creek Estates, the land at the centre of this dispute, was under development by Henco Industries to build a residential subdivision – originally part of 385,000 hectares known as the "Haldimand Tract." The Crown granted the Haldimand Tract to the Six Nations in 1784 in recognition of their service to the British cause in the American Revolutionary War. Henco claims that the Six Nations (Haudenosaunee) sold this land to the Crown in 1841; the Haudenosaunee deny this claim and have been fighting for its return.

The $26 million will be used in the following ways: $15.8 million will help fund the province's purchase of the Douglass Creek Estates properties from Henco Industries, and the remaining $10.6 million will go towards paying for the cost of policing (ibid.). According to Prentice, "Canada's new government is committed to providing the province, under these unique and extraordinary circumstances, with the financial support to foster economic stability and promote public safety" (ibid.). Meanwhile, the dispute remains unresolved.

Kitchenuhmaykoosib Inninuwug First Nation (KI)

The KI First Nation, a northern fly-in community, had been involved in a legal battle for two years with Platinex Inc., a Toronto-based mining exploration company. Platinex filed a $10 billion suit against KI after drilling was halted by protestors in February 2006. The KI had objected to Platinex's decision to ignore their 2005 moratorium on exploration and resource extraction. The moratorium has been instituted by the KI as a result of Ontario's failure to deal with environmental and economic issues in the north (*Windspeaker*, Dec.).

During this battle with Platinex, KI has incurred over $600,000 in legal fees. According to KI councillor John Cutfeet, "Platinex's presence was illegal, and now we're subsidizing Ontario's duty to consult." Chief Donny Morris wrote a letter to Premier Dalton McGuinty which stated that the KI "cannot further afford your justice system" and that the strain has affected basic programs in the community such as housing and food (ibid.). In late October the KI were forced to release their legal counsel because the costs had become prohibitive.

After the KI left the courtroom, the judge granted motions from Platinex and Ontario that granted the company access to the region, banned the community from interfering, and offered a schedule starting 2 November for the project (ibid.). The KI have announced they will continue to resist.

Ipperwash

The report of the Ipperwash Inquiry was released on 31 May. The inquiry was established by the government of Ontario on 12 November 2003 in order to investigate the events surrounding the shooting death of Dudley George by the Ontario Provincial Police during a peaceful occupation of Ipperwash Provincial Park in 1995. Sidney Linden was appointed commissioner of the inquiry. Linden's report found that George's death was the result of growing frustration over the failure of the federal government to return confiscated Aboriginal land; a desire on the part of the Ontario government to quickly resolve the issue; and mistakes and poor communication on the part of the OPP. Most significantly, the report found that while former Ontario premier Mike Harris did not interfere directly with police operations, he did push for a "speedy conclusion" to the conflict and made racist comments. During a meeting with senior officials Harris was quoted as saying that he wanted the "fucking Indians out of the park" (*National Post*, 1 June).

After the report's release Linden went on to note that very little has been done to diffuse ongoing tensions over land claims and that the "flash points for aboriginal protest and occupations are very likely as intense today as they were at the time of Ipperwash. No one can predict where protests and occupations will occur, but the fundamental conditions and catalysts sparking such protests continue to exist in Ontario, more than a decade after Ipperwash" (ibid.).

Ontario premier Dalton McGuinty made a formal apology in the legislature and acknowledged the province's role in George's death: "On behalf of the people of Ontario, we apologize for the events that led to the loss of life. We deeply regret the death of Dudley George" (*Toronto Star*, 1 June).

Aboriginal affairs ministry

In June the Ontario Secretariat of Aboriginal Affairs was replaced with the Ministry of Aboriginal Affairs. The mandate of this new ministry is to "promote collaboration and coordination across ministries on Aboriginal policy and programs; set priorities for and track the progress of Ontario's Aboriginal agenda; enhance government's awareness of Aboriginal people, issues and best practices for consulting and engaging with Aboriginal people; work with the federal government to find ways to make the most of federal funding; help Aboriginal people to access Ontario government programs, services and information; reform the land claims process to help address historical grievances; and encourage diversity, especially representation of Aboriginal people, in the Ontario Public Service."[15] Michael Bryant was appointed head the ministry in late October following a Cabinet shuffle (*Globe and Mail*, 1 Nov.).

Quebec

James Bay Agreement

On 16 July the Cree of Northern Quebec and the federal and Quebec governments announced they had reached a deal that resolved disagreements dating back to the original 1975 James Bay and Northern Quebec Agreement. The James Bay Project is a series of hydroelectric dams (the first phase was called La Grande Complex) built in northern Quebec by Hydro-Québec, over an area populated by 5,000 Cree people. The Cree had serious reservations about the project in regard to land degradation, especially since the project would flood large regions of their traditional territory where they continued to hunt and fish. The Cree took the Quebec government to court, and in 1973 the court ruled that Robert Bourassa, the premier of Quebec, had to negotiate a fair agreement with the Cree.

The James Bay Agreement reached in 1975 provided the James Bay Cree and northern Quebec Inuit with $225 million in compensation and a degree of control over education, health, and social services (*National Post*, 17 July). However, the Cree accused the Quebec and federal governments of failing to live up to their promises and took them to court. The agreement reached in mid-July is worth $3.5 billion over the next fifty years in resource revenues in exchange for the Cree's consent for the new hydroelectric project and the cessation of three ongoing lawsuits. This agreement, which takes place in two phases, establishes the groundwork for Cree self-government. The Cree will gradually assume administrative control over federal responsibilities in the areas of justice and economic and social development (ibid.).

15 http://www.ontario.ca/government/about-ministry-aboriginal-affairs, accessed 27 June 2011.

Nunavik Regional Government

On 5 December an AIP was signed between Quebec, the federal government, and the Makivik Corporation.[16] The AIP establishes the framework for the Nunavik Regional Government (Nunavimmiut Aquvvinga). The Nunavik Regional Government will have the same authority and responsibilities normally covered by municipal governments. Essentially the regional government will be the result of the amalgamation of three current organizations: the Kativik Regional Government, the Kativik School Board, and the Nunavik Regional Board of Health and Social Services (*Nunatsiaq News*, 14 Dec.). The Nunavik Regional Government will be subject to the authority of the Quebec National Assembly and the Parliament of Canada.

The Naskapi Nation of Kawachikamach, situated in northeastern Quebec and comprised of approximately 850 status Indians, has raised serious concerns over the AIP creating the Nunavik Regional Government. The Naskapi are worried an Inuit-dominated government will ignore their interests (*Globe and Mail*, 22 Aug.).

The Maritimes

Indian status

An agreement was reached between the federal government and the Federation of Newfoundland Indians (FNI) that grants the Mi'kmaq of Newfoundland formal status under the Indian Act. When Newfoundland joined Confederation in 1949 no provision was made for the Aboriginal population. Recognition under the Indian Act will provide the Mi'kmaq of Newfoundland and Labrador with access to federal programs and services. Canada has made funding available for social and health programs for the Mi'kmaq on an ad hoc basis (*La nation autochtone du Quebec*, 30 Nov.).

Atlantic Integrated Commercial Fisheries Initiative (AICFI)

In the federal budget the government earmarked $20 million to be spent over two years to "support capacity building in [the] Mi'kmaq

16 Makivik was established in 1978 in accordance with the terms negotiated in the 1975 James Bay and Northern Quebec Agreement. The organization is the legal representative of the Inuit people of northern Quebec and is responsible for land and financial management.

and Maliseet First Nations in the Maritimes and the Gaspe Region of Quebec (MMFNs) commercial fishing enterprises" affected by the 1999 Marshall Decision (*Turtle Island News*, 30 Nov.). The MMFN and Ottawa have been in discussion since March over how that money will be spent and what the programs will look like.

In late November the federal government announced a new program: the Atlantic Integrated Commercial Fisheries Initiative. According to the federal government the AICFI is intended to help Mi'kmaq and Maliseet First Nations "develop governance and business management skills, build capacity in their commercial fisheries operation and have a more effective voice in fisheries co-management. The long-term goal of AICFI is to integrate fully the commercial fisheries in Atlantic Canada, where all participants work cooperatively to achieve long-term resource sustainability."[17]

The North

Inuvialuit Final Agreement (IFA)

In late October Auditor General Sheila Fraser released a report criticizing INAC for failing to meet its obligations under the IFA. Signed in 1984, the IFA granted the region's Inuit (essentially the northernmost portion of the Northwest Territories) control over their own land and resources (*Globe and Mail*, 23 March). It has been twenty-three years since the agreement was signed and yet it remains only partially executed. In particular Fraser singled out the following: the failure of INAC to effectively coordinate federal responsibilities; the failure of INAC to develop a system for tracking how multiple government departments fulfil their obligations; and the failure of INAC to monitor the progress of implementing the agreement.[18]

17 http://www.dfo-mpo.gc.ca/fm-gp/aboriginal-autochtones/marshall/timeline-chonologie-eng.htm (accessed 20 June 2011).

18 Ibid. (accessed 29 June 2011).

CAREY HILL[19]

British Columbia

The year was a green one for British Columbia. The throne speech, budget, and many of the year's activities addressed climate change. It was also green if one equates that with prosperity. BC led Canada in job growth and opened the year with a 4.3 per cent unemployment rate. Finally, while the mining industry showed considerable promise, the forestry industry struggled with problems of attracting skilled workers and a protracted coastal strike.

A landmark Supreme Court of Canada decision regarding BC's Bill 29 affected the whole country and meant that collective bargaining was now recognized as a Charter right. Another landmark decision of the BC Supreme Court found that strikes for political purposes contravene the province's labour code.

Even though the Bill 29 decision was a major disappointment for the Campbell Liberals, the year was generally positive. For example, in April it was noted they had achieved a seventeen-point lead in the polls over the NDP Opposition party. BC premier Gordon Campbell attributed his party's popularity to the booming economy and willingness to consult on issues such as health care and climate change. Moreover, in the fall, the finance minister announced that BC's projected surplus for the year would be about $1.6 billion, a considerable increase over the $400 million originally projected.

The year was an important one for First Nations peoples in British Columbia. BC's first-ever Aboriginal lieutenant governor was named by Prime Minister Stephen Harper. The First Nations Education Act was passed, and the chief of the Tsawwassen Nation addressed the legislature, only the second non-government official to do so.

19 Thanks to Shannon Derrick for research assistance.

Throne speech

The throne speech was delivered on 13 February by Iona Campagnolo and focused on "securing the future" with a promise to tackle global warming, work in partnership with First Nations, and tackle persistent social issues such as homelessness.

The throne speech introduced the Pacific Leadership Agenda including the following actions:

- to lead Canada in partnership with First Nations;
- to tackle the challenges of global warming and unplanned urban sprawl;
- to increase affordable housing, reduce homelessness, and help those who cannot help themselves;
- to improve quality, choice, and accountability in our two most important public services – education and health care; and
- to open up Canada's Pacific Gateway and strengthen our economic competitiveness.

Budget

With revenue about $2.5 billion more than expected in 2006–7 and wearing old red shoes, the finance minister Carole Taylor offered a budget that moved the Campbell Liberals to the political centre. The budget offered a significant personal income tax cut, a housing strategy, and a green agenda, although the last was largely unfunded at budget time.

The largest portion of the budget was a personal income tax cut with a minimum 10 per cent cut in personal income taxes for those individuals earning up to $108,000. With this tax cut, BC became the Canadian province with the lowest personal income taxes for those earning up to $108,000. The budget also helped those on welfare by increasing the rates for single employable individuals (*Vancouver Sun*, 21 Feb.). The Opposition NDP criticized the governing Liberals for spending the largest portion of the budget on tax cuts, especially while at the same time noting that the $13.1 billion in health-care spending was unsustainable.

BC's overall health budget was called "Unsustainable" by the finance minister in her budget speech. It was noted that spending was up over 50 per cent since 2000. The $13.1 billion projected was a 7 per cent rise over the previous year (ibid.).

The budget also included a three-year plan to improve access to housing. The finance minister explained that the actions were meant to improve "access to a safe, appropriate and affordable place to call home." Commentators called this a "something for everybody approach" as the housing strategy involved an increase in shelter beds for the homeless, increased assistance for low-income renters as well as larger breaks for first-time home buyers and an increase in the upper limit of the homeowner grant to $950,000 (ibid.). Others such as BC Federation of Labour's Jim Sinclair contrasted the amount spent on housing and homelessness with the considerable tax cuts, calling the measures "a drop in the bucket" in comparison (ibid.).

The climate change strategy in the budget was largely unfunded with only $103 million over four years set aside. It was announced that a new energy plan would be unveiled in the weeks following the budget. A major component of the climate change strategy in the budget was a requirement that all new electricity projects in BC have zero net greenhouse gas emissions with 90 per cent of total electricity generation being clean or renewable (ibid., 29 Dec.). The BC Business Council was highly critical of the green agenda and the budget more generally. Spokesperson Jock Finlayson said there was little in the budget for business growth (ibid., 21 Feb.).

Disclosure requirements in BC's budget law required that the government complete paperwork and explain its reasons for not including all green program spending in the budget (ibid., 22 Feb.). It was explained that the decision to address climate change as a significant focus of the budget was made too late in the budget process for all spending to be included. Moreover, two health authorities' budgets were not signed off by the health boards as these authorities had new chairs. The reason for the new chairs was that Vancouver Coastal's chair, Trevor Johnstone, was fired and Fraser Health's Keith Purchase resigned in response (ibid.). Some $360 million was set aside for contingencies and necessary spending to be disclosed at the ministry's quarterly updates on the budget (ibid.). The rules also required the government to provide a three-year fiscal plan with the budget. In this case, the health budget did not receive this attention; it only addressed increased wages and benefits and did not address new services or increased costs in providing existing services. Finally, the budget did not include expected cost overruns for the Vancouver convention centre expansion project. By July the convention centre's budget had increased to $883.2 million, considerably more than the $565 million originally budgeted when the project began in 2004 (ibid., 29 Dec.).

Energy plan (climate change agenda)

An energy plan was introduced by the Campbell Liberals as part of their budget speech. While initially the plan appeared to be introduced with some haste, the details of the plan became clearer as the year went on. The plan included a reduction in greenhouse gas emissions by at least 33 per cent below current levels by 2020, putting BC's greenhouse gas emissions at 10 per cent below 1990 levels by 2020 (*Prince George Citizen*, 17 Feb.). In addition, the Campbell Liberals aimed to reduce greenhouse gas emissions from the oil and gas industry to 2000 levels by 2016, including zero flaring at producing wells and production facilities (ibid.).

As well, BC would be the first jurisdiction in North America requiring 100 per cent carbon sequestration for coal-fired projects. This requirement was expected to put an end to a $500 million coal-fired plant in Tumbler Ridge, near Prince George. In introducing the plan, the premier was optimistic and passionate, explaining, "Let's conserve, let's not be wasteful and, by doing that, I think we will find we get an economy that's more efficient, more effective and will have far, far less impact on our environment and we'll have an economy that's more productive and more competitive. I think if we're smart about this, I think we'll see this as being a major thrust of our economy that moves over the next couple of decades in British Columbia" (ibid.).

Concerns were raised that the energy plan did not mesh with other plans of the government including an expansion of transportation, mining, and the oil and gas sectors. Campbell remained optimistic, explaining that the challenge presented an opportunity to be green in the years ahead. Interestingly, Campbell personally changed some of his behaviours to address climate change, including his choice of hybrid car and low-energy lights (ibid.). Some on the industry side such as the president of the Mining Association of BC, Michael McPhee, suggested that the targets were unrealistic. By contrast, the BC Sustainable Energy Association applauded the plan (ibid.). West Coast Environmental Law was more cautious, suggesting the plan was a first step and that targets needed to be made legally binding.

Health

Health policy in BC in 2007 was characterized by a January announcement of an infusion of funds to the system, rising budget deficits, efforts to innovate, and consultations the Campbell government undertook across the province. As the finance minister warned in her budget speech, the health budget had increased by 7 per cent in just one year. This point was made against a backdrop in which the board chairman of the Vancouver Coastal Health Authority was fired and the Fraser Health Authority chair resigned in protest of the decision.

In January finance minister Carole Taylor announced an $885 million increase to the BC health-care budget, bringing the total to $13.1 million. Instead of waiting for budget day to make the announcement, Taylor said it was needed earlier as these were "extraordinary times" (*Vancouver Sun*, 25 Jan.). At the same time as new funding for health care was announced, Trevor Johnstone was removed as chair of the Vancouver Coastal Health Authority (VCH) because of the authority's deficit of $40 million (ibid.). In the lead-up to the announcement VCH had also started cancelling surgeries and closing some operating rooms before the health ministry said they were not allowed to reduce their deficit by reducing services to patients. Of the six health authorities, only Vancouver Coastal delivered a deficit budget. Johnstone's replacement was David Thompson, a former CEO of Teck Cominco and former co-chair of the BC Competition council with no health-care experience (ibid.).

In the budget the Liberal government set aside $100 million for a health innovation fund. The request for proposals addressed three main areas: (1) ways to reduce congestion in hospital emergency rooms; (2) improvements in primary care, particularly management of chronic disease; (3) and the use of budgetary incentives to improve productivity and outcomes within the system (ibid., 4 Aug.). Approximately one hundred proposals were received from across the six provincial health authorities. Chairman George Morfitt, former auditor general, and an independent committee reviewed the proposals after they were vetted by the health authorities. Fifty projects were funded from across the entire province.

An example of a successful project from the health innovation fund involved changing the way hospitals are paid, re-aligning incentives. Normally hospitals receive block funding and budgets are based on expected costs with limitations to services according to what the budget affords. One project tests the notion that performance bonuses for desired behaviour will lead to better and less expensive services. For example, hospitals would get paid based on what they do or produce such as finding a bed for a patient. This activity would entail a performance bonus.

Labour

While the health sector tried innovation, in labour it was another year of unrest and protracted strikes, this time by forestry workers and municipal workers. In late July, about 7,000 striking forestry workers shut down BC's $2 billion coastal forestry industry. The workers were demanding changes to hours of work and severance pay for partial closures and had concerns about contracting-out language. The strike finally came to an end in October with the narrowest of votes in favour of ending the strike and accepting the deal. The deal was struck between the United Steelworkers and Forest Industrial Relations, which represents thirty-one companies. The deal offered severance for workers losing their jobs in partial mill closings, as well as a 7 per cent wage increase over three years (*National Post*, 23 Oct.).

City workers in Vancouver also walked off the job in July. Vancouver's civic workers strike lasted three months, or eighty-eight days. The city saved $1.8 million on garbage collection during the strike (*Province*, 25 Nov.). Canadian Union of Public Employees (CUPE) Local 1004 – 2,000 members strong representing garbage collection workers as well as park employees – eventually settled for a 17.5 per cent wage hike over five years, a $1,000 signing bonus, improved benefits, and the establishment of a joint committee to address the assignment of overtime (Canadian Press, 15 Oct.). Once the strike was over, Mayor Sam Sullivan raised the possibility of contracting out garbage collection, stating that several citizens had come forward with this suggestion.

Vancouver's civic workers expressed some disappointment that the strike dragged out while other municipalities settled earlier with their unions. Mayor Sam Sullivan explained that CUPE had made it a personal strike, calling it "Sam's strike" and airing television ads valued at $30,000 (ibid.). He also explained that he had garbage thrown at his home and received negative comments from the picket line.

The other CUPE union local, Local 15, representing inside workers also agreed to a settlement. They, too, achieved a 17.5 per cent wage hike over five years and a $1,000 signing bonus. In addition, they also won contract language addressing contracting out, harassment, whistle-blowing, and job reclassification (*Times-Colonist*, 10 Oct.).

In addition to strikes, there were also significant court decisions in 2007 affecting labour unions and collective bargaining rights. In March the BC Supreme Court ruled that protests during working hours would be considered violations of the collective agreement. The BC Teachers' Federation and the Hospital Employees' Union argued that protests were protected speech. The Supreme Court found that strikes for political purposes contravene the province's labour code.

In June another landmark decision was issued, this time by the Supreme Court of Canada, regarding Bill 29, legislation passed by the Campbell Liberals in 2002. The ruling may have the result of giving some 8,000 former health-care workers including nurses, social workers, housekeepers, cooks, and security personnel back their jobs and costing taxpayers $1 billion. The Supreme Court ruled that the government should have consulted with unions before issuing Bill 29; the bill violated the workers' right to "good faith bargaining." This was the first time collective bargaining was enshrined as part of the Charter of Rights and Freedoms. The court gave BC one year to ameliorate the situation and address its concerns.

After losing in two lower BC courts, the Hospital Employees' Union (HEU) took their case to the Supreme Court of Canada backed by the BC Federation of Labour and the Canadian Labour Congress. The Supreme Court sided 6–1 in favour of the HEU. Judy Darcy, head of the HEU, explained, "This is a victory for public health care. Bill 29 was bad public policy and created chaos and havoc for patients and health-care workers" (ibid., 3 Aug.). Nevertheless Darcy also noted that as a result of Bill 29 privatizing, "In the past three weeks, 650 health-care workers have lost their jobs. We are calling on the government to impose an immediate moratorium on layoffs."

Bill 29 allowed health-care workers with legal union contracts to be fired and replaced with much cheaper workers who no longer worked for the government but for private business. For example, workers who were being paid $18 per hour in government wages were replaced by workers who were paid $10 by private companies, some multinationals. The bill effectively tore up the contracts of over 45,000 health-care workers.

In response to the ruling, the BC government met with unions in August to discuss next steps. Talks led by the associate deputy minister and including the Hospital Employees' Union, the BC Government and Service Employees' Union and the BC Nurses Union occurred.

For most of the year, union raids occurred within the film industry. International Alliance of Theatrical and Stage Employees (IATSE) raided the Association of Canadian Film Craftspeople (ACFC West) on four occasions, once successfully. One of the ironic aspects of these raids was that many members held cards in both unions. Thirty raids took place between the spring and late fall; most of them involving ACFC West and the BC Council of Film Unions, which represent

IATSE Local 891 (technicians), IATSE Local 669 (camera crews), and Teamsters Union Local 155 (drivers, animal handlers) (*Vancouver Sun*, 9 Nov.).

Aboriginal affairs

October was a month of several important milestones for First Nations peoples in British Columbia. The First Nations Education Act was passed, a chief of the Tsawwassen band addressed the legislature, and a First Nations person was sworn in as British Columbia's lieutenant governor.

In October the BC government passed the First Nations Education Act permitting all 203 First Nations bands in BC to take over jurisdiction of their on-reserve kindergarten to Grade 12 education systems. As long as their systems are consistent with the provincial curriculum for core courses leading to graduation, First Nations can make laws over education on their reserves and operate their own schools (*Province*, 20 Dec.). The First Nations Education Authority was also established by act. The education authority is a regulatory body for teacher certification, school certification, and curriculum and exam standards (ibid.).

Also in October, Kim Baird, chief of the 372-member Tsawwassen band, addressed the legislature to explain what BC's first deal reached through the BC treaty process meant to the band. Only one other non-government official, Joe Gosnell of the Nisga'a, had ever addressed the legislature in the same manner. In order to address the legislature in this way, MLAs must give unanimous consent for a "stranger" to approach the bar (ibid., 15 Oct.). One of the NDP MLAs, Michael Sather, said he would vote against the treaty and was suspended (ibid.). The treaty is valued at $120 million including cash, a share of the salmon fishery, and 724 hectares of prime agricultural land (ibid.). Sather's concerns with the treaty focused on issues surrounding the land as it removed land from the Agricultural Land Reserve (ibid.).

Perhaps the most auspicious event for First Nations peoples in British Columbia in October was the swearing in of Lieutenant Governor Steven Point, former provincial court judge and head of the BC Treaty Commission. He replaced Iona Campagnolo who had been in the post since 2001. He was the first Aboriginal person appointed to the post. At age twenty-three he had become BC's youngest chief ever, elected by the Skowkale First Nation. He graduated with a legal degree in 1985 and served as tribal chairman of Stó:lō First Nation from 1994 to 1999, when he became a judge. The legislature's lobby murals depicting First

Nations people as submissive and in potentially degrading ways were covered for the length of the ceremony (*Globe and Mail*, 6 Oct.). It was also noted that this was a historic event in light of the fact that the first lieutenant governor of BC, Joseph Trutch, was no friend of Aboriginal peoples. The change that this represented was remarked upon by federal Indian affairs minister Chuck Strahl, who explained that the moment sent "a great message … Symbolic things change people's perceptions. What it does is it put people's head in a different space" (*National Post*, 2 Oct.). A member of the leadership council and First Nations Summit political executive, Hupacasath chief Judith Sayers explained, "Iona was incredibly supportive of First Nations and I just love her for it but Steve is actually going to be First Nations" (*Times-Colonist*, 5 Sept.).

Forestry

While the protracted strike by forestry workers was challenging for the industry, it was also plagued by a labour shortage during the year that resulted in the decision to close two forestry education programs. Due to declining enrolment, the British Columbia Institute of Technology (BCIT) announced it would close two forestry programs. Demand for graduates from the forestry industry exists but there is a lack of interest on the part of students (*Vancouver Sun*, 3 Feb.). For thirty years, the two-year forest eco-systems program has been operated by BCIT and has seating for twenty-five students, but this year only fourteen students enrolled. Similarly, the one-year forest technician program has a capacity for sixty students but only twenty-two enrolled. A director at the Association of BC Forest Professionals explained that the need for forest technologists and technicians is at an all-time high as evidenced by the mountain pine beetle infestation (ibid.). The two programs will be terminated after the last of the current students graduate in 2008.

The BC Forest Safety Council ombudsman, Roger Harris, also noted the labour shortage in his report in January and expressed concerns about worker safety (*Province*, 18 Jan.). He emphasized the challenge of recruiting and suggested that there should be a classification and certification of job skills in the industry to address safety issues and attract new workers (ibid.).

The BC government announced $11.5 million in funding for the forest industry in April. Some $9.9 million of the total will be provided through Forestry Innovation Investment to a range of marketing activities with the funds distributed to several industry groups (*Vancouver Sun*, 14 April).

The Ministry of Forest released a report in September suggesting that 40 per cent of British Columbia's pine forest would be killed by the end of the year by the mountain pine beetle and that the pine beetle was moving into the southern half of the province. The infestation was expected to continue for the next twenty years and leave behind 445 million cubic metres of unharvested dead pine in the forests (ibid., 18 Sept.). The economic value of this dead pine and the associated costs to the industry represent $32.5 billion in direct losses while losses in stumpage fees to the province are estimated at between $4.5 billion and $6.5 billion.

Late in 2007 mill cutbacks and closures were announced. Canfor Corp laid off 300 workers as a result of its cutting back to two shifts from three at four interior sawmills. AbitibiBowater announced the closure of its Mackenzie newsprint mill and two related sawmills resulting in 300 to 400 job losses.

Mining

In sharp contrast to the forestry industry, the mining industry celebrated a year of gains. Companies spent almost $146 million on exploration in 2007, greater than the previous year. Spending in exploration investment was up 57 per cent over 2006 and over 1,300 per cent from when the Liberals first took office in 2001 (*Alaska Highway News*, 23 Jan. 2008). Twenty-three new mine development proposals had been received by the mining minister.

Trade, Investment and Labour Mobility Agreement (TILMA)

In terms of trade among provinces, BC and Alberta signed the Trade, Investment and Labour Mobility Agreement (TILMA) in 2006. It came into force in April 2007. Its purpose was to streamline business between the two provinces. Ontario expressed some interest in joining the agreement (*Vancouver Sun*, 29 Dec.). Critics of TILMA suggest it will negatively affect local governments' ability to make laws. Saskatchewan was invited to be a partner in TILMA, but it announced it would not sign on and would focus on achieving reforms to the Agreement on Internal Trade that applies across Canada (*Calgary Herald*, 2 Aug.).

Olympics

In July the RCMP announced that they will require more funds for the 2010 Winter Olympics security than the $175 million that was budgeted. In comparison the 2002 Salt Lake Olympics cost double that figure (*Province*, 29 July). Areas where additional funds may be needed included for the athletes villages in Whistler and Vancouver, where no money was set aside for security. This was not the first time this concern had been articulated. In 2003 the auditor general, Wayne Strelioff, warned that the Games may cost more than the figure that was budgeted. The RCMP made the announcement after the CBC obtained documents using Access to Information that noted concerns with the security budget for the 2010 Winter Olympics (*Vancouver Sun*, 27 July). The documents explained that originally the RCMP expected to protect twenty-one venues but there were more than one hundred under their jurisdiction (ibid.). Other factors that contributed to rising costs include the need to provide security clearance checks for more than 216,000 volunteers and employees associated with the 2010 Games (ibid.).

Pickton trial

The trial of Robert (Willie) Pickton began on 30 January 2006 and ended on 11 December 2007. Pickton was charged with twenty-seven counts of first-degree murder involving women sex-trade workers from Vancouver's downtown east side. In order to reduce the pressure and commitment on the part of the jury, the number of counts addressed in the trial was reduced to six counts of murder.

Pickton was found guilty in the second degree of all six counts and sentenced to life in prison without the possibility of parole for twenty-five years. The defence lawyer, Peter Ritchie, asked the jury to consider a parole eligibility of fifteen to twenty years as Pickton had no prior criminal record, had no history of violence, and was hard-working (*Times-Colonist*, 12 Dec.). BC Supreme Court justice Jim Williams explained the rationale for the sentence:

> This is the rare case that properly warrants the maximum. There were six separate events [murders] that took place over a period of four years. It necessarily follows that these events occurred serially. In that sense this case is markedly different from any other case to which I have been referred.

Speaking specifically to Pickton, Justice Williams said, "Mr. Pickton, there is really nothing that I can say to adequately express the revulsion the community feels about these killings" (ibid.). The trial revealed that Robert Pickton had "preyed on drug-addicted prostitutes he had lured to his isolated pig farm near Vancouver" (*Globe and Mail*, 11 Dec.).

The victims included Georgina Papin, Marnie Frey, Brenda Wolfe, Sereena Abotsway, Mona Wilson, and Andrea Joesbury who disappeared from Vancouver's downtown east side between 1997 and 2001. Their families cheered when the judge read the verdict from the jury in the case (ibid.).

In terms of next steps, a hearing was scheduled for 24 January 2008 to obtain a date for a second trial on an additional twenty first-degree murder counts. Late in the year, BC attorney general Wally Oppal suggested that a second trial might be redundant. He explained, "At the end of the day the governing question would be: Is it in the public interest to have a second prosecution given the fact that he is now serving six life terms?" (ibid.). He noted further, "These are difficult cases to run, they take a toll emotionally on all persons involved" (ibid.). The BC attorney general said that the decision on whether to proceed with the second trial would be made by the BC criminal justice branch (ibid.).

Economy

The economic outlook at year end was positive. The year had seen record mineral exploration and leadership in terms of job growth. For example, in January, the provincial unemployment rate hit a thirty-year low of 4.3 per cent (*Vancouver Sun*, 29 Dec.). On the downside, the hot economy meant that employers continued to have trouble finding skilled workers.

Business bankruptcies as well as consumer bankruptcies continued to fall in 2007. Business bankruptcies fell from 587 to 470 in 2007 while consumer bankruptcies fell from 7,022 to 6,661 (*BC Stats*). Notably, agriculture, forestry, and fishing bankruptcies were down significantly.

In terms of local successes, the yoga wear retailer lululemon athletica went public in July, selling shares for US$18 and closing on its first day at US$28. By year end the shares were trading at over US$47 (*Vancouver Sun*, 29 Dec.).

In September finance minister Carole Taylor announced that the forecasted provincial surplus would be four times what was originally estimated, $1.6 billion up from $400 million as tabled in February's budget. She explained that the extremely positive forecast was due to increases in corporate and personal income tax revenues, increases in federal transfer funds, money from federal trust funds, and the sale of a Vancouver mall by the Crown-owned insurance corporation (*Prince George Citizen*, 15 Sept.).

HAROLD JANSEN

Alberta

A quick glance at Alberta in 2007 would not have indicated that much was changing in the province. The province's economy continued to grow, the same party was in power, and there was no figure to challenge the government's grip on Alberta. Underneath the surface, though, things were in motion. The governing Conservatives appeared to be running into their first real political difficulties since the early 1990s, as Premier Ed Stelmach seemed to be having trouble connecting with voters, particularly in Calgary, Alberta's largest city. The province also engaged in a lengthy debate over the development of its signature oil and gas industry, asking about the fair balance between public and private shares of the proceeds from these resources. These developments indicated that there were some deep currents moving underneath the seemingly still waters of Alberta politics.

A shaky dynasty

For the governing Progressive Conservatives, 2007 brought a significant milestone. In September, the party passed the Social Credit government of 1935 to 1971 to become the longest-serving dynasty in the history of the province. The Conservative government celebrated thirty-six consecutive years in power. Although achieving this milestone was undoubtedly a noteworthy accomplishment, the celebration was relatively muted. The reason for this was that the party's popularity was diminishing and the Conservatives were suffering some setbacks that made their grip on power look surprisingly precarious.

The Conservatives' struggles could be traced back to the 2004 election, in which then premier Ralph Klein appeared tired and arrogant. After winning re-election, Klein's government appeared to be listless, with no clear policy direction. In particular, the government did not seem to know how to manage the unprecedented economic growth being experienced by the province. The government's reflex appeared to be to use its large surpluses to throw large sums of money at any problem that appeared. These concerns, as well as Klein's protracted departure from the top job, led delegates to the 2006 Progressive Conservative convention to only tepidly endorse Klein's leadership such that Klein had to hasten his departure. In December 2006, Ed Stelmach became leader of the party.

As premier, Stelmach was an interesting contrast with Klein. He seemed more adept and comfortable with the details of policy than his predecessor, but Stelmach lacked Klein's ease with the media and his communication skills. The result was a series of polls over the course of the year that showed the governing Conservatives declining in popularity. Early in the year, polls showed that roughly 50 per cent of voters intended to vote Progressive Conservative, but by the middle of the year, that number had dropped to around 40 per cent. In most other provinces with a multiparty system, that would be a respectable number, but in the context of Alberta's one-party dominant political system, this was noteworthy. At the end of October, in the heat of the debate over the royalty rates charged to oil and gas companies (addressed later), only one-third of Albertans indicated they intended to vote Progressive Conservative (*Calgary Herald*, 1 Nov.). The party rebounded back to the 40 per cent range a month later, but it was clear that the party's grip on power looked less dominant than it had in the past.

Stelmach's inability to project a powerful image for himself was at least partly responsible for the government's slide, as his mounting disapproval ratings through the year showed. The party's problems had a decidedly regional cast, however. Since the mid-1980s, Edmonton had been decidedly less hospitable territory for the governing party than Calgary. For twenty-eight of the thirty-six years the party had been in power, the premier had come from Calgary. Stelmach was from outside Edmonton and one common criticism of him and his government was that they were out of touch with the concerns of urban Alberta and particularly its largest city, Calgary. The polls throughout the year showed that Calgarians' opinions of the government were similar to those of their northern neighbours, a remarkable regional partisan realignment.

One Calgarian who certainly seemed to disapprove of the government's performance was Mayor Dave Bronconnier, who emerged as the government's most vocal critic in 2007. The issue of provincial funding for municipal infrastructure in April's provincial budget sparked the row between the city of Calgary and the province. In the budget, the province provided $127 million in additional infrastructure funding for the city but put certain conditions on the money, such as requiring a portion of it to be spent on affordable housing. Bronconnier said that the strings attached to the funding meant that Calgary could no longer go ahead and expand its light rail transit system to the city's west side as it intended. Bronconnier claimed that this broke Stelmach's promise to better fund infrastructure needs in cities. He dismissed the budget as "hocus-pocus, booga-booga economics" (ibid., 20 April). For his part Stelmach described himself as being "really ticked" at the mayor (ibid., 2 May). A meeting between municipal affairs minister Roy Danyluk and Bronconnier in late May did little to settle the dispute. It took a face-to-face meeting in early September between Bronconnier and Stelmach to settle the dispute as the two men agreed to a ten-year funding plan.

Another tangible issue that seemed to put the interests of city dwellers against those of the government was the thorny issue of rent controls. Calgary's booming economy and housing market had led to steep rent increases. The Canada Mortgage and Housing Corporation reported that the average rent increase in Calgary had been 18 per cent in 2006, the highest in Canada (ibid., 13 Feb.). Besides that, many tenants were seeing their units being converted into condominium units as landlords sought to cash in on low interest rates and the hot housing market. Premier Stelmach appointed an Affordable Housing Task Force to investigate the problem and to report back. The task force recommended temporary rent controls to alleviate the pressure on tenants. In April, the government rejected rent controls and promised instead to directly fund affordable housing. A poll done in May, however, demonstrated that both homeowners and renters in Calgary overwhelmingly backed the imposition of rent controls (ibid., 20 May). The government sought to limit rent increases to one per year and required landlords to give one year's notice before converting rental units to condominiums, but these reforms fell short of the demands of many in the cities.

At the height of this seeming conflict between the interests of the provincial government and the residents and government of its largest city, the province held two by-elections that served as a litmus test of the popularity of the provincial government. On 15 January former premier Ralph Klein and former deputy premier Shirley McLellan had both resigned their seats in the legislature. Premier Stelmach did not immediately call by-elections for their vacated seats but decided to hold off until May, when he called the by-elections for 12 June. Klein's Calgary-Elbow seat was the one of primary interest. The Conservatives first won Calgary-Elbow in 1971, when the party first came to power. Since then, the district had never once elected an MLA from any other party, even during the party's electoral difficulties in 1993. Stelmach's political troubles in Calgary, however, made this the district to watch.

The Conservatives nominated Brian Heninger, a local businessman. During the campaign, Heninger was often critical of Premier Stelmach and the direction of the government (ibid., 12 June). The Liberals nominated Craig Cheffins, an employee of Mount Royal College, as their candidate. Heninger took only 38.3 per cent of the vote, a significant drop from the 51.5 per cent Klein won in 2004. Cheffins, on the other hand, won 45.8 per cent of the vote and took the seat for the Liberals.

The election result in Drumheller-Stettler was never in doubt. The Liberals were so weak there that they had not even nominated a candidate in the district in the 2004 general election, when McClellan won 65 per cent of the vote. In the by-election, the Conservatives nominated Jack Hayden, a local politician. Hayden saw his vote drop from that enjoyed by McClellan, but he still won the seat easily with 57.6 per cent of the vote, well ahead of the 13.7 per cent of the vote earned by the second-place Liberals.

Taken together, the by-election results laid out the electoral challenge facing the government. In the rural areas like Drumheller-Stettler, the party appeared to be holding its support. Stelmach's rural background and largely rural Cabinet appeared to appeal to those areas. In the large cities, however, the Conservatives appeared to be in more trouble. The Calgary-Elbow by-election raised questions about whether the government could continue to count on the support of the province's largest city. Several Calgary-area Conservative MLAs publicly wondered as much in the days immediately after the by-election result (ibid., 14 June).

The clearest sign that Stelmach was getting the message came in an announcement of changes to Cabinet on 22 June. Stelmach appointed three new members to his Cabinet, two from Calgary and one from Edmonton. Calgary's Cindy Ady became the minister in charge of tourism promotion, while Yvonne Fritz became the minister in charge of housing and urban development. Edmonton's Gene Zwozdesky became the minister in charge of capital planning for the Stelmach government. Calgary's Ron Stevens assumed the post of deputy premier in addition to his existing responsibilities as minister of justice and attorney general. The moves boosted the representation from Alberta's large urban centres and also increased the number of women in Cabinet, another criticism of Stelmach's first Cabinet.

Despite the apparent difficulties Stelmach and his party were having in connecting with the electorate, the encouraging news for the party is that the Opposition parties were faring little better. In a poll taken at the end of November, the provincial Liberals managed to cross the 20 per cent threshold (ibid., 2 Dec.) for the first time in 2007. The rest of the Opposition support was fragmented between the New Democratic Party, the Alberta Greens, and the Alberta Alliance. The partisan landscape became even more crowded in October with the formation of the Wildrose Party, which sought to provide yet another right-of-centre alternative to the Conservatives. The failure of any of the Opposition parties or leaders to capitalize on the evident dissatisfaction with the Conservatives meant that the government's slump in popularity did not necessarily mean an imminent change in government. This had to be encouraging news for an otherwise beleaguered government as it faced the prospect of a likely election in 2008.

The royalty review

Without question, the single biggest public policy debate in Alberta in 2007 was over the royalty regime that governed the province's oil and gas industry. As oil reached record high prices in 2007, many Albertans began to question whether the provincial government – the steward of the resource on behalf of the people of Alberta – was getting its fair share of the profits. Despite the dramatic rise in the price of oil and the corresponding increase in exploration and oil development, Alberta was not seeing correspondingly large increases in its royalties. There were two issues that underlay the problem. The first was that much of the Alberta government's royalty revenue came from natural gas, not oil. Unlike oil, natural gas prices were relatively stagnant, and it was a depleting resource. The second problem was that most of the new oil production was coming from the oil sands, which was governed by a very different royalty regime than conventional oil. Oil sands companies only paid a 1 per cent royalty until they paid off the capital costs of their projects. This policy was brought in when prices were lower as an incentive for companies to make the huge investments in capital needed to develop the oil sands. As the world of $100-a-barrel oil approached, more Albertans began to question whether this type of royalty regime was in the best interest of Albertans.

During the 2006 Conservative leadership contest, Ed Stelmach promised to take a look at royalties if he was elected leader of the party and became premier. In February, Stelmach made good on that promise and announced the appointment of a panel to review Alberta's royalty regime. The six-member panel comprised three economists and three people drawn from the business community. The chair of the committee,

Bill Hunter, ran a consulting company and was the former president and chief operating officer of the Alberta-Pacific forestry company. The committee's terms of reference were fairly wide-ranging, covering the comparative competitiveness of Alberta, the potential impact of any changes, and a close look at the specific treatment of the oil sands sector.

The panel held hearings in Edmonton and Calgary, as well as in the important energy cities of Fort McMurray, Grande Prairie, and Medicine Hat, between April and June. In the hearings, energy companies argued that their businesses were not nearly as profitable as was portrayed in the media and that changes to income trust rules and looming federal efforts to combat greenhouse gases was going to further erode industry profits. They warned that the uncertainty created by the review itself made them hesitant to commit to new projects and that higher royalty rates might lead them to consider abandoning Alberta altogether.

On 18 September the panel released its report, entitled "Our Fair Share." It did not take much reading to find out the basic tone of the report, which was stated in the first line of the executive summary: "Albertans do not receive their fair share from energy development" ("Our Fair Share," 7). The panel recommended that the government's share of oil sands revenue go from 47 per cent to 64 per cent, that the take of conventional oil go from 44 per cent to 49 per cent and that natural gas go from 58 per cent to 63 per cent. The panel recommended that low-production conventional oil and natural gas wells see their royalties reduce while high-production wells see their royalties increase. On the thorny oil sands issue, the panel recommended that the 1 per cent royalty rate remain in place but that the government increase its share once the capital costs had been amortized. The panel also recommended a severance tax on oil sands production even in the startup phase of production. The panel noted that royalties and taxes in other jurisdictions in North America were higher and recommended the changes, which would result in an increase in revenue of about $2 billion per year. The panel recommended that all energy activity – existing and new – be treated the same by the new regime; in other words, the panel recommended that no existing companies have their royalty regimes grandfathered in. The report was also critical of the way the Alberta government had administered royalties in the past, arguing that there had been a lack of transparency and accountability.

Reaction was swift. The energy industry was predictably upset by what they saw as a giant tax grab that was going to come from their bottom lines. The stock market seemed to agree with that assessment as shares in major oil sands companies such as Suncor declined after the report was released. The energy industry publicly criticized the report and its methodology. Panel members, however, vociferously defended their analysis and conclusions. Oil industry giant EnCana threatened to cancel $1 billion in proposed spending if the government went ahead with the report's recommendations.

Just as the immediate furore over the report was dying down, provincial auditor general Fred Dunn reinvigorated the debate with the release of his annual report on 1 October. Dunn found several government reports from the previous three years that concluded that oil and gas royalties could be raised without unduly harming the industry but that the government failed to act on the recommendations. Dunn's report seemed to reinforce the panel's conclusions about a lack of transparency and accountability in the government's administration of oil and gas royalties in the province. In an interview a day later, Dunn argued that there was room to raise royalties even above the rates recommended by the panel (*Calgary Herald*, 3 Oct.).

On 17 October a group of about 500 oil industry workers protested at the legislature, urging the provincial government not to implement the report's recommendations. The problem for the workers, however, was that the oil industry did not appear to be successful in swaying public opinion on this issue in Alberta. Even though one in six jobs in Alberta could be traced to the energy industry, a poll done for the *Edmonton Journal* and *Calgary Herald* found that 88 per cent of Albertans agreed with the report's central conclusion that Albertans were not getting their fair share from the energy industry (ibid., 3 Oct.).

The one group that did not seem to react swiftly was the provincial government. Stelmach took his time to study the report and to respond. In the partisan landscape, Stelmach's government was being squeezed between the New Democrats and Liberals, both of whom were sympathetic to the panel's recommendations, and the Alberta Alliance and Wildrose Parties, who argued for the status quo. On 25 October the premier personally unveiled the government's response. The government's plan could largely be seen as a compromise, failing to fully implement the recommendations of the panel but increasing the government's royalty take by almost $1.4 billion. The government's plan created sliding royalty scales for conventional oil and natural gas that would see the rates change as prices and well production changed. On oil sands, the government announced it was changing the startup royalty rate from 1 per cent to a sliding scale that would start at 1 per cent when oil was at $55 a barrel and increase up to 9 per cent when oil got to $120 a barrel or higher. The government also announced a sliding scale for the post-payout royalty, going from 25 per cent to 40 per cent when oil was over $120 a barrel. The government announced it would not grandfather existing projects but would negotiate with Syncrude and Suncor to bring them into the new regime.

The compromise satisfied neither side of the debate. Those who supported the government receiving more revenue from the energy industry could see the government's decision as evidence that the government had bowed to the pressure of the oil and gas industry. The industry, in contrast, was outraged by the changes. A number of companies, particularly those with interest in natural gas, announced they were reviewing or suspending upcoming projects in light of the uncertainty created by the royalty changes. It was not always clear, however, how much of this was due to natural gas prices, which remained soft towards the end of the year, and how much was actually due to the new royalty regime. A poll done immediately after the government announced the plan seemed to indicate that the government may in fact have pleased neither side with the compromise. Only 47 per cent of respondents indicated they were happy with the plan, while 33 per cent were opposed. A total of 61 per cent of respondents believed that the oil and gas industry exaggerated the dangers of the plan (ibid., 31 Oct.).

For better or for worse, the debate over royalties defined Alberta's politics in 2007. It provided an opportunity for Premier Stelmach to provide leadership and set himself apart from the long shadow cast by Ralph Klein, his predecessor. By tackling an issue that Klein has let languish, he showed himself to be more adept at the details of policy and willing to tackle something with significant political downside. The royalty issue also revealed some ambivalent feelings in the province towards the oil and gas industry. Despite the fact that the energy industry was largely responsible for the prosperity enjoyed by the province over the previous half decade, Albertans demonstrated that they did not completely trust the claims of the industry and believed that the industry should be contributing more to provincial coffers. Although the industry was somewhat successful in getting the Stelmach government to back off from the most significant recommendations of the panel, it had much more work to do in the public relations battle for the allegiance of the people of Alberta.

Legislature

One of the places where the replacement of Klein with Stelmach might be expected to be most noticeable was in the legislature. Although

Klein had never shied away from a good verbal scrap, his tenure as premier would not be known as a time that reinvigorated the provincial legislature as the centre of political debate in Alberta. Indeed, Klein often seemed to want the legislature to meet as little as possible and preferred to deal with media directly through his own personal briefings rather than in the give and take of Question Period. The 2007 session of the legislature would be the first under Premier Stelmach's stewardship, and observers of Alberta's political process were keen to see what this might bring.

Stelmach made a couple of appointments before the legislature sat that suggested that in some substantive ways, things remained very much the same in Alberta. Stelmach appointed Paul Stanway as his director of communications and Tom Olsen as his director of media relations. What was remarkable about this is that prior to their appointments, Stanway has been the provincial political columnist for the *Edmonton Sun* and Olsen did the same job for the *Calgary Herald*. The sudden move of two supposed media watchdogs to the ranks of government public relations professionals raised questions about the critical stance of political journalism in Alberta. It also reflected significant continuities from the past where it was common for reporters to jump from journalism into the government's Public Affairs Bureau, which oversaw the government's relationship with the public and the media.

In other ways, however, Stelmach did seem intent on distinguishing himself from his predecessor. To that end, he took some steps to strengthen the legislature's ability to monitor the government and hold it to account. Under his leadership, the Conservative caucus strengthened the Public Accounts Committee, planned on holding regular fall sittings of the legislature, and announced intentions to hold to a schedule where the legislature would sit for three weeks then break for a week and to put an end to marathon evening sessions. Stelmach also announced an end to Wednesday evening receptions, where lobbyists and others could come and have a drink with Conservative members of the legislature.

Even more significantly, Stelmach's government established all party legislature standing committees on policy. Under Klein, the only policy committees were internal to the Conservative caucus and met privately. The legislature established four standing policy committees – Community Services, Managing Growth Pressures, Government Services, and Resources and the Environment – that would each have eleven members, eight from the Conservatives, two from the Liberals, and one New Democrat. The chair of each committee would be a Conservative MLA, but the vice chair would come from the Opposition.

Like their counterparts in other provinces, these committees would have the ability to study and report on their respective policy areas. What was less clear, however, was how these committees would fit into the process of passing legislation. Unlike in other jurisdictions, the standing committees would not automatically be given the opportunity to review legislation after it passed second reading; the legislature had to choose to send it to the standing committee, rather than to Committee of the Whole. Still, these changes represented some progress in reinvigorating the legislature's role in the political process.

Another measure of the changed nature of the legislature was the provincial budget. Klein's years as premier were marked by an obsession with eliminating the deficit and debt. Although Klein restored the province's budget to a balanced position, he was much less successful in managing the demands of Alberta's rapidly growing population. The emphasis in Stelmach's first budget was on infrastructure and keeping up with growth in the province. The budget saw a 10 per cent increase in overall spending, with both health and advanced education enjoying 10 per cent increases in spending. The province also committed to significant capital spending in both sectors. The provincial government also included an $18.2 billion capital plan to govern capital projects over the next three years. Even with the significant spending increases, the province was forecasting a $2.2 billion surplus in the 2007–8 fiscal year.

In terms of legislation, one piece of legislation that clearly reflected a new hand at the helm was the Tobacco Reduction Act, which passed third reading in the fall. The act banned smoking in all public places, including bars, casinos, and bingos, effective 1 January 2008; prohibited "powerwall" displays of tobacco products as of 1 July; and as of 1 January 2009 made it illegal for post-secondary institutions, health-care facilities, and pharmacies to sell tobacco. Klein had steadfastly opposed attempts to further restrict smoking.

The most controversial piece of legislation was arguably Bill 46, which split the Energy and Utilities Board (EUB) into separate entities, one of which would review energy projects, the other of which would review utilities projects. More controversially, the bill proposed to put limits on who could appear before public hearing over proposed projects, such as power lines. This was particularly controversial after it was revealed that the EUB had hired private investigators to spy on people opposed to a proposed power line between Edmonton and Calgary. The scandal significantly tarnished the reputation of the EUB. The move in Bill 46 to limit access to public hearings did little to appease concerns over the bill. In November, the government softened the bill in the face of public pressure. The amendments did little to mollify critics, who called for the bill to be scrapped in its entirety. Despite the opposition, the government invoked closure and passed the bill.

For its part, the Opposition sought to use its time in the legislature to try to exploit the rift between the Stelmach government and Calgary. In May the Liberals and New Democrats sought to amend the bill limiting rent increases to include rent controls, but despite an all-night legislature session, they were unsuccessful. In the fall, they used the legislature to pressure the government on royalties, but again made little progress.

Municipal elections

In Alberta 15 October was the day for local elections. Although there were some changes in the composition of city councils, in most of Alberta's cities, incumbents were overwhelmingly re-elected. In Calgary, Mayor Dave Bronconnier was handily re-elected with over 60 per cent of the vote. Given the intensity of his battle with Premier Ed Stelmach through the year, the renewed election mandate only served to strengthen his position, particularly after the Conservatives' by-election loss earlier in the year. In Edmonton, Mayor Stephen Mandel won a second term, winning almost two-thirds of the vote. In Lethbridge, Mayor Bob Tarleck won by acclamation, Red Deer's Morris Flewwelling won again, and Melissa Blake was re-elected as mayor of the Regional Municipality of Wood Buffalo, which included Fort McMurray. There were some changes, however. In Medicine Hat, Norman Boucher became mayor after Garth Vallely decided not to run for re-election. Of the larger centres in Alberta, Grande Prairie was the only city to see an incumbent go down to defeat, when Dwight Logan easily defeated Wayne Ayling, who was seeking a third term as mayor. The lack of close contests likely contributed to the low voter turnout, which was between 20 per cent and 30 per cent in most cities.

High-profile murder trials

Although the province's political evolution took most of the public attention, the most arresting human drama of the year came in the form of a pair of high-profile murder trials. In Medicine Hat, a 13-year-old girl stood trial for murdering her family in 2006. In horrifying testimony in June, the court heard how the girl – who was only 12 at the time of the murders – and her adult boyfriend killed her mother, father, and younger brother. Under the provisions of the Youth Criminal Justice

Act, the girl could not be identified. In July, the girl was found guilty of three counts of first-degree murder. In November, the girl was sentenced to the maximum ten-year sentence allowed for young offenders. On top of the year and a half she had already spent in custody, the girl was sentenced to four years custody in Alberta Hospitals' Intensive Rehabilitative Custody and Supervision program. After that, she would have to spend four and a half years in a group home. The girl's boyfriend, Jeremy Steinke, was scheduled to face trial for the murders in 2008.

In Edmonton, the lengthy process of trying Thomas Svekla in connection with the murders of Edmonton-area sex-trade workers began. Over the preceding several years, there had been a string of unsolved murders of sex-trade workers in Edmonton. In 2006, police had arrested Svekla and charged him with the murder of Theresa Innes. Just before he was about to make a January court appearance in connection with that murder, police also charged him with the murder of Rachel Quinney. Much of the year was tied up with procedural wrangling. A charge of sexual assault against Svekla was stayed after police lost some critical evidence. In October, the voir dire phase of the trial was held. At issue was the admissibility of wiretap evidence. The Crown argued that the police had exhausted all other investigative tools and that the wiretap was the only way to gather the evidence needed to secure a conviction. On 23 October the judge agreed with the Crown and admitted the wiretap evidence. Svekla would face trial in February 2008.

The economy

By any standard, Alberta grew rapidly in 2007, but coming off of the torrid pace of growth in 2006, it seemed like the economy was slowing. Still, Alberta's economy grew by about 3 per cent in 2007, a respectable number. The decline in growth was largely the result of the slowing US economy rather than anything that was happening in Alberta. Alberta's growth remained robust despite the warning signs south of the border largely because of the record high price of oil. The price of West Texas Intermediate Crude almost passed the $100 a barrel threshold and averaged over US$72 for the year. The high price of oil drove investment in Alberta's oil sands. Natural gas prices, on the other hand, remained relatively soft, leading to a decline in drilling and exploration in the province.

The labour shortage continued in Alberta as the economy continued to create jobs. Unemployment was around 3.5 per cent, essentially unchanged from what it was in 2006. The housing market continued its momentum from 2006, with housing prices increasing by an average of almost 23 per cent. By the end of the year, the average house price in Alberta was second only to housing prices in British Columbia. There were about 48,000 new homes started in Alberta, almost equalling the record set in the previous year. Although many Alberta homeowners were happy to see the value of their homes increase, the overheated housing market had some negative consequences. It significantly contributed to the 5 per cent inflation experienced in Alberta in 2007. It also likely played a role in the trends in interprovincial migration. In the second half of 2007, more people left Alberta than moved in from other provinces, a reversal of a trend in interprovincial migration over the past several years.

The year also saw an unprecedented labour agreement with teachers over future wage increases and unfunded pension liability. The teachers owed $2.1 billion to fund future pension commitments and the provincial government owed $4.3 billion. As the two sides began to negotiate a new collective agreement, this issue loomed large over the negotiations. The fear of a teachers' strike coinciding with an expected provincial election in early 2008 seemed to spur the province to action. In an astonishing agreement with teachers struck in November, the provincial government agreed to pick up and fund the teachers' share of the unfunded liability in exchange for a five-year agreement on wages that would see wages tied to an index of earnings in the province. The agreement needed to be ratified by all of the province's teachers and local school boards for it to take effect.

JOSEPH GARCEA

Saskatchewan

Saskatchewanians were able to celebrate both family and football in 2007. The family was celebrated near the start of the year during the first Family Day holiday, and football was celebrated near the end of the year when the Saskatchewan Roughriders won the Grey Cup.

The year started with concerted efforts by the New Democratic government, led by Premier Lorne Calvert, to foster economic and population growth. Towards that end, it launched a new multimedia advertising campaign targeted at youth in Saskatchewan to stay in the province and for those living in other parts of Canada to move to the province. The common message for all of them was that given the province's comparatively lower cost of living and the prospects of improved economic conditions, it would be possible for them to lay the foundations needed to achieve a productive and prosperous future for themselves and their children (*Leader-Post*, 27 Jan.). The campaign was based not only on policy rationality to help consolidate what seemed to be the start of a reversal of negative economic and demographic trends, but also political rationality in anticipation of a provincial election during the year.

Elections

The major electoral events in 2007 were the prospects of a federal by-election, a provincial by-election, and a general provincial election. An opportunity arose for a federal by-election when in the summer of that year the Liberal MP, Gary Merasty, resigned just eighteen months after he won the election for the northern riding of Desnethé–Missinippi–Churchill River by 67 votes (ibid., 31 July). Within one month of resigning as an MP, Merasty was appointed by Cameco Corporation as vice president of corporate social responsibility (ibid., 8 Sept.). As the year ended, it became clear that Prime Minister Stephen Harper's Conservative minority government would not call a by-election until it was confident that it would be able to win it or it was required pursuant to the election laws.

The provincial by-election was held during the first quarter of 2007, even though the vacancy occurred the previous fall when Saskatchewan Party MLA Ben Heppner died. The by-election was won handily by Heppner's daughter, Nancy (ibid., 2 March). The general provincial election, held in November, was also won by the Saskatchewan Party, approximately ten years after it was established. Under the leadership of Brad Wall, it defeated the incumbent NDP government led by Lorne Calvert by 38–20 seats. Considering that it received more than 52 per cent of the vote, the Saskatchewan Party did not win as many seats as some had predicted. The Saskatchewan Party won the election because of its ability to swing NDP seats in the major urban centres, including Saskatoon, Regina, Prince Albert, and Yorkton (ibid., 8 Nov.). Several of the seats were won by a very narrow margin of less than a few hundred votes (ibid.). In one case a judicial recount was required to confirm that the Saskatchewan Party candidate had won by approximately three dozen votes (ibid., 8 Nov. and 7 Dec.). The Liberal Party did not win any seats, including the one contested by its leader, David Karwacki.

Many policy issues emerged during the campaign. Several of these were focused on fiscal issues regarding taxation, annual budgets, and the debt. This included doubling the budget for education property tax rebates for agricultural, residential, and commercial properties in rural areas; eliminating the provincial sales tax (PST) on used car sales; mandatory balancing of the provincial budget; and a modest debt reduction plan. Other issues included increasing expenditures for infrastructure, families, health care, education, and policing; protecting the environment; increasing infrastructure funding to municipalities; doubling the family caregiver tax credit; a child tax benefit to help families cover the costs for children's sports, music, or art programs; expanding the budget for the provincial drug plan; constructing day surgery centres in Regina and Saskatoon; establishing a health ombudsman; continuing the existing tuition freeze; improving access to student loans for post-secondary education; increasing funding for school lunch programs; and removing clawbacks to social assistance recipients moving towards full-time work (ibid., 15, 16, 18, 23, 24, 25, and 26 Oct.).

Enhancing democracy also received attention during the election campaign. The notable proposal in this respect came from the Saskatchewan Party, which proposed convening a non-partisan and randomly selected Citizen's Assembly to explore some democratic reform issues, including fixed election dates, changes to the voting age, and possibly even electoral systems other than first past the post.

Two other major issues that received attention during the election campaign were also placed on the agenda by the Saskatchewan Party. The first was a commitment to provide incentives that would facilitate uranium refining and nuclear power production in the province (ibid., 24 May). The second was a commitment to explore the merits of signing the TILMA with British Columbia and Alberta (ibid., 9 June).

Political parties

Substantial political problems began to surface for the NDP in 2007. It began with a loss of a spring by-election. This was followed by media reports of a former caucus employee misusing caucus funds. In a letter addressed to the caucus chairman and caucus chief of staff she assured repayment provided the matter remained confidential. The letter was handed to the police two years later. This caused much criticism and resulted in the resignation of the two members before the spring session ended (ibid., 28 and 30 April). Eventually the premier asked the Conflict of Interest Commissioner to investigate the matter and submit a report by 15 June (ibid., 1 May).

Another major setback for the NDP was that it lost several of its notable incumbents prior to the general election (ibid., 5 May and 24 Aug.) and others in the election (ibid., 11 Oct.). While some believe that these veterans saw the election defeat coming and decided to get off the sinking ship, others believe the loss of these veterans weakened the profile of the party and ultimately contributed to its defeat. Immediately after the election loss the outgoing NDP premier, Lorne Calvert, stated his party would go through a rebuilding process that focused on several objectives including regaining support in rural areas, strengthening their support in cities, and attracting Liberal supporters (ibid., 9 Nov.).

Whereas things were not going well for the NDP in the spring, things started to go very well for the Saskatchewan Party. In addition to improvements in the polls, it was also making substantial improvements in fundraising not only in Saskatchewan but also in Alberta, where Brad Wall spoke at $300-a-plate dinners in Calgary and Edmonton (ibid., 16 March). By the fall of that year, the party had managed to win the election and form a majority government. This occurred just ten years after the party was established and just three years after Wall had become party leader.

The Liberal Party had hoped that this would be the year when its leader, David Karwacki, could win at least one seat in the legislature. Despite the party's efforts to concentrate its resources in potentially winnable constituencies, it failed to achieve its objective. Within one month after the election loss, Karwacki announced that he would be resigning as party leader (ibid., 19 Dec.).

The existence of the Green Party of Saskatchewan was only evident to the public during the provincial election. In that election the party managed to nominate more than twice as many candidates and to garner almost four times more votes (2 per cent) than in the previous election, but it failed to win a seat (ibid., 11 Oct.).

In 2007 the Progressive Conservative Party (PCP) was attempting to revive and re-establish itself. This was happening on the tenth anniversary since it was placed in hibernation to make political room for the newly created Saskatchewan Party in 1997 (ibid., 17 Oct.). The PCP remained irrelevant during the provincial election, fielding only a few candidates and collecting only 0.18 per cent of the vote. Most of the energies and resources of senior party officials were devoted to a legal dispute with the Saskatchewan Party over the control of a $2.9 million trust fund (ibid., 1 Nov.).

Legislature

In 2007 there were two legislative sessions, one in the spring while the NDP was still the governing party and one in the fall after the provincial election when the Saskatchewan Party took control of the legislature. The spring session was described as one of the most bitter in recent years as both parties were posturing and positioning themselves for a provincial election expected to be called some time during the year (ibid., 18 May).

In anticipation of a provincial election, the NDP government made special efforts to improve its electoral positioning through several means. This included averting a strike in the health sector (ibid., 12 July). The prospects of an election and a shortage of skilled labour also led the provincial government to be more generous than in some other years in funding various programs, including the apprenticeship program, which received approximately $400,000 to provide an apprenticeship stipend for 154 individuals (ibid., 11 Aug.). It also included a $26 million investment in funding for a project that would lead to the building of a $4 billion polygeneration plant at Belle Plaine. The funding was drawn from the carbon capture portion of the New Green Fund and the sale of its share in the NewGrade heavy oil upgrader in Regina by the provincial Crown Investment Corporation (ibid., 6 Oct.).

The fall session was the quickest to be held following a provincial election and one of the shortest. The newly elected Wall government seemed intent on reminding people what it had promised during the election and that it was very committed to implementing some of those things very quickly (ibid., 21 Dec).

In the throne speech it committed itself to several key sets of initiatives (ibid., 13 Dec.). The first of these was the enactment of a special act to govern provincial budgeting that included a balanced budget each and every year; a formula for allocating budgetary surpluses; the inclusion of a four-year financial projections in every budget; and paying down the provincial debt. A second set of initiatives targeted at retaining young people included tuition rebates for students choosing to stay in Saskatchewan and tax incentives of up to $10,000 annually for five years for young entrepreneurs under 30 years of age. A third key initiative was a plan for the creation of Enterprise Saskatchewan, a semi-autonomous agency designed to facilitate constructive interaction between the private sector and government in fostering and sustaining economic growth.

The Saskatchewan Party government also made several commitments in relation to other policy sectors. Some of the most notable ones were for the health, municipal, and education sectors. For the health-care sector it committed itself to hiring 800 nurses over four years and to training more doctors, a "patient first" review of the entire health system, an improved prescription drug plan, and a tax benefit to encourage active lifestyles. For the municipal sector it committed itself to produce a new and more generous revenue-sharing agreement with municipalities, and for the school sector it promised increases in operating grants.

Government

There were probably more changes in the composition of Cabinet this year than in the recent past. The changes resulted from the resignations of several NDP Cabinet ministers prior to the election and the addition of an entirely new crop of Cabinet ministers that were appointed by the newly elected Saskatchewan Party government (ibid., 22 Nov.). Despite the changes, the size of the Cabinet was only reduced by one member. Approximately half of the thirty-eight-member caucus, including five women, were appointed to Cabinet. The Cabinet was carefully constructed to reward most of the original caucus members. One of the original caucus members, Don Toth, became Speaker of the legislature (ibid., 7 Dec.). The change in government also produced a change of senior administrative posts. In addition to criticizing some of those appointments, the NDP also criticized the decision to increase salaries in senior roles by $30,000 while other public servants saw limited increases (ibid., 10 Nov., 27 Nov., and 4 Dec.).

Budget

In 2007 two important sets of budget documents were produced by two different governments. Whereas the NDP government produced the budget submitted in the spring session, the Saskatchewan Party produced the revised and updated budget documents in the fall session after it won the election.

The calculations of the spring budget produced the perennial debate on whether Saskatchewan's budget was balanced. Whereas the NDP government claimed that it had produced its fourteenth consecutive balanced budget, the provincial auditor indicated that the summary financial statements suggested that the province had a $701.3 million deficit if several hundred million in financial transfers from the province's Crown corporations and the Fiscal Stabilization Fund (FSF) were included. The Chartered Accountants of Saskatchewan provided their own analysis and concluded that the real deficit was closer to $500 million, with revenues at $7.87 billion and total expenditures at $8.39 billion (ibid., 23 and 24 March).

The NDP government had increased expenditures in that budget for several sectors, including health, education, infrastructure, agriculture, and justice and corrections (ibid., 24 March). In the case of education the government created an annual $10,000 tax exemption for five successive years for new graduates who maintained a residence in the province. The government also cut some taxes including business taxes, corporate capital and income taxes, and education property taxes on some categories of properties. The business tax cuts were welcomed by the business organizations and opposed by some of the major unions and associations who maintained that they were not necessary (ibid., 28 June).

The budget documents produced after the election in the late fall by the new Saskatchewan Party government provided some good news for the government and residents of the province. The major piece of good news was contained in the supplementary estimates, which indicated that the size of the projected surplus was increasing (ibid., 29 Nov.). The excitement was somewhat tempered by the provincial auditor's remarks a couple of months earlier that despite some improvement in the fiscal position of the province, the government should be prudent in its spending because the finances remained vulnerable to potential fluctuations in the economy (e.g., drops in natural resource revenues, increased interest rates, increased crop insurance, etc.) (ibid., 7 Sept.).

Economy

In 2007 Saskatchewan's economy started to show signs of strong and sustained growth largely as a result of rising resource and commodity prices (ibid., 28 March). The initial projection of 3.3 per cent growth for the year, which was above the national average, was revised upward to 4 per cent approximately halfway through the year, and reached approximately 4.4 per cent during the latter part of the year (ibid., 28 March, 23 June, and 14 Sept.). The economic growth was evident in the continuing strong performance of the job market in which the surprising growth of 2006 continued in 2007 (ibid., 6 and 26 Jan.). Areas of job growth included agriculture, mining, oil and gas, construction, and the trade and service industries.

Although the job growth percentage had been rising during the year, in the week leading up to the provincial election campaign the leader of the official Opposition, Brad Wall, tried to minimize credit that could be claimed by the NDP government by pointing out that the actual numbers were small compared to the jobs created in each of the other Western provinces (ibid., 3 Nov.). Nevertheless the growth was sufficiently impressive to lead the Fraser Institute, which had been a perennial critic of the NDP government, to praise the NDP for achieving what it referred to as a historic transformation of economic policy and for having the third-best climate for investment behind Alberta and British Columbia as a result of some strategic cuts to income and corporate taxes designed to make the province more competitive.

Saskatchewan's economic growth started to have a positive effect on the size of its population. After nearly a decade of decline, the population started to surge as more people stayed in the province, others immigrated to the province from abroad, and still others either returned or relocated to the province from other parts of Canada in search of jobs and lower housing prices (ibid., 23 June).

Intergovernmental relations

The most prominent issue was the ongoing equalization saga between Ottawa and Saskatchewan. The provincial government, along with the official Opposition, complained that the federal government's decision to renege on its election promise of excluding non-renewable resources from the equalization formula would result in an $800 million to $1 billion loss in equalization payments to Saskatchewan. Both parties felt Saskatchewan had been betrayed and were ready to fight the federal government in the political and judicial arenas. Under the federal government's formula, Saskatchewan would receive $226 million in equalization funding for 2007 and no funding for 2008 (ibid., 20 March). Despite cooperating with the NDP government in its fight against the government while in Opposition, when it formed the government the Saskatchewan Party adopted a more conciliatory attitude towards the federal government (ibid., 23 Nov.).

While the federal and provincial governments were sorting out their issues on fiscal federalism, municipal governments in the province reminded both of them that they continued to face substantial infrastructure deficits that had to be addressed sooner rather than later (ibid., 21 Nov.).

The Trade, Investment, and Labour Mobility Agreement, which came into effect in April, was the dominant issue in interprovincial relations. The NDP government decided not to be a co-signatory to this agreement, leaving Alberta and British Columbia as the sole signatories (ibid., 15 Feb.). The Saskatchewan Federation of Labour (SFL) and municipal associations largely opposed the agreement in Saskatchewan (ibid., 29 June). They were concerned about the effect the agreement would have on Crown corporations as well as the ability to engage in preferential purchasing. While the Saskatchewan Party did not agree with the SFL's arguments, they shared the municipalities' sentiments. In 2007 only business associations supported TILMA largely on the belief that it would boost the provincial economy (ibid., 13 June).

Aboriginal affairs

The Aboriginal dimension of the province retained a prominence and centrality in public affairs. Saskatchewan became the first province to proclaim June as Aboriginal History Month (ibid., 12 June). It did so in response to the request by the Regina Aboriginal Professional Association (RAPA), which had been lobbying the provincial as well as the federal government to make such a declaration (ibid., 31 May). Other notable initiatives related to Aboriginal issues include the co-sponsorship by the Aboriginal, provincial, and federal governments of the following: the national conference titled Excellence in Action: Best Practices in First Nations, Metis and Inuit Economic Development (ibid., 8 Jan. 2010); a major job fair for Aboriginal youth; the signing of a trilateral intergovernmental partnership for youth job creation; and the creation of the Saskatchewan Police Aboriginal Recruitment Committee mandated to increase applications by Aboriginal applicants (ibid., 21 Feb., 2 Mar., 26 April).

The importance of Aboriginal governmental leaders in the province was clearly evident in the meeting by Saskatchewan Party leader Brad Wall, with the executive of the Federation of Saskatchewan Indian Nations (FSIN) to discuss issues of importance to them and to assure them that if his party formed the next government it would want to build constructive lines of communication with them (ibid., 20 June).

Saskatchewanians became more familiar with the significance of the "duty to consult" Aboriginal governments on resource exploration and extraction projects. The chief of the Clearwater River Dene First Nation chose to block road access to two mining camps operated by Oilsands Quest because of the inability to produce a mutually acceptable agreement. Oilsands Quest subsequently moved its operation across the border to Alberta (ibid., 28 Aug.).

The casino partnership between the provincial and First Nations governments made the news again. The Battlefords Tribal Council (BTC) and the Golden Eagle Community Development Corporation sued the government of Saskatchewan and the FSIN over their decision to recognize the newly formed Battlefords Agency Tribal Council as the host tribal council for the Golden Eagle Casino in North Battleford (ibid., 20 Sept.).

This was also the year that the First Nations Bank (FNB) based in Saskatoon moved closer to becoming an independent financial institution by raising $14 million in new capital among Aboriginal investors that would permit it to buy back some shares owned by the Toronto-Dominion Bank (TDB) and to use the rest as working capital. The FNB was established in 1996 as a joint venture between TDB and two Saskatchewan Aboriginal entities, the Federation of Saskatchewan Indians Inc. and the Saskatchewan Indian Equity Foundation Inc. (ibid., 30 Oct.).

The year 2007 was a significant one for governance and politics in Saskatchewan's Métis sector on at least two major interrelated issues. The first of these was the issue of fixing the problems that had emerged in the Métis electoral system during the 2004 elections. Those elections were marred with electoral tampering that resulted in criminal charges against several Métis leaders and members (ibid., 25 May) and the withdrawal of federal and provincial government funding for the Métis Nation Saskatchewan until proper elections were conducted (ibid., 24 Jan. and 3 Feb.). The matter was eventually resolved when the recommendations of the Independent Oversight Committee for an independently managed and monitored electoral process were approved by the Métis Legislative Assembly and the Metis General Assembly, after they had been rejected by the majority of members of the Provincial Métis Council (PMC) (ibid., 23 April). The election for the PMC was eventually held later in the year and a new president and executive were elected (ibid., 7 Sept.).

The other major issue in the Métis sector was the decision of the board of governors of the Métis National Council to ouster Clem Chartier, a Métis from Saskatchewan, as president just nine months after it had extended his term in office for at least twelve months. The extension to his term as president had been approved in light of the complications that would have been caused to the national electoral process because of the aforementioned electoral problems of its Saskatchewan provincial affiliate (ibid., 4 Aug.). Chartier sought a court injunction to allow him to complete the additional one-year term that had been bestowed on him by the MNC board of governors (ibid., 25 Aug.).

The other major development in the Métis sector was a court decision that upheld Métis fishing rights across the province. This occurred when the court found Donald Belhumeur not guilty of fishing without a valid licence in southern Saskatchewan. He challenged the fine he had received on constitutional grounds, arguing that it was unfair for Métis in the northern part of the province, but not those in the southern part, to exercise their fishing and hunting rights (ibid., 19 Oct.). By the end of the year the provincial Crown appealed the court's decision (ibid., 23 Nov.).

This was also the year that the Métis Nation Saskatchewan asserted the principle of duty to consult Métis governments in relation to Enbridge's major oil pipeline development that would run through "traditional Métis territory" in Saskatchewan. The MNS accused Enbridge of failing to consult them and asked the National Energy Board to withhold the company's application to build the proposed pipeline (ibid., 6 Dec.).

GEOFFREY LAMBERT

Manitoba

The NDP was re-elected to office in May 2007, winning a third consecutive majority. This unprecedented result was a tribute to their competent management of affairs and, to a large degree, the popularity of their leader, Premier Gary Doer. However there were dissenters, and not everyone was enthusiastic about Doer or his regime.

The economy

The gross provincial product for Manitoba passed $38 billion this year, and the growth rate was just over 3 per cent, about average by national standards. Private investment was strong, although public investment had slowed down.

This was to be only a temporary pause, however, since the government had announced a major building program in the budget, which was not coincidentally called the Building Budget. The main elements in this program were the expenditure of nearly half a billion dollars on new schools and health-care facilities, as well as an extension and upgrading of the floodway ("Duff's Ditch"), which had so often come to the defence of Winnipeg when the Red and Assiniboine Rivers threatened to burst their banks. The 1997 flood had perhaps taught decision-makers that Winnipeg was still not immune from the deluge. The absolutely catastrophic state of the province's roads was a strong reason for them to be put on the list of building priorities.

There were a number of major projects already approved or underway in 2007. Manitoba Hydro was moving its headquarters to downtown Winnipeg, just south of Portage Avenue and close to the eminently successful M.T.S. Centre, opened in 2004. It was home to the Manitoba Moose of the American Hockey League and had been host to numerous shows and concerts.

Typically news that someone was building close to the intersection of Portage and Main is sufficient to garner excitement about the prospect of "reviving downtown" Winnipeg. The fact that several thousand Hydro workers would soon be disgorged onto Portage Avenue in search of food, booze, or some other diversion proved a huge incentive to the speculators. In reality a long series of disappointments shows optimism tends to dissipate fairly quickly. The M.T.S. Centre was the latest case in point, although the building itself was a great success. The Centennial Concert Hall, City Hall, and the Portage Place mall could not tell similar stories.

All trade and business associations in the area had invested in polls to find out how to draw more people downtown. According to poll results, people were reluctant to go downtown, particularly after dark, because they felt bothered by aggressive panhandlers. So the question became one of how to rectify the problem. There had been success along Corydon Avenue, in the south end, which is full of Italian restaurants and other businesses where one is seldom bothered. But close by on Osborne Street, heart of Osborne Village and home to a variety of trendy businesses and high-rises, it is like Portage Avenue. The solution remains a mystery.

Two other projects attracted a lot of attention this year. One, perhaps the most glorious of them all, was the extension and renewal of the Winnipeg International Airport. The aim was to fulfil the need for another twenty-four-hour airport in Canada, of which there are very few. There would be more offices and commercial space, including a hotel. The new airport was to be called the James Armstrong Richardson International Airport, after the former president of Richardson Securities of Canada, who had lived in Winnipeg and had been a flying enthusiast before his death in 1939.

Winnipeg's second family is, arguably, the Aspers. They were intimately involved with the Museum of Human Rights, which was to be built at the Forks. After a design had been approved and money collected, progress seemed to stop. Some blamed it on the opposition of central Canadian interests, opposed to any national museums outside Ottawa. Others pointed to the financial problems of the family empire. Those in a position to know reassured us that all was well.

With the aforementioned projects and more, construction was a significant part of the healthy performance of the Manitoba economy in 2007. Closely allied to it was the boom in manufacturing. Whether it was machine tools, processed food, clothes, or furniture, manufacturing came out a winner. The effects of this strong performance were felt in several other areas. For example, the housing demand continued longer than it had in most other cities, Regina and Saskatoon excepted.

The vacancy rate in Winnipeg was 1 per cent. Prices of resold properties reached new heights, and the cost of individual properties reached record levels. The number of applications for building permits continued to rise, and consumer demand for household goods was heavy.

Growth was by no means as good in other sectors of the economy but still enabled practitioners to feel content. Agriculture had a good year. Its performance in recent years had been marred by climactic and political factors (such as mad cow disease), but it was catching up to other sectors. Grains and oilseeds were in a good position, and cattle had come from a long way back. The crown jewel of agriculture, however, was the hog industry. For particular reasons, its position was being undermined, or so it seemed, in part, perhaps, because of pollution. So breeders are always on the lookout for government intervention.

The sale of hydro power was also good, and bold plans were afoot to elevate it into the clean green power source that would be appropriate in a world with the environmental characteristics and concerns this one has. Finally, mining reflected all the up-and-down price habits of the world marker. Fishing was satisfactory. Tourism felt the impact of a smaller share of the film industry. Other aspects of the tourism industry were flat, suggesting there is a finite number of times visitors wish to be photographed with a polar bear.

Anyone looking in Manitoba for work was therefore in a good position. Indeed there may even be reason to argue that there was a labour shortage, for a historically high number of immigrants came to the province in 2007 and the few years preceding it. It has been estimated that, for several years, between 10,000 and 13,000 immigrants moved to the Keystone province every year. These figures were close to the historic highs recorded in 1913.

The unemployment rate in Manitoba in 2007 was a 4.3 per cent average month by month. One group clearly benefiting were the youngest workers, aged 15 to 24. In many previous years they would have had to leave the province to build a life for themselves. With improved conditions, the population of Manitoba grew to above 1.2 million.

Immigrants to the province have come from just about everywhere, especially from Asia, India, and Africa. Maple Leaf Foods in Brandon has made a point of hiring from the Chinese mainland. The home care system in Manitoba would be even more stretched than it is without the participation of Filipinos. Apart from the ethnic backgrounds of the workforce, one can make a few observations about gender as well. It is a widely recognized fact that women have enjoyed a greater access to the glittering prizes than used to be the case. Thus, for example, for a short period in the first decade of the twenty-first century, the presidents of all three Manitoba universities were women. It is also well demonstrated that the gender ratios of entrants into universities and professional schools was tipping slowly in favour of women.

Nonetheless, despite these gains, figures for the first years of the century suggest a high degree of continuity in the structure of the workforce. First, according to Statistics Canada, over half the jobs held by women are in service fields. Indeed fully 33 per cent of women in Manitoba in 2007 were in health and education jobs. On the other hand practically none of them were in utilities, construction, oil and gas, or fishing. But perhaps the most telling data in the set are those which deal with farming. The proportion of the labour force engaged in what was a foundational activity of the province by 2007 was 9 per cent, 3 per cent among women – an apt commentary on the impact of technical and human forces.

The government's major tool in dealing with economic issues is through the budget, and it is to this topic that this chapter now turns.

The budget

The budget was brought down on 4 April. It was finance minister Greg Selinger's eighth budget and also the eighth where he announced a surplus and satisfaction on all counts. Selinger holds a PhD from the London School of Economics and was a member of the social work faculty at the University of Manitoba. He is widely respected, and his earnestness is regarded as a useful tool in contrasting to the ebullient premier. Many thought he would have an excellent chance of success should he seek the leadership once Gary Doer retired.

He frequently muses on philosophical issues, such as the role and purpose of the New Democratic Party. The basic principles were making sure that Manitoba was not too expensive for people to live. That meant keeping down costs, including taxes; supporting young families; ensuring that the First Nations were respected and honoured and provided with opportunities to make the best of themselves; reviving rural life, as too many towns and villages were suffering from the ills of too few people; making hydroelectric power a mighty source of driving the West; making a commitment to turning Manitoba into a "truly green" province; ensuring that Manitobans had access to the best health-care system in the country, if not the world; making sure that the province's schoolchildren had education and training of the very best quality; and caring for seniors, materially and in terms of the respect they are owed.

Selinger, always well prepared, was able to cite chapter and verse in support of his contention that the NDP was carrying out its mandate.

As outlined in this budget, Selinger intended to spend $9.2255 billion. The largest expenditure would be on health, some $3.8866 billion, or 42 per cent of the total budget. Support for the health-care system had been at this level for a number of years. Although there was sporadic discussion of finding new ways to pay for or pass off health-care costs, all but the doughtiest right-winger seemed to accept the status quo with regard to health-care: namely that it is a right, not a privilege, and no one should have easier access than anyone else. There was no "hallway medicine," or so claimed the NDP. One has to say that it certainly looked like hallway medicine when one first walked in.

The education system was to come second, receiving $1.7833 billion. It was not enough, of course, complained professionals in the field. School trustees cried foul and passed off their shortfalls to the tax-paying public. The universities and colleges, made up of wily types, also protested. Their major grievance had been the government's stubborn support of a tuition freeze without a compensating increase in their operating grant. Education minister Diane McGifford gave a few indications that this might be lifted.

The entire idea behind the frozen grant was that college education would be cheaper in real terms and hence more accessible. The government argued that overall registration would increase as a result, which would make up the ground lost by freezing the level of grant support. The level of enrolment went up, but so did the level in almost every other province. This increase was not incompatible with a tuition freeze. Who won the dispute? It is probably best to call it a tie.

The government's third priority was debt reduction, then all the other functions of government (agriculture, the arts, transportation, etc.), sharing a pot which had started off much bigger.

As for revenue, Selinger expected to raise $9.305 billion, leaving him, ostensibly, with a small surplus of about $80 million. This was the era of surpluses, and surpluses which were always bigger than the size predicted. This gave the double impression of paper-clip austerity to save public money, on the one hand, and of generosity (more cash to hand out at the end of the year) on the other. The finance minister indicated that his primary sources of revenue would be income tax ($3.315 billion), other taxes (including sales tax of $1.336 billion), and other fees ($453 million). A final item from local sources would be $488 million transferred from the liquor ($263 million) and lotteries ($225 million) commissions. The federal subvention would be $3.241 billion, of which $1.876 billion would be equalization grants. There was, thus, a faint irony in the province's lining up with other "have-not" provinces like Ontario to collect their dole from rich ones such as Saskatchewan.

No new taxes were raised in this budget, although there was a general 1 per cent cut in certain business taxes. The government also brought in rather generous tax credit proposals to help out students, simultaneously easing the limitations on the operating grant. What inevitably became the major focus of controversy was the proposal to provide students with a 10 per cent tax credit designed to encourage them to remain in or return to Manitoba. It applied whether or not they studied in Manitoba, whatever discipline they majored in, or whether or not they actually graduated. Supporters saw it as a means of promoting access and of providing a solid incentive for staying in the province. Opponents saw it as a toy for the rich. The legislation was pushed through briskly in light of the upcoming election.

The Right and Left

The NDP played the political game well, being able to read public moods aptly. The legislative Opposition appeared inept. But there was an element of effective criticism of the administration.

By this time the New Democrats practically "owned" the left-wing vote. The old Communist Party, which had played an honourable role in the history of Winnipeg's north end, had, to all intents and purposes, disappeared. The Green Party had yet to shape an identity. The Liberals were in search of a role.

But there was impressive potential opposition at the right and left of the spectrum. The classical Liberals on the right had as advocates much of the Tory caucus and some of the professoriate. However, perhaps the best, most reasoned critique came from think tanks such as the Frontier Centre for Public Policy and its indefatigable head, Peter Holle. The Frontier Centre was a regular critic of the government from what would normally be called "the Right." They suggested that the province's alleged prosperity stood on brittle glass – in particular that the government was highly dependent on federal government favour. The tax burden they regarded as monstrous and suggested that the government's numerous taxes and impositions were a burden on the business community and a deterrent to productivity. Written in a lively style, the centre's publications and pronouncements had some influence.

The Left naturally saw things differently. The province's universities were their main centres of operation, but they also had a voice through such journals as the Winnipeg-based *Canadian Dimension*. A former editor had been University of Manitoba economist Cy Gonick.

The NDP is itself sometimes regarded as a coalition of elements. And occasionally these elements would dissent and possibly push the government in a direction it did not wish to go. One element of the party is labour, which bears the label "radical" with pride. However the movement has been quite content to go along with the centrist orientation of the contemporary leadership. Another element are the intellectuals, the civil servants, journalists, Protestant clergy, and teachers one finds at party policy meetings. One suspects many of them would prefer a more ideologically based politics but will make do with issues of foreign policy, aid and development, and the like. In fact one suspects the party's greatest potential difficulty may come with women and Aboriginals. In the first case, a posture of "be forever vigilant" is likely appropriate, just to remind the rest of the party not to take them for granted. And Aboriginals bring to the table such a mixed bag of grievances that the good feeling between them and their NDP confrères sometimes seems brittle.

The sessions of the legislature

The legislature met for, effectively, three mini-sessions in 2007. The first was a continuation of the one that had originally convened in fall 2006. Very little legislation survived the hurry to pass the budget and to get into the streets for the campaign. Private members' legislation all died on the order paper.

After the election the slightly amended House (very few seats changed hands, although there were a few retirements) met to elect a Speaker (George Hickes, an Aboriginal from Point Douglas, the very oldest part of the city of Winnipeg, was re-elected), organize themselves, and then return home until the fall. November saw a reconvening, with a throne speech, followed by a few weeks of normal activity and then home for Christmas.

The volume and the content of legislation were therefore quite light. There were plenty of amendments to statutes, incorporations, and so forth, but there was little of the epic variety issues to stir people's souls. This is not, though, to suggest that some of the legislation did not have significance for the audience towards which it was directed. For example, there were amendments to the Workers' Compensation Act and an extension to the mandate of Steinbach Bible College to enable it to offer a few degrees. The government's desire to restrict the cheque-cashing outfits, which had sprung up, was obviously well-intentioned if a little intrusive. Of greatest general application, perhaps, was the government's notion of curbing one's freedom to drive and use a cell phone at the same time.

Any problems the government might have were on the human side of the ledger. The NDP was now in its third term, and there were a fair number of caucus members who had been around since the party had taken power in 1999 or even longer. There was also the need to refresh and rejuvenate the Cabinet. The fact that there was fresh talent available made some changes easier. The Cabinet already contained more women than any previous Cabinet. A number of MLAs had been elected from different multicultural communities (Indian, Filipino), and this suggested a more diverse Cabinet in the near future. Doer had thirty-six members now, for a majority of fifteen. There was a possibility, therefore, that the coalition might start to crack, since some party elders might be less easy to control.

And then there was the question of how much longer Gary Doer might stay on. He had been party leader now for an astonishing twenty-one years and had won three elections in a row, putting him in a league with few others. Hugh McFadyen, leader of the Manitoba Progressive Conservative Party, would probably survive. He was young, energetic, and eager. He deserved the chance to show he had the "royal jelly." Those who thought he should be ousted because the Tories had fallen below the "magic number" of 20 seats in the legislature were not being very helpful.

The election

The election was held on 22 May. It was expected to be an NDP sweep right from the beginning, according to polls taken by Probe Research and published in the *Winnipeg Free Press* and on the CBC. What was nearly missed, however, was the fact that there was an actual swing of 1.3 per cent from the government to the Tories.

The New Democrats won 47 per cent of the vote (down 1 per cent from 2003) and 36 seats (a net gain of 1 seat). The Tories won 37 per cent (up 1 per cent) and 19 seats (a net loss of 1). The Liberals held the 2 seats they had held before, with the leader, Dr John Gerrard, holding on to River Heights, and Kevin Lamoureux once again winning Inkster, which was turning into a personal fief. If there was an explanation for the small anti-government swing, it was probably due to turnout. At 58 per cent, it was indicative of a turnout which is skewed somewhat to the old and affluent, a slightly pro-Tory group.

The seats which changed hands were three. Two others, which had been held by short-term independents (for one reason or another, they did not receive their party's nomination and so crossed the floor), returned to their initial parties. The two MLAs leaving the Progressive Conservatives and going to the NDP represented Southdale and Kirkfield Park. These were suburban seats that had been Tory for a long time. Whether or not this switch is a sign that the suburbs are turning NDP remains to be seen. The seat that was won by the Progressive Conservatives was Brandon East, which had been held by Cabinet minister Stuart Smith. The winner was Rick Borotsik, one-time mayor of Brandon and for several years the only Tory MP in western Canada. He had never lost an election.

The NDP won because of the adequacy of their record and the quite astonishing popularity of their leader. Even though he skipped the bulk of all-leader forums, he remained the most popular head of government in the country. McFadyen was seen as callow and inexperienced, and his embracing of such issues as crime in the streets and the possible return of the Winnipeg Jets seemed opportunistic. Many people commented that this was probably the most boring election they had ever endured. It was hard to disagree.

KEN COATES AND GREG POELZER

The territories

The first decade of the twenty-first century saw the steady emergence of the Canadian North as an international political battleground and as one of the most hotly debated areas in the world. Throughout 2007 the North's profile continued to grow, through the continued engagement of Aboriginal and territorial leaders on the world stage and growing confusion and concern about the broad questions over Arctic sovereignty. For decades the North operated in relative obscurity, but the unique combination of debate about climate change, the opening of the Northwest Passage to commercial navigation, resource development plans, and the increasing important of Indigenous and regional governance pushed the region to the forefront of national politics and international affairs.

The Arctic jumped onto the world stage in 2007, largely through Russian interventions. Russian scientists claimed that they had identified the precise location of the Lomonosov Ridge, which runs between Ellesmere Island and Siberia, and claimed that this delineation supported their claims to the continental shelf in the area. With the exception of the United States, which is not a signatory of the United Nations Convention on the Law of the Sea (UNCLOS), the circumpolar nations had a time-limited opportunity to make a case for the shelf to the commission established under UNCLOS. Canadians quickly discovered that Canadian scientific exploration now required a ramped-up effort to keep pace with circumpolar nations, to avoid the possibility that the country could forfeit its claim to potentially resource-rich territories.

The Russians played a symbolic card to assert their dominance over the region. A submarine commanded by Artur Chilingarov headed to the North Pole in July 2007 and deposited a titanium flag on the sea floor. The Russians greeted Chilingarov with a hero's welcome when he returned. The stunt gathered international attention and drew angry rebukes from Prime Minister Stephen Harper and Peter MacKay, defence minister. The Russian claim riled Canadian nationalists, who feared that poor preparedness on the government's side had left the country vulnerable. The prime minister had a soft spot for the Arctic, however, and insisted on immediate government attention to its scientific and territorial responsibilities. The 2007 episode fed into Canadian worry about the Arctic that ran in a strait from the Manhattan voyage (1969), Polar Sea (1985), and the dispute with Denmark over Hans Islands (2004).

The emphasis on Arctic sovereignty was not new. Canada and the circumpolar world have been the focus of earlier national, North American, and international debates about the future of the Far North. What made the debates raging through 2007 so interesting and intense was the manner in which the Arctic issues connected internal northern issues, national priorities, and global concerns. Prime Minister Harper, for example, had made Arctic defence a key priority in the 2006 election and followed through in 2007 with visits and ongoing commitments to the region. He promised a military training centre for Resolute, a port for Nanisivik, and new Arctic patrol vessels, while also acknowledging the need for urgent investments in housing and local infrastructure. Indigenous leaders and territorial politicians, at the same time, lobbied aggressively for attention to such fundamental issues as northern infrastructure, housing, employment, and cultural programming. Proposals from mining and energy companies to intensify the exploration and development of the North played into both regional plans for greater economic activity and the prime minister's confidence in the commercial future of the region.

The focus on internal and national needs for the region aligned very nicely with Canada's need to become more assertive about its Northern Territories. Pressure from the United States about the legal status of the Northwest Passage, concerns about drilling rights in the Beaufort Sea, and growing Russian assertiveness on the delineation of the continental shelf combined to increase Canadian interest in the North. The Conservative government did not move as aggressively on domestic issues as the Liberal and New Democratic Party Opposition wanted, but there was a significant improvement in short- and long-term policy and planning related to socio-economic conditions in the region. The transition for the emphasis on international affairs, through the Arctic Council in particular, and military considerations was subtle but perceptible. The Canadian public seemed increasingly concerned about improving conditions in the region and responding to territorial demands for attention to their top priorities.

One sign for the growing attention to northern matters came through the nomination of Sheila Watt-Cloutier for the Nobel Prize. The award, eventually shared by the Intergovernmental Panel on Climate Change and former US vice president Al Gore, is perhaps the world's most high-profile recognition. Watt-Cloutier, born in northern Quebec but a resident of Nunavut, was a credible candidate, both for her work on behalf of Inuit and Indigenous issues and for raising the profile of the Arctic on matters connected to climate change. She is widely connected with the compelling assertion that Northern Indigenous peoples have a "human right to be cold," a statement that garnered international attention as environmentalists and politicians debated the potential impact of human-generated climate change (*Globe and Mail*, 28 Dec.). Watt-Cloutier emerged in 2006–7 as one of the world's most important spokespersons for environmental matters and drew international attention to the fact that the Inuit, in particular, would be among the first peoples to experience the full effects of major climate change. The vulnerability of Arctic peoples – as shown by the impact of warmer temperatures on permafrost and, therefore, northern buildings, changes in temperature and related shifts in bird, animal, and fish populations, and the increasing dangers of travelling on the ice – attracted external interest in a way that few northern issues had previously.

Northern politics

If 2007 saw the continued presence of the North on the national political agenda, it was a year with relatively little movement at the territorial level. With only one territorial election (in the Northwest Territories) and no federal campaign, the year in politics passed quite quietly. One trend – the high rate of turnover in local Aboriginal politics – spoke to a continuing challenge in northern governance. Aboriginal politicians, particularly those operating at the local level, work under extreme pressures. Financial and human resources are limited, political and administrative structures for self-government are still evolving, and social and cultural pressures are intense. The combined forces place exceptional hardships on local politicians, and it is hardly surprising that the effort to keep abreast of complex files takes a major toll. At the same time, the demands of local governance often sparked local controversies and bitter personal disputes over council spending, management, or priorities.

Consider a series of developments in the Northwest Territories in 2007. Chief Ron Pierrot of K'asho Got'lne Community Council (Fort Good Hope) resigned suddenly in January, indicating that he was suffering from alcohol abuse. The Pehdzeh Ki First Nation (Wrigley) lost its third leader in a year when Chief Tim Lennie stepped down, claiming exhaustion after only six months in his position. Chief Robert Sayine did not seek re-election as chief of the Deninu Ku'e First Nation (Fort Resolution), although he did stay on the band council. Chief Jim Schaefer, citing personal reasons and conflicts with the council, resigned his post with the Salt River First Nation (Fort Smith), claiming that his forward-looking agenda of education and business development was at odds with the council's short-term plans. The government of Canada pulled the financial and administrative control from the West Point First Nation and ordered a new chief and council election. Deninu (Fort Resolution) chief Bill Norn ran afoul of his council colleagues, who suspended him from his leadership role. In one of the more bizarre twists that reveals the challenges of local level politics, Freida Martselos became the chief of the Salt River First Nation. Within a week, she was dismissed by her council, which rejected her allegedly autocratic ways. Martselos and others then occupied the band office for more than a week. Hay River lost its entire council in 2007, following a court ruling that forced the existing council to step aside in the middle of their term. When the new elections were finished, five new members and three incumbents took up seats on the eight-member council.

The growing pains associated with devolution and emerging governments presented yet again in 2007 through two reports by the auditor general of Canada, Sheila Fraser. In her first report, she drew attention to challenges with the monitoring and management of the student loan portfolio. The effective management of students' loans is essential to longer-term goals of ensuring the development of a skilled workforce in the North and its overall capacity building. In November she unleashed a scathing report on the Nunavut Business Credit Corporation (NBCC). The NBCC provided business loans and was responsible for oversight of the lending program. Fraser, by taking the aggressive step of refusing to accept NBBC's financial statements for the previous year, drew attention to a series of serious problems, including poor records management, ineffective monitoring, and the mismanagement of individual loans. The NBCC lost the majority of its staff during the audit process. Fraser even questioned the appropriateness of leaving the NBCC as a separate government agency.

The core issue – the preparedness of the territories for province-like powers, which the Yukon gained in 2003 – came to the head for Nunavut with the release of a report commissioned by Indian and Northern Affairs Canada. The document, prepared by ministerial representative Paul Mayer, examined the suitability of negotiating a transfer of land and resource control to the territory. Mayer took some of the wind out of Nunavut's sails, indicating that slow steps would be better than large leaps into the unknown. The report focused on territorial capacity and, particularly, Nunavut's ability to manage the large and important land management files. Mayer concluded that Nunavut lacked the critical mass necessary to tackle the responsibilities and had to achieve greater administrative stability before proceeding. He urged the government of Canada to work with the governments of Nunavut and Nunavut Tunngavik on the development of professional expertise and experience on resource-related matters.

The government of Nunavut continued its efforts to put an Inuit stamp on the still-young jurisdiction. Two laws, Bills 6 and 7, reached the legislature after months of community consultations, putting in place regulations that would elevate Inuktitut and Innuinaqtun to the same legal level as English and French. Perhaps predictably, both sides criticized the proposed legislation, including those favouring strong Indigenous language laws and those, principally in the small business sector, who worried about the costs and consequences of the pro-Inuktitut and Innuinaqtun legislation. The bills called for mandatory language instruction from kindergarten through twelfth grade, a major step towards rebuilding youth connection to regional cultures. The laws called for the creation of a government agency to support and monitor language usage and for basic government services to be provided in the official languages and for signs, advertisements, and other public documents to follow the same requirement. Store owners worried about the challenges of finding people proficient in multiple languages, particularly among the skilled workforce. The introduction of the language bills (they would pass in 2008) represented a major step forward towards the ideal of developing Nunavut as a truly Inuit jurisdiction.

Although the Yukon did not enjoy the glamour of an election, politics were as dynamic as ever. The impact of land claims settlements and devolution to the Yukon Territorial government were reshaping politics in the Canadian North. The release of the North Yukon Land Use Plan in 2007 had the potential for shaping the future development of the territory, which was home to important caribou and wetlands habitat and the site of potential oil and gas development. Without waiting for the release of the report, the territorial government proceeded with the controversial oil and gas dispositions. However, it was anticipated that the Land Use Plan would end the "road-by-road and valley-by-valley battle" over development priorities in the North Yukon.

Within the territorial legislature, the report revealed that Yukon MLAs were the worst paid in Canada at $38,000 annually. The report recommended that salaries should nearly double to $65,000, which would still put Yukon MLAs as the fourth poorest paid in Canada. Interestingly, the salaries of Yukon Cabinet ministers were lower in 2007 than in 1979. All parties recognized the importance of the issue, as well as the need to balance concerns of not making pay too high, only to attract people who were in it for the money, and not too low, only to discourage good candidates. As the author of the report and former clerk of the Assembly, Patrick Michael, pointed out, "You could get to the point where the only people running are at the beginning of their careers or retirees at the end of theirs" (*Yukon News*, 2 Nov.).

The Yukon was also the centre of national political attention. Governor General Michaëlle Jean visited the Yukon between 17 and 21 June 2007, presiding over citizenship ceremonies as well as visiting various art studios. The emphasis by the governor general on the arts made sense as the Yukon is the highest per capita recipient in arts funding, at $113.33 per person, which was $100 more than the second-best-funded jurisdiction in Canada, the Northwest Territories. In December of that year, former Liberal Party leader Stéphane Dion paid a visit to the Yukon in part to lend support to local Liberal MP, Larry Bagnell. Local reports acknowledged that Dion had done his homework on many of the key issues in the Yukon, but his ability to connect with voters was limited: "Stephane Dion gets it. But his ability to communicate it needs work" (ibid., 10 Dec.). Dion's Northern foray may have been a harbinger of his Canada-wide political future.

Northwest Territories election

In a year otherwise devoid of a great deal of northern political change, the 1 October 2007 election in the Northwest Territories (NWT) provided a reminder of the unique nature of regional electoral politics. The NWT, like Nunavut, operates on a consensus-style form of government, meaning that voters are not faced with political parties and the electoral processes that accompany partisan politics. Instead, electors focus on constituency issues, selected local representatives who, as a group, pick the premier (government leader) and the Cabinet. Given that the government does not operate in a standard party-based format, the NWT amended their electoral laws to provide for fixed election dates. The 2007 election was the first fought on the basis. The election promised considerable turnout, with Premier Joe Handley deciding not to seek re-election, one of five incumbents who did not place their name before the voters.

Northwest Territories' elections are qualitatively different than any in Canada, save Nunavut. Three candidates were acclaimed (two fewer than the previous election), finding no one willing to stand against them in their constituency. The thirty-four candidates who stood for election included, again, a group quite distinctive from the Canadian North, reflecting the fact that these were intensely local elections, won and lost on community-based concerns. There is also a high level of forgiveness in territorial politics. Four of the candidates went into the campaign with criminal records (including one with a conviction for releasing crickets in the legislature). Peter Liske registered to run and then withdrew after drawing international attention (and a critique from American television personality Jay Leno) to his pledge to seek help for his alcohol problem if he was elected. One incumbent, Bobby Villeneuve, ran afoul of territorial regulations when he claimed, erroneously, that he lived in Fort Resolution and therefore warranted a housing allowance. His bid for re-election fell well short. Another candidate, Bryan Sutherland, claimed to be the leader of a territorial political organization, the NWT Party, but electors were unimpressed and gave him little support in his campaign for a seat.

The election itself attracted little media attention, if only because the absence of territory-wide parties meant there was little debate about NWT issues. Instead constituency elections focused on personal qualities and networks and local issues, reinforcing the increasingly acknowledged reality that consensus-style government works relatively well for day-to-day governance but interferes with long-range planning and the focus needed for major decisions. The campaigns did not draw a great deal of attention in the territory. Around 55 per cent of eligible voters cast a ballot – a number that underestimates the total, given that no voting occurred in three constituencies. Six new members entered the legislature, to go with the ten incumbents (three by acclamation). All four candidates with criminal records lost. Two incumbents, Calvin Pokiak and Bobby Villeneuve, lost badly, Pokiak finishing with little more than one-quarter the number of votes of winner Jackie Jacobsen and Villeneuve with a tiny 12-vote turnout, coming fourth behind winner Tom Beaulieu, who polled over 252.

The most critical decision came after the official voting. When the results were finalized, the members of the Territorial Assembly met in mid-October to select the NWT's next premier. Two incumbents, Michael Miltenberger and Floyd Roland (elected in his riding by acclamation), ran for the premier's seat. Roland won. He held elected office at the municipal level in Inuvik before running for the NWT assembly in 1995. Roland had been re-elected twice before 2007, the second time, in 2003, by acclamation. In statements following the selection of Roland and his Cabinet, the new premier vowed to continue to press the government of Canada to increase funding for the NWT and to accelerate the campaign for province-like status for the territory. Premier Roland joined his counterparts, Yukon premier Douglas Fentie and Nunavut premier Paul Okalik, to form a strong territorial front in demanding major change in federal-territorial relations. Former Yukon premier John Ostashek, who led the newly formed Yukon Party to office in the Yukon and was premier from 1992 to 1996, passed away on 10 June 2007.

The northern economy

The economy of the territorial North continued its upward trend in 2007, with major resource projects and promises of further development spurring investment and employment. A surging Canadian dollar, which exceeded US$1 in September 2007, created problems across the North. Mining companies saw the rising dollar hurting exports and making their operations less competitive. Tourism operators and wilderness outfitters, working largely with American customers, saw their prices escalate, harming the always-sensitive sector. For consumers, of course, the higher dollars reduced prices somewhat. Overall, however, 2007 was a generally positive river, driven by continued optimism in oil and gas and a continuing surge in the mining sector.

While the Mackenzie Valley Pipeline project remained mired in the review processes, optimism continued in the energy field, even with the projected cost for the pipeline ballooning to $16.2 billion from the previously forecast $7.5 billion. Supporters of the pipeline signed a major agreement with the government of the Northwest Territories in January 2007, committing themselves to significant employment and training benefits for NWT residents if and when pipeline construction proceeded. Included in the accord were assurances of opportunities for local businesses. Exploratory activity continued in 2007, with Chevron and BP continuing to drill in the Beaufort Delta and Paramount working its Cameron Hills property. MGM Energy (an affiliate of Paramount) launched a substantial exploration south of Fort Good Hope and Husky Oil/International Frontier Resources (near Tulita), BG International (near Colville Lake) commencing exploratory work in the NWT, and BGI also working International Frontier Resources near Fort Good Hope.

The northern diamond boom continued, with exploration expanding into Nunavut and with the potential for several large-scale operations coming online. The NWT saw its economy leap forward 13.1 per cent, a major improvement over the 29 per cent growth the previous year, driven largely by construction activity at Snap Lake. This was the highest growth rate in Canada. Nunavut, just grabbing onto the initial stages of a regional diamond expansion, was second in the country at 13 per cent, compared to a national average of 2.7 per cent (and only 3.3 per cent in Alberta). The NWT GDP exceeded $4.2 billion, led by mining and oil and gas developments. In the latter case, an exploration plan calling for the expenditure of $585 million in the waters off Tuktoyuktuk buoyed the regional exploration sector. The regional harvesting economy – fishing, hunting, and trapping – remained much the same. In the Yukon, the economy expanded at a healthy 3.8 per cent pace, attributable to the opening of a new mine, the construction of several large government projects (including the Canada Winter Games facilities), and higher copper and gold prices. The territory's GDP rose almost 9 per cent, to finish at $1.8 billion in 2007. Nunavut experienced comparable growth – 13 per cent in 2007, almost a 10 per cent improvement over the previous year. Mineral activity accelerated, capped by the start of work on the Meadowlake gold mine.

Mining continued to lead the northern economy on several fronts, particularly in the Northwest Territories. Companies flipped territorial properties with considerable regularity. Agnico-Eagle took over control of the Meadowbank property located close to Baker Lake; Zinifex, an Australian firm, acquired Wolfden Resources, assuming control of the Izok and High Lake mine sites in Nunavut. Miramar, working to bring the Doris North mine (part of the Hope Bay development south of Cambridge Bay) into production, sold its holdings in the area to Newmont, one of the world's largest gold producers, for $1.5 billion. The announced plans to proceed with the Doris North property failed to materialize, despite rising gold prices that reached a twenty-seven-year peak late in the year (gold rose 8.2 per cent in 2007, a substantial slowdown from the 27.6 per cent increase of the previous year).

Other major projects moved into production or expanded operations. The Mary River iron mine run by Baffinland, touted as one of Canada's largest base metal mines in decades, inched forward, as did the Churchill diamond mine under development by Shear Minerals. Snap Lake, a large-scale diamond mine run by De Beers, commenced full operations in summer of 2007. Concerns emerged about future prospects, however, as prospecting permits in the Northwest Territories fell by close to half from 2006 – still covering 2.9 million acres – while 150 permits were signed in Nunavut, opening up 6.3 million acres for exploration. Industry representatives attributed the NWT decline to regulatory issues, although there were broader signs, including throughout Nunavut, that the land and development management systems implemented through strong territorial controls and with broader engagement by Indigenous communities and organizations were proving effective in ensuring local participation in the evaluation of proposed projects.

Uranium remained hotly contested. A proposed exploratory venture by Ur-Energy in the Thelon Basin was withdrawn because of concerns about safety and the cultural impact on the people of Lutsei K'e. The government of Canada held firm on the recommendations of the Mackenzie Valley Environmental Impact Review Board, even following sharp protests from mining interests. An old mine site, at Port Radium, re-emerged as a focal point for activity. The local Deline community claimed that serious health problems lingered after the mine closed. Remediation efforts, undertaken by Aboriginal Engineering and using a substantial amount of local labour, continued in an effort to ensure the long-term safety of the site. In Nunavut, the Mineral Exploration and Mining Strategy, released by the government in March 2007 and approved by the Nunavut Tunngavik Inc., included a provision supporting responsible uranium mining. The provision, part of a mining friendlier strategy in the territory, emphasizes maximizing returns for the Inuit and mitigating negative effects on the land and wildlife.

Northern employment continued on an upward trajectory. In the Northwest Territories, unemployment fell to 5.4 per cent, while the employment rate stood at 73.6 per cent, the highest in Canada. The Yukon experienced a small decline in overall employment, but over 70 per cent of all people over 15 years old reported that they were working in 2007. The unemployment rate in the Yukon fell to 5.2 per cent, slightly below the NWT. Employment growth in the largest settlements in Nunavut continued to show healthy year-over-year improvement, jumping 10 per cent in 2007. The territorial employment rate of almost 65 per cent was higher than the Canadian average, and unemployment fell to 8.7 per cent. The Inuit continued to encounter greater problems in the workplace than other Nunavut residents, with employment rates of 55 per cent compared to 90 per cent for non-Inuit. This improvement in economic performance translated into healthy personal incomes. The NWT had the highest personal disposable income in Canada, $41,490 compared to a national average of $27,244. The Yukon ranked second at $38,627. Residents of the territories also had impressive savings rates, with Yukoners holding back almost 17 per cent of their pay, well behind Nunavut at 39 per cent and the NWT at 23.8 per cent. For the country as a whole, the national savings rate was a small 2.7 per cent. Former Yukon premier Tony Penikett used to say that workers came north to "make a killing, not to make a living" (GlobeandMail.com, 26 July). The savings patterns reflect this continuing reality. Workers did not reinvest or spend in the North. Rather, they held onto their money, it appears, to save for an eventual relocation to the south.

General economic conditions changed little in 2007 compared to the previous year. In the Yukon, weekly earnings rose 3.4 per cent, a healthy jump over 2006 but little more than 1 per cent higher than the 2.5 per cent inflation rate. Personal income – a broader figure than the wages – jumped a full 8.4 per cent to reach $46,700, the highest growth rate in the country and the second-highest personal income. Real estate values jumped a full 14 per cent across the territory and 16.5 per cent in Whitehorse. Building permits, conversely, fell off 4.1 per cent, primarily because of the completion of major projects related to the Canada Winter Games. Positive indicators could be seen throughout the economy, with the number of travellers coming to the Yukon jumping 4.7 per cent, again because of the games, with retail sales climbing almost 11 per cent.

Northern and Indigenous-owned companies became increasingly prominent across the North, continuing to fulfil one of the promises of the land claims agreements and capitalize on new partnerships with the private sector in the region. The Arctic Cooperatives remained active and well connected to the national and international cooperative movement. The Inuvialuit Development Corporation and Nunasai used their company NorTerra to buy up Northern Metalic Sales centres in the NWT. The government of Nunavut maintained its support for soapstone carvers, hiring a sectoral coordinator to assist with the provision of tools and to ensure a steady supply of soapstone. Similar assistance was available for cultural organizations and heritage activities, including film, music, and cultural programming, in the hope that these sectors would raise the profile of Nunavut and support a growing tourism industry.

The harvesting economy remained important, particularly in Nunavut and the NWT, although 2007 proved to be a financially difficult year. Fur prices and sales peaked in 2006, only to fall sharply the following year. The price for marten pelts, one of the key commodities, plunged a full 42 per cent from the high of $115 to slightly more than $67. Prices for fisher and mink also declined sharply, with slight increases for lynx and marten and improved trade in wolf and wolverine. A major commercial operation, the Kitikmeot (Cambridge Bay) muskoxen hunt, was hit by bad weather, with the harvest falling from 287 animals in 2006 to 246 in 2007. Northern hunters continued to protest European and southern efforts to block the sale of seal products and, in 2007, there arose a new threat, namely the proposal under discussion in the United States to place polar bears on the threatened species list, a move that would severely undercut the commercial polar bear hunt.

Deh Cho Bridge and northern transportation

Transportation remained a critical issue throughout 2007. Debate over the construction of the Deh Cho Bridge project near Fort Providence stirred again this year. On September 28, the government of the NWT and the Deh Cho Bridge Corporation entered into a $150 million contract for the bridge, designed to cross the Mackenzie River and eliminate the need for the ferry and ice bridge combination that controlled shipments to Yellowknife, approved by the government of the NWT just days before the territorial election. The bridge, over 1 kilometre in length, would operate year-round (there are spring and fall gaps between the operations of the ferry and winter road) and would be paid for by federal subsidies and tolls on commercial trucks. It appeared at one point that the project would founder. Transport Canada halted the permit when oil companies raised questions about the possibility of shipping supplies from Asia to Fort McMurray, using the Mackenzie River. The large ships being considered for the trip would not have been able to move under the proposed bridge. Federal approval came in November.

There were, likewise, increasing demands for the completion of a Mackenzie River highway lining Yellowknife and Inuvik and the development of road access in Nunavut, the latter a particularly costly and uncertain venture. The ice roads that lined Yellowknife to the diamond mines attracted a great deal of attention. The road system, which runs between 400 and 600 miles, depending on the mines in operation each year, was immortalized on the television series *Ice Road Truckers*, which started shooting in 2007, generating considerable debate in the region and resulting in the company blocking future filming along the road. The main ice road system, the Tibbitt to Contwoyto Winter Road, built annually by Nuna Logistics and RTL-Robinson, allowed for supplies to be delivered by truck to widely dispersed mining camps. The ice road broke records in 2007, remaining open for seventy-three days

(27 January to 9 April) and experiencing fewer than one hundred hours of closures, largely because of blizzards. A remarkable 700 drivers were registered to use the road, delivering almost 11,000 loads heading north and another 818 moving loads south. Not all of the regional transportation worked so smoothly. Northern Transportation Company Limited (NTCL) supplied many NWT communities by barge. In 2007, the barges could not get into Aklavik and Fort Good Hope because of low water, forcing communities to airlift in supplies at considerable expense and inconvenience.

The northern society

The social profile of the northern territories did not change profoundly in 2007. In the past, a resource boom such as was experienced in 2007 would have brought a sharp increase in overall population, demands for schooling, housing, and medical assistance, and other major infrastructure and service commitments. In the resource economy, built around fly-in camps and temporary workers, a major increase in mining activity need not result in substantial changes in local populations. At the same time, the greater involvement of northern and Aboriginal firms on the resource supply and support side meant that major expansions in activity resulted more in improved employment prospects for locals than a mass influx of workers from outside. The demographic stagnation felt across much of the North continued in 2007. Consider the case in the Yukon. Indeed, in the decade from 1997 to 2007, the Yukon's total population fell by 1,243, or a total of 3.7 per cent. School enrolment dipped slightly, falling under 5,000 students and showing an 18.8 per cent decline since 1997. The sharp decline in student population was due, in large part, to the territories-wide pattern of seasonal labour and flying workers in for construction and resource projects. Families, in these settings, typically remained in the south. Roughly a quarter of the population in the Yukon was Aboriginal.

Perhaps the dominant social issue of 2007, particularly in Nunavut, related to violence and crime. Crime, including murder, had become quite commonplace across the North, with most of the violence and harm kept within ethnic and community groups. (The level of interracial crime in the territories has been, and remains, very low.) Drug trafficking and alcohol abuse remained a topic of much debate in dozens of communities and a focal point for demands for government action. A survey of policing and crime, released in 2006 and debated over the following year, concluded that residents were pleased with the services provided by the Royal Canadian Mounted Police but were increasingly nervous about the level of crime and violence in their communities. In one of the most frank and open conversations in Canada about the causes and consequences of criminal behaviour, the survey documented sexual and domestic violence, alcohol-related offences, and a perceived jump in property-related crime. Residents blamed the spread of drugs and illegal alcohol use for the rise in crime and wondered why the police did not intercede more often, particularly when the offenders were generally well known within the communities. Residents of smaller communities appealed for more police officers and indicated that they feared reprisals if they assisted police with prosecutions.

The situation in the North was not unrelentingly bad, although the NWT, Nunavut, and the Yukon ranked first, second, and third in overall crime respectively in the country. Nunavut's crime dropped by 5 per cent in 2007, making for two consecutive years of improvement. Violent crime, however, increased significantly over the year, with homicides spiking from two in 2006 to seven in 2007. This, once more, gave Nunavut the highest murder rate in the country. Sexual assaults jumped even more, by 12 per cent, while assaults grew less dramatically. On the positive side of the ledger, property crime fell substantially, with the largest drop coming in the theft categories. Drug-related crime fell impressively, down 26 per cent from 2006 and coming in at the lowest of the territories. Crimes committed by youth continued a welcome and significant downward trend, indicating that the territory's investments in youth and cultural programming were working.

Two high-profile shootings – of Constable Douglas Scott (Kimmirut) and Officer Christopher Worden (Hay River) – pushed the generally good news on crime off the front pages and drew national attention to the challenges of violence and policing in the Far North. The former case, occurring in a tiny, predominately Inuit hamlet of some 450 people, revealed the difficulties small police detachments face in communities that are increasingly the sites of violence and substance abuse. Both officers attended to calls on their own, in an environment where drunkenness and domestic violence are commonplace. In the case of Constable Scott, debate swirled around the North following suggestions that he had not called in a second officer to assist for fear of running up overtime expenses for the detachment. The two cases highlighted the vulnerability of northern police offices and the growing culture of violence and substance-related crime in the region.

Education attracted continuing attention in 2007 as well, sparked in part by the Canada-wide settlement of the residential school compensation question. The debate over the early failure of formal education in the Canadian North focused attention on the current shortcomings of the system. While graduation rates in the NWT had edged over 50 per cent by 2007, they still stood well below the 78 per cent national average. Education achievement in the smaller communities jumped ever more, from 17 per cent in 2005 to close to 60 per cent by 2007. Critics pointed out that grade completion did not equate to educational achievement. Teachers pointed out that the pattern of granting social passes rendered high school graduation less meaningful in terms of substantial educational outcomes. Educational success varied widely across the NWT, often reflecting the effectiveness of school boards and the level of commitment from local politicians. Communities like Behchokǫ̀ (near Yellowknife) demonstrated impressive educational achievement and provided additional evidence that the emphasis on local control was starting to show returns.

Canada Winter Games

Whitehorse hosted the Canada Winter Games in 2007, the first time that this important national event had been held north of 60°. An impressive Pan-Northern Torch Relay preceded the event. The torch was lit in Ottawa and then transported to Alert, at the top of Ellesmere Island. From there, the torch was used to light three territorial torches, each of which toured throughout one of the territories. By the time the torches were reunited in Whitehorse, they had visited over eighty communities, sparking region-wide interest in the games. Over 4,500 athletes and officials came to the territorial capital for the event. The games, which attracted five television stations (English, French, and Aboriginal), included traditional sports and the Inuit Games and Dene Games, adding an Aboriginal flavour to the competition. The pan-northern approach to the games, as exemplified by the torch relay, continued throughout the competition, with advertising, cultural events, and coverage highlighting the Yukon, NWT, and Nunavut.

The Yukon capital benefited significantly from the investment in new sporting facilities, including a major improvement of the local ski hill, an impressive sporting complex for the city, and new residences for Yukon College. Capital investments totalled more than $69 million, a healthy contribution to the city and territory. The total economic impact of the games stood at close to $95 million, with the 7,500 visitors to the territory flooding the territory's hotels and spending another $8.7 million. Airline traffic more than doubled that of February and March

2006. The Winter Games tapped the Yukon's much-vaunted volunteer culture, with over 4,000 local residents (out of a local population of under 28,000) supporting the activities and the athletes. The southern athletes got a taste of the Canadian sub-Arctic winter, with extreme cold interfering with some of the outdoor events, forcing delays and cancellations. In the end, Quebec topped the standings, winning 122 medals, followed by Ontario, Alberta, and British Columbia. All provinces and territories won at least one medal, with the Yukon getting one gold (cross-country skiing) and three bronze (leading Newfoundland and Labrador in the process), the NWT securing a single gold (cross-country skiing), and Nunavut winning one bronze (Judo).

Conclusion

By the end of 2007 the territorial North had secured a firm foothold in the national consciousness. Where for the previous two decades attention had focused largely on the Indigenous struggles for land claims settlements and the emergence of regional governments, the new North focused on the re-emergence of two familiar themes: Arctic sovereignty and northern resource development. The latter grew substantially in 2007, with only the failure to launch the Mackenzie Valley Pipeline project holding the North back from a full-stage boom. And while Canadians remained genuinely concerned about the social problems in the Aboriginal communities in the North, it was debate about control of the continental shelf and Russian claims on the Arctic that really got the nation's attention. From playing a leading role in the global climate change debate through the growing sense that the North held the key to Canada's economic future, the Yukon, NWT, and Nunavut held onto and improved their standing as a region of note and importance to the country as a whole. It was fitting that the Canada Winter Games were held in Whitehorse in 2007. The country, it seemed, was once more coming to terms with its northern obligations, asserting its standing as a circumpolar nation, and awakening to the potential of the Arctic.

ROBERT DRUMMOND

Ontario

Issues of health, education, energy, and the environment continued to capture the attention of Ontario political actors in 2007, as did concerns about the provincial economy. This last issue was conflated with continued disputes about the distribution of federal funds to the provinces and Ontario's claim that it was not receiving fair treatment. The occupation by native protestors of a building site in Caledonia continued, the inquiry into the Ipperwash incident of 1995 filed its report, and the provincial government recognized a need to enhance its involvement in Aboriginal affairs. All of these matters were however overshadowed, or at least encompassed, by the general election campaign which began officially in mid-September but informally took up much of the preceding eight months as well. There was much speculation in the press throughout the spring and summer about Premier McGuinty's prospects for a renewed majority mandate. At the same time the election was held, the province's voters were invited to choose in a referendum between the electoral system then in place and a new system recommended by a citizens' panel that had been convened to consider electoral reform.

The legislature met for the first time in 2007 on 19 March, continuing the second session of the thirty-eighth Parliament. It received the provincial budget almost immediately (on 22 March) but then embarked on a relatively light legislative agenda, passing only fifteen public bills before being prorogued on 4 June, some three weeks ahead of the time originally expected. The lawmakers' output included acts related to civilian review of police, promised changes to the Safe Schools Act, protection of endangered species, regulation of water purification, and an omnibus bill making mainly housekeeping amendments to several laws related to the health-care system. When the legislature commenced the first session of the thirty-ninth Parliament in late November (following the re-election of the Liberal government) its legislative agendas was even slimmer, with the passage of only one public bill (related to employment standards and health insurance for military families). The new Parliament of course began with a throne speech, and the government also tabled an economic update but, perhaps fatigued by a long campaign, it appeared that they were content to reserve their main legislative priorities for 2008.

Health

Much of the action around health care was concentrated in the early part of the year, although clearly the record of the government in health matters was not ignored during the election campaign as it gathered steam in the late summer and into September. On 9 January the Commission of Inquiry into the SARS epidemic of 2003 issued its final report. It called on the provincial and municipal governments to provide better protections for health-care workers in the event of a large-scale outbreak of communicable disease, and that led health-care workers to ask that they be included in the right to refuse unsafe work under the Occupational Health and Safety Act. The commission concluded that there had not been any political interference in the fight against the disease, and therefore the spread and persistence of the outbreak was not attributable to self-serving barriers erected by governments. The province had already taken steps to create a new public health agency, and there was no further action taken immediately on the final report's recommendations.

Later in the month the province introduced a new colorectal cancer screening program. In addition to encouraging high-risk patients to have a colonoscopy at frequent intervals, the province undertook to fund under the Ontario Health Insurance Plan (OHIP) a wide-ranging (nearly universal) opportunity for people to have the less invasive faecal occult blood test that looked for evidence of blood in stool samples. The initiative was part of the province's cancer care strategy, targeting a cancer without noticeable symptoms in early stages, but one that was highly preventable (and treatable if caught early) and with a high risk of fatality if diagnosis was late. The aim was for everyone over fifty years of age to take the test every two years.

On 24 January the Registered Nurses' Association of Ontario (RNAO) organized a one-day session at Queen's Park where approximately one hundred nurses met with members of Provincial Parliament (MPPs) and ministers to discuss health issues. The lobbying effort was partly to enhance awareness among politicians of nurses' importance in the health-care system, but it also served to allow some exchanges of views about possible improvements to care. On 9 May the government announced it would commit $60 million to add 1,200 nurses to the long-term care sector. Doris Grinspun of the RNAO applauded the action but observed that some 9,000 nurses would be needed by 2010 to meet the needs of the health-care system.

The day following the nurses' visit to Queen's Park (25 Jan.), it was reported that 1,000 patients a day were spending seven hours or more in emergency rooms throughout the province. The report opined that emergency room visits should not ordinarily require more than four hours. In some cases, patients were spending long hours in emergency rooms because acute care beds were not available for them to be admitted to hospital. In other cases, the delays could be attributed to shortages of nurses and emergency room doctors. The report made it clear that the backlog was *not* a result of facilities' being overburdened by people with minor ailments.

On 26 January the province pointed to one area in which access to care was being improved. They announced that waiting times for cancer care had declined for the third year in a row. However, in early May, the province's cancer care strategy came under fire on the issue of access to high-cost drug treatments. Cancer patients complained that they had to pay (out of pocket or by private insurance) for cancer-fighting drugs that were not covered by OHIP, despite their being administered in hospitals. NDP critic Shelly Martel claimed this barrier to access was a violation of the Canada Health Act, although a court challenge was not immediately pursued.

In early April, the issue of organ donation, which had arisen around a private member's initiative in 2006, resurfaced with renewed calls for a "negative option" for organ donation on driving licences – that is, unless one declared that one's organs should *not* be made available for donation in case of accidental death, consent would be presumed. However health minister George Smitherman indicated there would be no legislation in that area until after the fall election, and the issue remained in abeyance for the remainder of the year.

When the Liberals campaigned for election in 2003, they had been highly critical of the public-private partnership (or "P3") model for building hospitals – financing of construction for a public facility by private investors. However, soon after coming into office, Premier McGuinty had described P3 as "the right way to go" (Canadian Press, 8 April). In early April, Conservative leader John Tory accused the government of having caused significant cost overruns because of the delay their initial hesitation had engendered. Quoted by Tobi Cohen of Canadian Press (8 April) he said, "All of this was caused by

Mr. McGuinty playing politics instead of just getting on with what was best and building the hospital." He pointed in particular to a North Bay hospital project whose cost, he said, had almost doubled as a result of interest charges. The government countered that the cost of the facility (and its value) to taxpayers had not changed and that borrowing costs were always treated separately and always paid. If some of the increased cost was a result of construction delays, the contractor would be responsible. Other critics saw the interest costs as the major fault of the P3 model. Ontario Health Coalition director Natalie Mehra was quoted by Tobi Cohen (Canadian Press, 8 April) as saying that private borrowing costs were bound to be higher than public ones and that the province would be better off building its own facilities. She described the P3 model as "a very destructive" way to build hospitals and feared that interest costs would siphon money from the health-care system for the next thirty years. The province did not indicate any willingness to abandon the P3 model; neither did they suggest there would be many more such projects. The Conservative criticism – almost the opening shot of the early campaign – did not capture much public attention after the initial flurry.

In September the Ontario Medical Association sought to make health care a major focus of the election campaign when they launched an effort to impress on the parties their four top priorities. First they called for fixing the shortage of health-care professionals, saying 2,000 more doctors and 8,000 more nurses were needed to meet the province's needs properly. Second they asked for implementation of a patient electronic record. Third they sought to ensure the "right care" when and where needed. And finally they asked for a commitment to raising a generation of healthier children. Since the third and fourth priorities contained no specific proposal, they were easy to agree with but gave little guidance on assessing performance. By the time the doctors launched their campaign, election attention had largely turned to a different issue – funding for private, faith-based schools – and health care, despite its importance, probably did not decide many people's votes.

Education

In addition to the steps taken to amend the Safe Schools Act (to add "bullying" to the list of offences and to provide a system of progressive discipline to replace mandatory suspensions), issues of education were quite diverse in 2007 and ranged across the primary, secondary, and post-secondary systems.

In 2005 the government had moved to require that students remain in school until age eighteen. At the time it was recognized that some special programs would be needed to make school – now required – more meaningful for those who would have preferred to drop out. Among the programs proposed was a pilot study that would allow young people between sixteen and nineteen years of age who had dropped out of four high schools in Toronto, Windsor, and Ottawa to earn credits towards their high school diploma while working part-time for the Ontario public service. The program, begun in one school and expending to three others 16 January, would allow eighty participants to earn ten high school credits and get up to twenty-seven weeks of experience while working in clerical jobs in the public service for minimum wage. Teachers were concerned that the scheme not devalue the diploma. Chinta Puxley of the Canadian Press (16 Jan.) quoted Ontario Secondary School Teachers Federation (OSSTF) president Rhonda Kimberley-Young: "We'd like to see more students leave with diplomas but they need to leave with meaningful ones." Conservative critic Frank Klees said the way to ensure higher graduation rates was to change the way Ontario schools were funded, and NDP critic Michael Prue suggested the "pilot" should immediately be extended to many more students.

January also saw the OSSTF stepping outside the school arena to consider international politics when two members of the District 12 (Toronto) local sought to introduce a motion for the OSSTF convention to censure Israel for its treatment of Palestinians. The move angered many Jewish organizations (as well as several union members) but the OSSTF defended the right of its members to move any motion they wished. The local defeated the motion the following day and it did not go to the convention, but the issue highlighted divisions in the union's ranks over the heated conflict in the Middle East.

Access to education for students with autism continued to be an issue, and the province committed to a further $3 million for treatment and for training new therapists. The extra money would ensure over 200 more students would be served, but there remained over 1,000 on a waiting list for intensive behaviour therapy.

The issue of collective bargaining rights for part-time instructors in Colleges of Applied Arts and Technology (CAATs) returned in February, when a group seeking to organize the CAAT part-timers announced they had petitions signed by some 11,000 people calling for bargaining rights. It was estimated that there were approximately 17,000 part-time instructors in the CAATs. When the Supreme Court of Canada ruled in June that the Charter of Rights and Freedoms protected collective bargaining rights, those organizing the campaign for CAAT part-timer collective bargaining reportedly believed the decision was apposite to their case. On 30 August the government acknowledged that part-time and seasonal college employees should have collective bargaining rights, but they indicated their intention to hold a consultative review to provide guidance on how the rights should be given. For example, would work-study students (holding about 30 per cent of part-time jobs) be included among those given union rights? The support for collective bargaining from the College Student Alliance suggested some thought such students would be included.

On 24 May the issue of school safety was given a sad and dramatic spotlight as a 15-year-old boy was shot and killed in a school in the northern part of Toronto. He was the first student ever to be killed by gun violence inside an Ontario school, and his death led to renewed calls for bans on handguns and more attention to safety in schools. It was perhaps a sad coincidence that the government passed its Safe Schools Act amendments less than two weeks later, just before the legislature was prorogued. Proponents of the reforms argued that the zero-tolerance policy of the original act had been ineffective and in fact encouraged gang affiliations among those suspended or expelled, as well as engendering anger over perceived inequities in the application of penalties. Opponents stressed the desire to keep schools safe for those who wanted to be there and argued that suspension or expulsion might be appropriate in many cases. Neither side could say with certainty what would have prevented the incident that cost a young man his life.

In late June there was a foreshadowing of the school-related election issue that would dominate the campaign – faith-based school funding. A group called the Multi-Faith Coalition for Equal Funding of Faith-Based Schools, together with eight families with disabled children, filed suit against the Ontario government alleging discrimination in funding for children with disabilities. In 2000 the government had agreed to extend funding from the health ministry to assist students in private, faith-based schools who required speech therapy, nursing services, occupational therapy, or physiotherapy. As health services, they were to be made available regardless of the educational context. However, funding to assist blind, deaf, and learning-disabled students fell within the budget of the education ministry and as such was restricted to schools within the public or separate school systems. The coalition and the families filing suit argued that this somewhat artificial distinction resulted in discriminatory treatment of blind, deaf, and learning-disabled students in faith-based schools. As a consequence, while the government had set aside $14.4 million for disabled children in faith-based schools, it had spent only $4.5 million. In some quarters it was observed that the discrimination would not occur if faith-based schools were eligible for all Ministry of Education funding. By the end of the summer, John Tory had made the public funding of faith-based schools a signal plank in his election platform, and it would come to dominate the campaign, ultimately to the detriment of Conservative fortunes and Tory's own electoral prospects.

In late July, the Canadian Union of Public Employees elected to target the Liberal government in the election campaign on the issue of school layoffs, principally among the support staff and educational assistants they represented. On 14 August their attack was somewhat blunted by the government's announcement of a new funding formula that would permit the preservation of many such jobs. CUPE was complimentary about the change but took the position that the funds were still insufficient.

In early September, John Tory sought to make an election issue of the standardized tests the Conservatives had introduced when they were in power and which the Liberals continued to employ. Tory claimed the tests were being rigged to boost scores so that the government could point to improvements in education. Both education minister Kathleen Wynne and Charles Pascal, head of the Educational Quality and Accountability Office (which administered the tests) rejected the claim somewhat indignantly. For his part, NDP leader Howard Hampton also suggested the tests were more about government re-election than about improving education, but unlike Tory he undertook to scrap the tests if his party formed the government.

On 5 September the *Globe and Mail* reported that the Canadian Jewish Congress was launching an advertising campaign to persuade the government to fund all faith-based private schools on the same basis as they funded Roman Catholic separate schools. The issue clearly had salience for parents who had chosen their children's schools on religious grounds but found they bore expenses for their choice that Roman Catholic parents need not bear.

That same day Howard Hampton announced the NDP's proposal that tuition fees in post-secondary institutions be reduced to more affordable levels and frozen for a period of four years. The proposal resonated well with students in post-secondary institutions, but there was no estimate of the costs of replacing tuition fees with increased provincial grants.

In the end the biggest contribution of the education portfolio to political life in 2007 was undoubtedly the impact John Tory's commitment to public funds for faith-based schools had on the electoral successes and failures of the Progressive Conservative Party.

Energy and environment

The need to find alternative sources of electric power, if the province was to honour its commitment to close all coal-fired generating stations, remained a priority in 2007. On 11 January a consortium of Portlands Energy, ARISE Technologies, and the University of Toronto opened a solar power research facility on the Toronto waterfront. Canada's largest solar research centre, it would produce between 500 kilowatts and 1 megawatt of power, but it was hoped it would also produce some practical ideas for harnessing solar power for the province's electricity grid. As conservation was seen to be an additional means of addressing the challenge of leaving coal, the province announced a plan 25 January to provide $2.9 million to assist low-income householders to improve the energy efficiency of their apartments. In April, the Coalition of Large Distributors (involving six major electricity distribution firms) reported they had used conservation measures to remove several hundred million kilowatt hours of usage from the grid.

The need for additional generating capacity to replace coal-fired generators remained a concern however, and in mid-April Conservative leader John Tory made his own position clear at a PC fundraising dinner. As quoted by Keith Leslie of Canadian Press (18 April), he accused the premier of having "dithered for four years" in not building more nuclear plants, and he pronounced nuclear power to be "safe, reliable, affordable and it is greenhouse-gas-free."

However, a Toronto conference organized in mid-June by Great Lakes United, an international coalition of environmental lobbyists, heard reports that governments were being irresponsible in pursuing nuclear power. According to a report from Greenpeace (quoted by Christopher Maughan, Canadian Press, 16 June) tritium levels in Lake Ontario (on whose shores there were several nuclear reactors) were three times as high as those in Lake Superior (where there were no reactors). Canada's standards for acceptable levels of tritium were reported to be ten times less strict than those in the United States and seventy times less strict than those in Europe. The same day the CEO of Ontario Power Generation (OPG), Pierre Charlebois, wrote a letter to the editor of the *Globe and Mail* in which he said OPG would not operate its facilities if the operation were unsafe and claimed that radiation levels were voluntarily maintained well below regulatory limits.

Environmentalists did not seem inclined to trust such assurances of voluntary restraint.

With the widespread opposition to nuclear power in some environmental groups, the issue had the potential to be featured in the election to come, but it did not capture significant press or public attention when the writ dropped.

On the conservation front, CanWest News announced 19 April that Ontario was considering a ban on incandescent light bulbs by 2012. Compact fluorescent bulbs were more expensive to buy but used significantly less power and thus were cost-neutral or even produced positive savings in the long run. Despite that fact, reliance on incandescent bulbs was still very widespread and a wholesale conversion to fluorescent was clearly going to be a challenging goal.

In July the Power Workers Union questioned the report of the chief energy conservation officer for 2006, saying the report contained insufficient detail to allow a judgment on whether Ontario was making significant progress in energy conservation and demand management. Moreover, they said, the report did not allow an assessment of the costs of those conservation and demand management efforts. The controversy about how much conservation (as compared with alternative energy sources) would contribute to maintaining the province's energy self-sufficiency remained a live one.

The principal environmental issue that the legislature addressed in 2007 was water quality, following efforts over the past several years to respond to the recommendations of the inquiry into the Walkerton contaminated water tragedy of 2000. In late May the government passed new legislation to safeguard Ontario drinking water (it was given royal assent on the last day of the session), but on the day it was being given third reading, advisories were posted around the legislature building telling people not to drink the tap water in the venerable structure because of lead contamination. Quoted by Unnati Ghandi of the *Globe and Mail* on 31 May, environment minister Laurel Broten observed that the advisories were a poignant reminder of the importance of safe drinking water and a demonstration of the need to reinvest in infrastructure as buildings aged. According to Minister Broten, the legislature had long provided filtered water for staff, but she acknowledged that would not have stopped people from unthinkingly drinking the tap water.

The challenge of achieving good water quality was highlighted a couple of days later (2 June) when the *Globe and Mail*'s Karen Howlett quoted Harry Swain, chairman of the Water Strategy Expert Panel, who was calling for more resources to be provided to small municipalities so they could meet water quality standards. He estimated that a utility would need some 30,000 customers to have economies of scale that would allow them to meet provincial standards without undue hardship. However, there were over 600 utilities operating in the province with fewer than 10,000 customers each.

First Nations

The occupation by Aboriginal protestors of a building site in Caledonia, begun in February 2006, continued throughout the year. The land claim that had given rise to the occupation remained unresolved. In January it was announced that the Ontario Provincial Police would receive a grant of $22 million to offset the additional costs of policing the stand-off between the protestors and other local residents.

As protestors marked the one-year anniversary of the occupation in February, Six Nations chief Allen MacNaughton accused the federal and provincial governments of stalling the land claims talks in the hope that the Six Nations would tire of the process and walk away. He warned that if the pace of talks did not pick up, there might be occupations of other disputed sites around the Grand River. A spokesperson for Indian affairs minister Jim Prentice denied that Ottawa was stalling. Deirdra McCracken (quoted by Chinta Puxley, Canadian Press, 28 Feb.) said, "Absolutely there is political will on behalf of the federal government to see this dispute come to an end." But she added, "I don't think any of us went in thinking we could solve it overnight." The Ontario government – now owners of the disputed land – called on the federal government to come up with a solid proposal to settle the land claim; otherwise, they said, the dispute would continue. The OPP commissioner complained that the federal government had been "missing in action" while their officers were caught between the protestors and the local residents. Haldimand County mayor Marie Trainer complained that Caledonia residents were being held hostage and wondered how the settlement of the claim could take so long.

In early April a complaint was lodged with Solicitor General Monte Kwinter, alleging that OPP commissioner Julian Fantino had sent a "threatening" email on 7 April to Haldimand County politicians in connection with the Caledonia dispute. Fantino apparently warned politicians that he would hold them responsible for any injuries to OPP officers resulting from anti-occupation protests to which Haldimand political figures had lent verbal support. The protests were led by a group called "Caledonia Wake Up Call" headed by Gary McHale, a counter-protestor from Richmond Hill. If further violence resulted from McHale-led demonstrations, Fantino said, he would support officers launching civil suits and would pass additional policing costs on to the county. He also suggested he would recommend not renewing the OPP contract with the county when it expired. Mayor Trainer described the email as "very inappropriate," but the commissioner declined to discuss it, saying it was a private correspondence (even though it had been copied to at least eleven senior provincial officials, including the premier's chief of staff). Minister Kwinter refused to comment on the complaint, which seemed to be mainly a further indication of the frustration felt by all those closely involved in the stand-off. A couple of days after the complaint against Fantino was lodged, twenty-two OPP officers filed their own suit against McHale alleging that he had defamed them on a Web site he had created to represent his views of the Caledonia situation.

In late April Mohawks of the Bay of Quinte area blockaded train lines near Desoronto, saying they intended to remain for forty-eight hours despite an injunction calling for their immediate removal. In the end the band removed the barricades earlier than planned because they feared a violent confrontation. The fact that cooler heads prevailed was welcomed, but the band did warn that further protests were likely unless land claims were settled. A blockade near Desoronto in November 2006 had resulted in the January 2007 arrest of two men, one of whom was charged with uttering death threats while the other was charged with assault and mischief.

A few days before the Desoronto blockade in April, the provincial government had signed an agreement with Grand Chief Stan Beardy of the Nishnawbe Aski Nation (NAN) to create a new forum for dialogue with First Nations of Treaty Five and Treaty Nine. The aim of the forum would be to address implementation of the Provincial Parks and Conservation Reserves Act in NAN territory, as well as natural resource permits and land use planning issues. The issue of resource management on northern reserves had arisen pointedly in January, when the Grassy Narrows First Nation called for a moratorium on all industrial activity on their lands without their permission. They were particularly objecting to clear-cut logging, a practice defended by the natural resources ministry but one that environmental groups opposed along with Grassy Narrows' band members. The band had already blocked logging trucks from entering its territory via Highway 671 for five years. The new forum might provide a means of addressing such concerns, and it appeared to be somewhat easier for the province to engage in collaborative planning with First Nations where land claims were not the main issue.

On 10 May Chief Angus Toulouse (of the Ontario Region of the Assembly of First Nations) joined Premier McGuinty in calling on the federal government to create an independent body to settle hundreds of outstanding land claims. Clearly the Ontario government felt some pressure from protests around land claims, but they asserted the federal government had principal responsibility for finding resolution of those claims.

On 31 May Mr Justice Linden issued his report on the Ipperwash incident of 1995. The report – 1,500 pages based on the testimony of 140 witnesses over 25 months – concluded that Ottawa's neglect of Aboriginal land claims, together with an impatient provincial government and a culturally insensitive police force, had contributed to the death of Aboriginal protestor Dudley George. Federal Indian affairs minister Jim Prentice blamed previous governments, saying that his government was working to improve the land claims system. Premier McGuinty apologized to the George family on behalf of the province, and Aboriginal leaders spoke of the importance of the events at Ipperwash in representing the hopes of First Nations for resolution of their claims and improvement of their conditions and opportunities. Phil Fontaine, national chief of the AFN, was quoted by Chinta Puxley of Canadian Press (31 May) on the futility of force: "We must implement the alternatives – education, new government structures, and respectful negotiations – the peaceful constructive strategies that include meaningful consultation and engagement of our people in order to avert these situations in the future."

Although Mr Justice Linden concluded that former premier Harris had probably employed an obscenity in expressing his frustration with the occupation of the park, he stopped short of blaming the government for the reaction of the police officer who had fired the fatal shot. Through his lawyer Harris indicated no apology would be forthcoming from him or any member of his government. He issued a statement in which he said the inquiry had completely absolved him and his government of the charges he called "malicious and petty political allegations" (Canadian Press, 31 May). However, Conservative leader John Tory said he supported the apology issued by Premier McGuinty and hoped it would allow closure for the George family.

In late June a National Day of Action was called by First Nations groups and protests were held throughout Ontario. John Tory called on the government to ensure strict enforcement of the law in the event, despite his sympathy for many of the protestors' goals. In early September Angus Toulouse pointed to the Day of Action, as well as protests such as the Caledonia occupation, as signalling the need of the government that would be elected in October to rebuild shattered relationships with Aboriginals.

The complexity of the issue for the province was highlighted by the fact that a week later the *Globe and Mail* reported on a suit filed by two residents of Caledonia whose home was adjacent to the occupied site. The residents alleged that they had been harassed by protestors who trespassed on their land, barricaded their home, and threatened them, to the point that the husband had lost his job, the wife had been unable to sustain her home business (a hair salon), and their son had been forced to live at a friend's house in order to concentrate on his school work.

Following the election the government's throne speech was applauded by First Nations. In particular the government moved to implement one of the Ipperwash inquiry's recommendations by appointing Michael Bryant as a minister responsible for Aboriginal affairs. When the Conservatives called in December for a legislative committee to hold hearings on Aboriginal land disputes, Bryant countered that there had already been an extensive hearing (the Linden Commission) and said that the recommendations of the inquiry constituted the government's "road map" for future action (Chinta Puxley, Canadian Press, 18 Dec.).

Federal-provincial relations

In addition to the question of responsibility for resolving land claims and other Aboriginal issues, the province and the federal government had a number of confrontations over the year.

In March the federal government announced grants of $1.548 million for transit (including previously promised matching funds for a Toronto subway extension to York University and the town of Vaughan) as well as for a transmission grid to facilitate importing electricity from Manitoba. Although these funds were welcome, the province insisted they did not significantly alleviate the fiscal imbalance in financing for established programs. While Ontario acknowledged the need for interprovincial redistribution through equalization payments, they questioned some of the recent adjustments to that program, as well as the fairness of allocations in support of health care, post-secondary education, and social services that were independent of equalization.

In November the Ontario government was critical of the federal redistricting proposals for the House of Commons, saying they were discriminatory against Ontario and favourable to western provinces where the federal Conservatives had been more successful.

In both the fiscal and electoral cases, the federal authorities disagreed, and a continuation of hostilities into the new year seemed inevitable.

Election campaign

In early January the Conservatives indicated they had successfully retired their $10.5 million debt and were beginning to raise money for the October election. In the meantime, the government called three by-elections to be held 8 February. When the votes were held, the Liberals' Michael Chan retained Markham (and was subsequently appointed minister of revenue). The Conservatives' Joyce Savoline kept Burlington, but the NDP's Paul Ferreira took York South–Weston from the Liberals.

On 8 February the chief electoral officer responded to the observation that the originally scheduled election date was a Jewish holiday (when observant Jews would not be able to vote). He changed the date to 10 October to the approval of all parties.

In the months leading up to the vote several MPPs declared their intention not to run again. Among those stepping down were NDP member Shelley Martel and Liberals Jennifer Mossop, Marie Bountrogianni, and Mary Anne Chambers. The loss of so many women from the House led to renewed concerns that the legislature – with its evening sittings and lack of on-site daycare – was not a "family-friendly" place. The situation was not improved by a Web site entry from Liberal strategist Warren Kinsella in July which jokingly attributed a comment about wanting to be home baking cookies to Conservative member Lisa McLeod.

Despite (or perhaps because of) the fact that the October election actually resulted in more women entering the House, in December the legislature (on a motion from McLeod) agreed to create a non-partisan committee to investigate ways of making the body more amenable to retaining women (and men) who wanted to combine public service with family responsibilities. Such good intentions, however, did not deter Finance Minister Duncan from getting in hot water in November when he told an audience that his colleague Sandra Pupatello had better legs than he did and that he was the "non-sexy" member from the Windsor area.

As early as 12 February the Conservatives unveiled their plans for the fall campaign. Their focus was to be on John Tory whom they labelled a "different kind of leader," perhaps hoping to distinguish him not only from Premier McGuinty and NDP leader Howard Hampton but also from former premier Mike Harris.

When the Liberals brought in their budget in March, it was scrutinized for what it might portend in terms of the Liberal campaign. Most observers noted the attention to the province's most vulnerable citizens, with a child benefit plan for low-income families, a promised increase in the minimum wage, and a new housing allowance for low-income residents. Canadian Press (22 March) described the budget as having "borrowed heavily from the political playbook of left-leaning critics after three Liberal by-election loses to the New Democrats." The government projected a surplus, and some critics complained that the proposed spending was insufficient to meet the needs supposedly addressed. Others, including John Tory, favoured more tax cuts instead of the proposed expenditures, which Tory described as "a political spending buffet" (ibid.). Whether because of the budget or for other reasons, Tim Peterson, younger brother of former Liberal premier David Peterson, announced 29 March that he would leave the Liberal caucus and sit as an independent. He indicated he would run as a Conservative in the coming election.

In April *Globe and Mail* columnist Murray Campbell described the campaign as being in a "phony war" period, with no party revealing details of their platform until the auditor general had reported on the state of the province's finances, expected in June (12 April). On 9 June however, John Tory announced his plan for providing funding to faith-based schools, on a basis similar to that for Roman Catholic separate schools. In mid-July, there were proposals from the NDP to ensure that revenues collected from industries in northern Ontario should remain in the north, while the Conservatives focused on their proposals to end the tax on diamond mining and to move 10 per cent of the provincial government workforce to the north. The Liberals argued that they already put much more money into the north than they took out in taxes. The environment was apparently seen as an important issue by voters, although the *Globe and Mail*'s Murray Campbell expressed his view at the end of July that the concern would not translate into support for the Green Party.

By 20 August polls were indicating the Liberals might be headed for a minority government because they were losing support to the NDP and the Greens. Polls showed them around 40 per cent, with the PCs near 35 per cent, the NDP at 18 per cent, and the Greens at 8 per cent. Premier McGuinty announced that day that the province would "upload" to its books a number of municipal disability and drug programs at a cost of some $935 million. It was not a campaign promise, he insisted, but merely existing government policy. On 4 September the premier did make an election promise – the creation of a new statutory holiday (Family Day) in February. Small business owners complained that they would bear the cost of lost work time and that the holiday made no economic sense. Employees for the most part were, however, favourably disposed. The same day a coalition of broadcasters announced there would be one televised debate among the leaders on 20 September, although Green Party leader Frank DeJong (unlike his counterparts in PEI and BC elections) would not be included, on the grounds that his party was unrepresented in the current assembly.

When the debate was held, Premier McGuinty was forced to confront accusations of broken promises, Conservative leader Tory was rebuked by the premier for his plan to give public funding to private religious schools, and NDP leader Hampton found it difficult to be heard in what Canadian Press (20 Sept.) called "free-for-all moments." Hampton was critical of the government's record and regretted that faith-based school funding was creating a distraction from what he called the chronic underfunding of public schools. Tory pointed to the health tax, the failure to close coal-fired generators, and the waiting list for treatment of autism as weaknesses in the government's record. McGuinty pointed to the efforts his government had made to achieve lower class sizes, labour peace, and expanded health care. In the end as is so often the case, no one could point to a "knock-out blow" or turnaround moment in the debate, and all sides claimed victory (or at least a favourable showing). Some independent observers credited John Tory with the best performance but ironically concluded it would not be enough to alter his position in the polls.

The Liberals promised increased spending in several areas of education, as well as for transit and other municipal infrastructure. They proposed a "denticare" program for low-income families, costed at $45 million; the NDP proposed a similar program but said it would require $100 million. The Conservatives promised to roll back the health-care levy (as did the Green Party) but increase health spending. They claimed they could find "efficiencies" to save $1.5 billion, and they too proposed increased spending on education. They would review the property assessment system and cap increases at 5 per cent. And they would pursue a zero-tolerance approach on occupations and blockades in Aboriginal land claims disputes. Public funding for faith-based schools was however the cornerstone of their campaign. The

NDP promised an increase in the minimum wage to $10 an hour and a ban on replacement workers during strikes. They (and the Greens) would end public-private partnerships in building infrastructure, and they proposed caps on industrial hydro rates, residential property tax assessments, and transit fares. They and the Greens proposed freezing post-secondary tuition, although the Greens opted for a lower cap. More money for autism treatment, some extra supports for northern Ontario, and reversal of $3.6 billion in costs downloaded to municipalities rounded out the NDP platform.

On election day the voters of the province handed the Liberals another majority mandate – 72 of the legislature's 107 seats. The Conservatives won only 25 seats, and leader John Tory was unsuccessful in his effort to unseat education minister Kathleen Wynne. The question of his continuing as leader was immediately raised, as the campaign's focus on faith-based school funding had been largely his decision and it had proved distinctly unpopular in most ridings. Since he had lost his own seat, it was hard to see how he could easily continue, although he pointed to support from the caucus and the party executive. The NDP won 10 seats, and while Howard Hampton indicated his intention to stay on, there were bound to be challenges to his leadership, given what many in his party described as disappointing results. The turnout for the vote had been the lowest in Ontario history at 52.8 per cent.

The voters had also soundly rejected the opportunity provided them by the Citizens' Assembly to reform the province's electoral system. The Assembly had recommended a mixed-member proportional system which would have increased the size of the legislature to 130 seats, of which 70 per cent would be elected in constituencies by plurality vote, while the remaining 30 per cent would be distributed from party lists to bring parties closer in proportion of seats to their proportion of the popular vote. Parties would need at least 3 per cent of the vote to get any seats.

To be approved, the new system would have needed 60 per cent of the vote in the province *and* majority support in 60 per cent of the provincial ridings. The recommended reform met neither of these standards; indeed, over 60 per cent of voters preferred the existing system. If the recommended system had been in place for the 2007 election, and if people had cast their votes in the same proportion for the parties, the result would have been a minority Liberal government, with 59 or 60 seats; the Conservatives would have had 38 or 39, the NDP 21, and the Green Party 10. Electoral reform seemed likely to be abandoned for a time, although proponents insisted that not enough had been done to inform voters of the character of the reform, and they pledged to continue the fight.

The newly elected government set about crafting a new Cabinet, bringing in ten new members, shifting Michael Bryant into the new portfolio of Aboriginal affairs, and moving Dwight Duncan to finance, owing to Greg Sorbara's decision announced 26 October that he would resign his Cabinet seat in order to spend more time with his family. Because of decisions by some Cabinet members not to run again (and the defeat of one member in the election) only four veterans were dropped in the shuffle. The government met the House in late November, clearly saving most of their throne speech agenda until the coming year.

In mid-November Murray Campbell of the *Globe and Mail* reported the province would not appeal a judge's ruling that struck down the recently approved adoption disclosure legislation. Instead they would redraft to allow parents and children involved in past adoptions to veto the disclosure of their information. Supporters of the veto right were pleased with the ruling, and former NDP MPP Marilyn Churley (who had been a driving force behind adoption disclosure reform while in the legislature) was reluctantly content with the loss of automatic disclosure and pleased that the retroactivity of the bill's continuing provisions would be maintained. The ruling (and the decision not to appeal) was a vindication for privacy commissioner Ann Cavoukian, who had argued that the right of veto was required in the law.

In December just before the Christmas recess, the government introduced a fall economic statement that promised increased funding for municipal infrastructure and some tax measures to assist manufacturing and resource industries. Action on those items would come in 2008.

Writing in the journal *Policy Options* (Nov. 2007, vol. 28, no. 10), political consultant (and former federal NDP campaign director) Robin Sears wondered at the low turnout and soporific character of the campaign. He pointed to the challenges faced by the new government – energy shortages, increasing air pollution, possible unrest among public-sector unions as numerous contracts came due, comparatively poor statistics in child poverty and post-secondary education funding, property tax concerns among middle-class voters, a declining manufacturing sector, and a serious municipal revenue shortfall in its largest city – and wondered whether the Liberals could cope. Conservative senator Hugh Segal, writing in the same issue, bemoaned the failure of electoral reform and wondered at the complacency of voters. He noted that proponents of change had not yet addressed the trade-off apparently motivating voters between "the risks of illegitimacy, vote distortion and false majorities" and "the risk of system change."

Despite an election that had firmly renewed the status quo, there remained the prospect of serious challenges and significant debate – albeit perhaps with new leaders in Opposition – as the year wound to a close.

DANIEL SALÉE AND RICHARD BISAILLON

Quebec

The year 2007 in Quebec's history will be remembered for two distinct episodes with important political and policy ramifications. First Quebecers elected a minority provincial government on 26 March. It came as quite a surprise; minority governments are unheard of in Quebec politics. One has to go back to 1878 for the last time this happened. Jean Charest's Liberals were re-elected, but the message was clear: Quebecers meant to keep them on a tight leash. Their confidence in the Charest government and the policies it had implemented during its first term in office had none of that resounding vitality politicians like to see. The other surprise of this election was the downgrading of the Parti Québécois (PQ) almost to third-party status as Mario Dumont's Action démocratique du Québec (ADQ) passed ahead with a 13 per cent gain in popular vote and 37 additional seats in the National Assembly (up from only 4 in the 2003 election) to become the new official Opposition.

The second memorable episode of 2007 of course is the controversy over "reasonable accommodation," that long-standing policy designed to facilitate the inclusion of individuals from minority groups into the mainstream of Quebec society. The mounting backlash, which had been stirring for some time, against state-sanctioned practices meant to accommodate cultural and religious differences brought to the fore the anxieties of Quebecers over political concerns related to identity and minority integration, and it spurred the government into setting up a commission of consultation to look into the matter. Although other policy issues called out for the consideration of the public during the year, none will match the attention reasonable accommodation garnered or the political energy it mobilized.

The election: reconfiguring the political landscape

First pundits and those in the know maintained that Jean Charest would call an election for the fall of 2006. The rumour persisted through the summer and part of the fall until October when it became clear that the idea of a fall election was premature. "A regular term is five years," declared Monique Jérôme-Forget, president of the Treasury Board. "[W]e've only been in power for three and a half years. There is no compelling reason for us to call an election at this point."[20] By January 2007 the tide started to turn. For the first time in three years, some public opinion polls were showing a slight advantage to the Liberals over the Parti Québécois. On 21 February, hoping to capitalize on apparently more favourable winds, Jean Charest announced that he was calling an election for 26 March, about a year earlier than was necessary. It was a bit of a gamble. Most observers thought that he was going to go down in history books as a one-term wonder because large segments of the population (the labour movement and community groups in particular) were so dissatisfied with the unequivocally neoliberal policy agenda his government had put forward since 2003.

But like other gambles Charest took in his political life, he won that one too, however bittersweet the victory. The Liberals squeaked by with a 13 per cent drop in popular vote (from 46 per cent in 2003 to 33 per cent in 2007) and a loss of 28 seats in the National Assembly (going from 76 in 2003 to 48 in 2007) to form a minority government. The ADQ secured an unexpected 31 per cent of the popular support and brought in 41 representatives in the National Assembly, the vast majority of them with little or no political experience, while the PQ with 28 per cent of the votes – its worst performance in thirty-seven years – had a hard time clinging to 36 of the 45 seats it had prior to the election. The 2007 general election was remarkable for the crisis of voters' confidence which was faced by the two major political parties that have alternately dictated the nature and contents of Quebec politics for the past four decades. Both lost significant portions of their traditional basis of electoral support. The PQ was clearly at its lowest ebb, and the Liberal party's pyrrhic victory constituted for all intents and purposes a thinly veiled setback.

This dramatic outcome is attributable to a combination of factors. Jean Charest's rocky first term in office no doubt diminished his chances of keeping his party's showing at a level approaching the results of the 2003 election. Dubbed by detractors the worst government Quebec had since the Taschereau administration in the 1920s and 1930s, Charest's Liberals had, by any account, an uneasy relationship with the Quebec

20 Translated from the French. Quoted in Denis Lessard, "Pas d'élections hâtives," *La Presse*, 11 Oct. 2006.

population almost from day one (André Pratte, *La Presse*, 16 May 2010). Intent on "re-engineering" the Quebec state and stressing individual responsibility to the detriment of social solidarity in most aspects of public policy, their initiatives regularly met with intense opposition, forcing them to backtrack on quite a few occasions, seeming rudderless and indecisive. Although their fortune improved slightly in early 2007, their image as a vacuous and insipid government stuck and certainly did not help their case going into the election; Charest's uninspired defence of his record during the televised debate of the party leaders on March 13 did little to change that.

Thankfully for Charest, the Opposition leader, the PQ's André Boisclair, also had to contend with an image problem – his own to begin with: since his election as party leader in 2005, Boisclair has had to defend his reputation against references to his openly gay lifestyle and substance abuse during his time as Cabinet member. His television appearance, not long after he took the helm of the PQ, in a comedy sketch depicting a homosexual relation between Stephen Harper and George W. Bush also raised doubts about his judgment and his ability to act properly and with dignity as a political leader.

More importantly though, Boisclair had to grapple with the PQ's steadily declining popular support since the 1995 referendum and the waning political appeal of the sovereignist option by which the party mainly defines itself. Through the better part of the past decade, the party has been plagued by internal strife over leadership issues, ideological squabbles between its left and right wings, and very public shows of angst over the proper strategy most likely to lead to the sovereignty of Quebec, all of which have had a dispiriting effect on an electorate increasingly less convinced that the politics of sovereignty matter as much as PQ stalwarts proclaim. Boisclair did reasonably well during the electoral campaign and held his own during the televised debate. His opponents engaged with him on issues and did not seek to impugn his private lifestyle choices. Still, his declared commitment to the party policy of holding another referendum on sovereignty as soon as possible after taking the reins of power kept at bay many voters who despite their disgruntlement with the Liberals would not consider the PQ as a valid alternative precisely on account of its continued insistence on sovereignty. They sided with the ADQ instead. Finally, Boisclair's neoliberal leanings rubbed the wrong way many leftist sovereignists for whom the sovereignty ideal is intimately linked with a social-democratic and even socialist social project. While they may have voted for the PQ in the past, with Boisclair in charge, they preferred to redirect their vote this time around to political formations whose ideology is closer to their own, namely the new, socialist sovereignist Québec Solidaire (QS) party and perhaps even the Green Party, who together garnered over 7 per cent of the vote.

Mario Dumont's and the ADQ's surge in popularity was certainly owed in part to the Charest government's sketchy record and the PQ's complicated internal dynamics. In fairness, though, the ADQ's electoral success in 2007 also reflected Dumont's undisputable abilities in the political arena. Despite his relative youth, he is a seasoned politician with a strong and well-honed populist streak in him. In the months leading to the election, he managed to increase his and his party's political capital quite substantially by latching on and indeed fuelling the reasonable accommodation controversy that had been brewing in the media for about a year. Following a string of news reports about some Muslim men insisting that their wife be examined only by a female doctor in emergency wards, a Montreal YMCA agreeing to frost its windows looking into the courtyard of a neighbouring Hassidic school so as to prevent the exposure of its pupils to the sight of women bouncing about on exercise machines in gym apparel, or again the decision of a local centre of social and public health services to offer prenatal classes for Muslim, Sikh, and Hindu women where men are not allowed, Dumont made strong statements on a television show in November 2006, echoing public ill-feeling about such cases of "unreasonable accommodation" and laying the blame on the government for its inaction in the matter. He was quite successfully riding in the process a growing wave of increasingly vocal concerns among Quebec's French Canadian population regarding the integration of immigrants and what many perceived as their imposition in Quebec society of cultural and religious values foreign to Quebec's mainstream social norms and rules of public behaviour. By the time the election was called, the ADQ had more than doubled its popular support, from 11 per cent the year before to nearly 25 per cent.

The reasonable accommodation debate did not quite become the focal point of the electoral campaign, but it unquestionably helped Dumont and the ADQ bring their particular agenda into fuller view. It provided the ADQ an opportunity to occupy centre stage in public debates and be more visible, which, as a small third party, it seldom enjoyed. Dumont had enough savvy to parlay that opportunity into votes. Beyond the reasonable accommodation debate, the ADQ owed its success as well to the growing presence in Quebec society of a strong and fairly well-rooted strain of conservatism. Despite the progressive, left-liberal and social-democratic aura that has emanated from Quebec society since the days of the Quiet Revolution, undercurrents of ideological conservatism have continued to pervade the public sphere. In recent years especially, intellectuals and policy experts who quite boldly assert their admiration for ideas of the New Right (distrust of the state, strong faith in the market as key instrument of social and individual accomplishment, suspicion towards ethnocultural diversity and multiculturalism, return to traditional gender roles, etc.) have come to take a central and influential place in public debates.[21] Their views resonate well with large segments of the white francophone, suburban middle class as well as with rural and semi-rural populations who are unhappy with the way Quebec society has evolved and readily point the finger at what are, to them, sources of frustration and dissatisfaction, namely the burdensome state expenditures they are largely financing out of their income and consumer taxes with little or no evidence of return; the multiplicity of state regulations; the assault on the Western values they hold dear; the laxness with which criminals are dealt with on account of Charters of Rights; the deterioration of family bonds; and unending, unproductive constitutional and administrative bickering between Quebec and Ottawa. Mario Dumont's discourse, strongly tinged with New Right tenets, well translated the sentiments of that particular, demographically significant constituency and literally spoke to them. They were ready for him. Without the growing and increasingly assertive presence of the neoliberal conservatism they espoused in Quebec's political landscape, the ADQ might well have never emerged as forcefully as it did.

Reasonable accommodation

Mario Dumont's decrying of Quebec's reasonable accommodation practices came on the heels of a widely unpopular ruling of the Supreme Court released in March 2006 authorizing a young Sikh teenager to carry his *kirpan* on the premises of the Montreal-area high school he was attending, against the school's own rules prohibiting the possession of knives within its confines.[22] In the months that followed, public forums, including radio and television public affairs programs, newspapers

21 Well-known figures include Mathieu Bock-Côté and neoliberal think tank Institut économique de Montréal. See Frédéric Boily, *Le conservatisme au Québec: retour sur une tradition oubliée* (Québec: Presses de l'Université Laval, 2010).

22 The *kirpan* is a ceremonial dagger that Sikh males are required to wear at all times as a sign of their religious faith.

op-eds, and weblogs were replete with remonstrations denouncing the "excesses" of reasonable accommodation and calling for an end to state-sanctioned socio-institutional asymmetry. Dumont's fall 2006 intervention certainly added a significant voice to the chorus, but the outcry reached a fevered pitch at the end of January 2007 when the town council of Hérouxville felt compelled to issue an edict, a code of conduct for immigrants who might consider settling in its midst. Hérouxville is a small, rural, socially homogenous municipality, located off the beaten path, 160 kilometres northeast of Montreal; its people are firmly rooted in Quebec's majority culture; it has no recent history of immigrant settlement and does not anticipate any immediate influx of newcomers from abroad. The town's code, which was widely reported by global news outlets, emphatically warned prospective immigrants that they are coming to a country with customs that are appreciably different from theirs, where men and women are considered equal and can freely and unrestrictedly interact in public settings, schools do not provide special venues for prayers, headscarves and face coverings are not accepted, and special dietary habits are not accommodated in public institutions. This unexpected initiative was unequivocally meant to suggest that any cultural and religious manifestations that do not accord with the norms and values of the host society were not welcome. Despite jeers and sneers dismissing the people of Hérouxville as narrow-minded country bumpkins, town officials persisted in their way and even lobbied the government to amend the Charter of Rights and Freedoms in order to abolish reasonable accommodation. Many applauded Hérouxville's action and a number of towns in the region stated their intention to follow suit.

Dumont had touched a raw nerve. His position cannot be simply written off as the right-wing rant of a conservative demagogue. Different public opinion polls taken at the time of and after his November 2006 declaration consistently showed that, like him, a significant majority of Quebecers (between 60 and 75 per cent depending on the survey) were against most or any form of socio-institutional accommodation for immigrants and ethnocultural minorities. What might have seemed at the time like the calculated, opportunistic pronouncement of a politician on the rise quickly turned into a deep-reaching and broad-based social debate over immigration, Quebec identity, and civic rules of intercultural coexistence in the public space, with a strong potential for unsavoury twists and turns if unmonitored.

The government reacted to the situation by setting up on 8 February a commission of consultation on practices of accommodation related to cultural differences, composed of fifteen academics and specialists of intercultural relations headed by two prominent Quebec intellectuals: award-winning sociologist and historian Gérard Bouchard and world-famous political philosopher and social theorist Charles Taylor. The commissioners were instructed to take stock of accommodation practices related to cultural differences and assess concomitant social stakes in light of other experiences outside Quebec; conduct an extensive consultation among individuals and organizations wishing to state their views on accommodation practices related to cultural differences; and make recommendations to the government with a view to ensure that accommodation practices related to cultural differences conform to Quebec's values as a pluralistic, democratic, and egalitarian society.

The co-chairs of the commission toured Quebec during the fall of 2007 (from 17 Sept. to 13 Dec.), holding twenty-two generally well-attended, televised public hearings and citizens' forums in seventeen regions and municipalities where ordinary citizens were invited to present briefs and speak their mind freely about reasonable accommodation. In addition, four province-wide forums were organized by the Institut du Nouveau Monde, a left-of-centre think tank, at the request of the commission. Overall the process attracted 3,423 participants and generated 901 written submissions and 761 requests for testimony (241 of which were heard by the co-chairs). Although regrettable and reprehensible remarks about immigrants and minority cultures were voiced on a number of occasions, the unpleasant collective spleen-venting that some observers dreaded did not really occur. The co-chairs discouraged and did their best to deflect any hint of disrespectful or ill-informed comments.[23] Still the end result essentially confirmed what numerous letters to the editor, weblogs, and public opinion polls had widely suggested during the months preceding the commission's public hearings: most Quebecers would rather do away with reasonable accommodation insofar as it applies to ethnocultural diversity.

What exactly was at stake? The principle of reasonable accommodation implies in essence that for social justice to be served it may sometimes be necessary to treat certain individuals differently or with special attention. It has been regularly and successfully invoked by the Quebec Human Rights Commission and by Quebec and Canadian courts since the 1980s to ensure that the particular needs of individuals belonging to minority social groups will not be adversely affected

23 For a full account of the commission's work and related events, see Jeff Heinrich and Valérie Dufour, *Circus Quebecus* (Montreal: Boréal, 2008).

and will be respected in accordance with the fundamental rights and freedoms guaranteed by the Quebec and Canadian Charters of Rights and Freedoms. Practices of reasonable accommodations have thus been designed and implemented in keeping with the state's legal and constitutional obligations to avert a broad range of potential situations of discrimination. They may include, for example, special allowances made in the workplace for people suffering from a physical handicap or incapacity that could preclude them from fulfilling all the requirements of their job description; dispensations for individuals with recognized religious requirements preventing them from working or attending school on certain days or at certain times; or the relaxation of dress codes in public schools (in the case of the *hijab*) or institutions (in the case of the turban for Sikh police officers) for the benefit of individuals whose commitment to their religion forces them to wear garments or symbols that do not conform with established norms.

Basically, then, a reasonable accommodation stems from a state prescription enjoining public institutions as well as private organizations to offer special arrangements, when possible and if requested, to individuals who might be discriminated against by rules or norms that are initially meant to apply to everyone. Practices of reasonable accommodation are usually negotiated on a case-by-case basis following a request for singular treatment by one or several individuals. It is generally understood that they cannot contravene accepted principles of social interaction (such as gender equality for example) or the stipulations of a labour contract; they cannot be enforced to the detriment of public safety or the efficient operation of the organization from which accommodation is sought; nor can their implementation entail the obligatory provision of additional human and physical resources at a cost that could prove financially adverse for the organization. As the name suggests, a reasonable accommodation should be offered only when such a request can be easily met within the operational parameters of the institution or corporation and does not force it to deviate significantly from its usual mode of operation or mission.

Practices of reasonable accommodation have by and large proven to be a useful tool of intercultural relations management favouring social cohesion and a relatively smooth integration of members of ethnocultural minorities into the mainstream of Quebec society. Despite media coverage portraying the accommodation of difference as a thorny social issue, the implementation of reasonable accommodations has worked well for many years and without much fanfare to ensure the generally harmonious and unproblematic coexistence of the francophone majority with growing and increasingly diverse ethnocultural minorities in innumerable situations (Katia Gagnon, *La Presse*, 29 May 2006). Notwithstanding the impression that requests of dispensation and privileged treatment on account of religious or cultural claims have multiplied and become harder to manage, only a very small proportion of members of ethnocultural or religious minorities avail themselves of accommodation policies in reality. Of the 5,482 grievances submitted to the Quebec Human Rights Commission between 2000 and 2005, barely 2 per cent had to do with religious discrimination, and only one-third of those pertained directly to requests for accommodation. The majority of grievances for religious discrimination came from Christian (mostly Protestant) communities and not from Jews or Muslims as the media's intense focus on the latter might lead one to believe – which also indicates that, contrary to popular belief, the bulk of grievances and requests for accommodation do not necessarily originate from immigrant groups.[24] In reality, the application of the principle of accommodation benefits just as much members of the majority Christian culture as it does outside-of-mainstream individuals: a day off on Sunday, the exemption granted religious Catholic and Protestant students from taking part in an introductory course on sexuality in elementary schools, nurses being excused from assisting in clinical abortions on account of their religious belief on that issue, civil registrars refusing to officiate at same-sex unions on grounds of conscience – these are all everyday examples showing that reasonable accommodation transcends imperatives of immigrant or minority integration.

In-depth studies into the reasons why established and generally unproblematic practices of reasonable accommodation were suddenly called into question by Quebecers have yet to be done. Preliminary insights have blamed the whole episode on the media's sensational and deliberate extrapolation of otherwise isolated and insignificant incidents; others chalked it up to the influence of undercurrents of Islamophobia allegedly running through the Western social imaginary since 9/11. Whatever the explanation one favours in the end, it is clear that the strong feelings expressed against reasonable accommodation before and during the hearings of the Bouchard-Taylor Commission shattered the image of intercultural harmony Quebec likes to project of itself. In this respect, though, Quebec is not unique. It is part of a growing tendency observable in Western liberal democracies to retreat

24 Yolande Geadah, *Accommodements raisonnables: Droit à la différence et non à la différence des droits* (Montreal: vlb éditeur, 2007), 23–25.

from the pluralist ethos they have cultivated over the past few decades.[25] Quebec's open reasonable accommodation debate stressed unequivocally the perennial dilemma facing liberal democracies about what to do with foreigners and bearers of otherness: make them more like mainstream society and ensure that they will not contaminate the dominant culture and institutions, or open a wider democratic space in which they can also feel at home on terms that are more familiar and more amenable to them?

The general narrative that emanated from a majority of the briefs presented at the commission made clear which side of this dilemma a good chunk of Quebec's population felt the state ought to privilege. At least four threads made up this narrative: (1) Current practices of reasonable accommodation open the doors to religious and cultural norms that stray too far away from Quebec's defining and fundamental value set. If we are not vigilant they will eventually transform Quebec society in ways that will not be recognizable or acceptable to mainstream Quebecers. (2) The cultural majority group is doing a favour to immigrants and other ethnocultural minorities by letting them in and letting them share the benefits of a great way of life: they should be grateful, adapt to the mainstream, and not ask for any special privilege. (3) Most non-Christian religions (Islam was singled out regularly as the most problematic) are against gender equality and are potentially deleterious to women: they must be reined in and their most objectionable practices be kept in check. (4) At the end of the day, formal equality is the only way to go; no one should enjoy prerogatives and privileges which do not apply in the same way to others.

The message was unambiguous. The diverse ethnocultural fabric of Quebec society is not at issue, but the presence of the *Other* must be more strictly regulated. Without the imposition of some exacting code of social conduct, without clear guidelines of what is expected of immigrants, particularly those whose cultural mindset differs markedly from the majority's, Quebec as a French-speaking, egalitarian, democratic, and secular society risks disappearing. Practices of reasonable accommodation only foster the development of a space of cultural and normative indeterminacy. They fail at integrating immigrants properly into the mainstream of Quebec society, confuse them as to what is socially acceptable behaviour, and create resentment among the cultural majority group.

25 See Christian Joppke, "The Retreat from Multiculturalism in the Liberal State: Theory and Policy." *British Journal of Sociology* 55, no. 2 (2004): 237–57.

Life in a minority government

Outside the reasonable accommodation debate, life went on of course, but not quite as usual. The minority situation in which the Charest government found itself after 26 March had a sobering effect on it. In his inaugural address in the National Assembly on 9 May Charest humbly recognized that the electorate's message was clear: Quebec voters wanted to see a different way of governing whereby the government and the Opposition would work together to promote and implement policies that would benefit all Quebecers.

Charest's willingness to work with the Opposition – and conversely, whether the Opposition would be disposed to support the government – was soon put to the test. The budget speech by the new finance minister, Monique Jérôme-Forget, on 24 May immediately raised the ire of the Opposition and triggered a week-long political crisis, which came very close to bringing down the government barely two months after the election.

Among the main objectives of this budget, the minister proposed to lower the income tax by $950 million, a significant sticking point for the Opposition. The ADQ accused the government of being irresponsible by doing away with much-needed income and transferring onto future generations the onus of paying for its recklessness. The PQ found this income tax reduction illogical and inappropriate: how can the government deprive itself of such an important sum when it anticipates having problems financing the health system? The ADQ also reproached the government for proceeding in a way that will increase the public debt by nearly $7 billion over the next two years in spite of its balanced budget. In this context, the ADQ further charged, the government's insistence on presenting a balanced budget was totally deceiving as it did nothing to lower the public debt. The PQ's other criticisms focused on what it called the government's lack of vision in the fields of education and health. It deplored the fact that while at least $450 million of new money, according to its estimation, needed to be invested without delay in those key areas, the government did not share its sense of urgency. Indeed, there was no room in the budget for new investments in education and only $55 million was earmarked for health. For their part, unions, community organizations, and Québec Solidaire denounced the government's plan to eliminate the capital tax for all enterprises by the end of 2010 and its failure to make good on its electoral promises of creating new places in day-care centres, recruiting up to 1,500 new doctors, and massively reinvesting in post-secondary education as telling indications that the government had no consideration for ordinary people.

The government fought back, insisting vehemently that its budget was good because it was purposely designed to ease the tax burden of the middle class – a rather loosely used concept bandied about in mainstream political discourse to refer (erroneously) to the bulk of the Quebec population – and protect its interests. Despite the government's initial reluctance to amend its budget in any way, both Opposition parties' intention to vote against it (and implicit threats of bringing the government down), and much political posturing on all sides, a deal was finally brokered between the government and the PQ at the last minute before the vote scheduled to take place in the National Assembly, one week after the budget speech. The government maintained its $950 million tax relief but agreed in the end to add $60 million more for health, $30 million targeted for students with learning difficulties, and $21 million for resource-rich regions – in all, $111 million the government was to draw from increasing the income tax of banks and oil companies by 2 per cent two years earlier than planned. This move did not sit well with the ADQ, who accused the government of hypocrisy, arguing that whatever tax increases were imposed on private corporations like the banks and oil companies would inevitably trickle down to the consumers and could hardly be seen as a gesture to protect the middle class. The ADQ refused to take part in any discussion to make changes to the budget and unequivocally voted against it. The PQ, still unhappy with the revised budget because the government maintained the income tax cut, but reeling from its recent electoral rout and painfully aware that it was in no position to go into – and win – a new election, arranged so as not to defeat the government: only three of its members of the National Assembly (MNAs) were sitting in the National Assembly at the time of the vote; they too voted against the budget, but it went through nonetheless, 46 yeas against 44 nays.

Political observers and commentators have argued that the outcome of this tension-filled political drama played ultimately to no one's advantage. The Liberals' stubbornness had them painting themselves into a corner, looking inflexible and arrogant. The ADQ's adamant refusal to take part in negotiations over possible ways of amending the budget, risking in the process to bring down the government so soon after the election, raised doubts particularly about the judgment of its leader. Finally, it was clear to everyone that the PQ was only bluffing, for it had no intention of facing another election; this episode showed how politically weak it still was.

The fracas over the budget set the tone. In the months that followed, a more explicitly adversarial and electorally driven political dynamic within and outside the National Assembly was to become the norm. Mario Dumont's ADQ rarely missed a chance to push Charest up against the wall, reminding him that he could easily be made to fall should he not toe the line.

Charest found himself – too often, in all likelihood, to his and his party's taste – having to back-pedal on decisions after a scathing public critique from Dumont. Political observers could not help but notice that the government seemed to borrow from the ADQ's program to the point where some wondered openly who, between Charest and Dumont, was actually leading the government (Josée Legault, *Gazette*, 6 July; Michel David, *Le Devoir*, 24 May; Denis Lessard, *La Presse*, 24 May). By the end of June, despite the budget's income tax relief, the rate of satisfaction towards the Charest government had gone down seven percentage points from the previous month to 36 per cent; and voters' intentions for the Liberals were at 27 per cent, 6 per cent lower than what they had achieved for the election, three months earlier. Had there been another election at that time, the Liberal party would have come in dead last, behind the ADQ and the PQ (Vincent Marissal, *La Presse*, 27 June).

Clearly, the government was in an uncomfortable position. More unpopular than ever, under constant attacks from the Opposition, Charest and his Cabinet were almost paralysed, gingerly moving about, reluctant to instigate new policy initiatives or legislative proposals for fear of being brought down. The action plan presented by the premier in his inaugural address in May was relatively light and, some thought, unimpressive (Michel David, *Le Devoir*, 10 May; Jean-Jacques Samson, *Journal de Québec*, 10 May). In fact, the government spent most of the year dodging bullets. At that, it did not do too badly on the whole. After narrowly defeating a non-confidence motion tabled by Dumont in early November, it was still standing as the year came to a close.

Meanwhile in the sovereignist camp: Quebec nationalism on the edge?

Small consolation perhaps for Charest, but the very political party and ideology he purposely came to Quebec politics to stave off were also facing significant challenges of their own. On 8 May, a little more than a month after the election, André Boisclair stepped down as leader of the Parti Québécois. He would later resign as MNA for Pointe-aux-Trembles on 15 October, bringing an end to a bright political career that spanned nearly two decades. Boisclair was first elected to the National Assembly under the PQ banner in 1989 at the age of 23, the youngest parliamentarian ever in the history of Quebec politics. He would later be invited to join the Bouchard and Landry Cabinets in which he held several portfolios, including relationship with citizens and immigration, social solidarity, environment, and municipal affairs. Following Bernard Landry's resignation in 2005, and after an eighteen-month eclipse from active politics, he successfully ran for the leadership of the PQ, finishing well ahead of his closest rival, Pauline Marois. His relative youth certainly played to his advantage as party militants hoped to rejuvenate the party's image. Although Boisclair's sovereignist credentials were strong and undisputed, he did not necessarily belong to the *purs et durs* (hardcore) nationalist bloc of the PQ. Much more of a civic rather than an ethnic nationalist, he had a widely pluralist view of Quebec diversity and leaned on the side of caution when it came to formulating a political strategy for the achievement of Quebec sovereignty. He was in favour of holding another referendum as soon as possible but did not want an eventual return of the PQ to power to be considered an automatic licence for a unilateral declaration of independence, much to the dismay of the PQ's ultra-nationalist elements who, in the end, never ceased to call his moral authority over the party into question.

The resignation of Boisclair triggered yet another political crisis within the PQ – the second one in two years – exposing further the party's vulnerability and revealing again the same fault lines that keep reappearing between radicals and moderates every time doubts about the depth of the leader's sovereignist convictions are raised. Pauline Marois soon emerged as the only contender to replace Boisclair (Bloc Québécois's Gilles Duceppe announced his intention to run almost simultaneously but quickly withdrew his candidacy) and was acclaimed as the new leader of the PQ on 27 June, the first woman ever to be chosen as the head of a major political party in Quebec. She temporarily led the party from outside the National Assembly until she easily won a by-election in the riding of Charlevoix on 24 September. Marois is one of the party's key players whose history with the PQ goes back to the early 1980s when she joined the Cabinet of René Lévesque as minister for the status of women. She would later go on to hold a variety of high-profile Cabinet posts in all the other PQ governments, including education, finance, and health and social services.

The arrival of Marois at the helm of the PQ had a calming effect and improved the party's ranking in voters' intentions. Different public opinion polls conducted in late August and early September showed that the PQ led by three or four percentage points over the ADQ and 7 per cent over the Liberals; among francophone voters the PQ stood at close to 40 per cent, in comparison with roughly 34 per cent for the ADQ and 20 per cent for the Liberal Party. Similarly, at 37 per cent, Marois came significantly ahead of Mario Dumont (25 per cent) and Jean Charest (22 per cent) as the political leader Quebecers would prefer to see as their premier.[26]

The outlook was good for Marois and her party, but it did not automatically translate into unqualified support for Quebec sovereignty, the PQ's main raison d'être. One public opinion poll released in the last week of June revealed that only 32 per cent of Quebecers would vote in favour of sovereignty had a referendum been held at that time (André Pratte, *La Presse*, 27 June). Another one, published a few days earlier, stressed that while there was still a relatively solid core of Quebecers supporting sovereignty (around 40 per cent), the vast majority (84 per cent) did not think it likely to happen within the next decade and proclaimed their pride in being Canadians (Hélène Buzetti, *Le Devoir*, 23 June; Lysiane Gagnon, *Globe and Mail*, 20 Aug.).

Just as Marois was taking over the PQ, the sovereignist flame was clearly vacillating; nearly half (48 per cent) of PQ supporters even thought it might be best to put the sovereignty option on the back burner (André Pratte, *La Presse*, 27 June; "Le choix…"; Lysiane Gagnon, *Globe and Mail*, 20 Aug.).

While this probably reflected in part the changing, more cooperative dynamic of federal-provincial relations between Quebec and Ottawa since Charest came to power, Quebecers had other policy priorities in mind – the sorry state of highways and road infrastructures, the inefficiency of emergency wards, the declining economic health of regions, and reasonable accommodation, to name but a few – which were of a more immediate concern than the elusive goal of an independent country. They no longer seemed to harbour that crucial and urgent sentiment of outrage at being undermined or disrespected within Canada – a sentiment without which it is unavoidably harder to mobilize people for sovereignty. Their move away from the PQ in the March election, in continued support of an avowedly federalist party (Liberals), and their new enthusiasm for an emerging party (ADQ) keen on defending Quebec's interests but unequivocally within the Canadian federation,

26 http://www.radio-canada.ca/nouvelles/Politique/2007/08/29/001-quebec-sondage-pq.shtml, accessed 24 June 2011; http://www.quebecpolitique.com/2007/09/sondage-leger-marketing-de-septembre-2007-intentions-de-vote, accessed 24 June 2011.

sent the PQ a clear message: keep the lid on the idea of a sovereign Quebec for some time to come; provincial autonomy is good enough for now; sovereignty can wait.

Marois took note and elaborated a political strategy that downplayed sovereignty and emphasized instead *Québécois* identity. In October as the hearings of the commission of consultation on practices of reasonable accommodation were in full swing, she introduced in the National Assembly the Quebec Identity Act, Bill 195, designed to create and assert Quebec-based citizenship and a constitution, while her colleague, the constitutional scholar Daniel Turp, MNA for Mercier, presented Bill 196, a Quebec Constitution, with the specific purpose of entrenching the paramountcy of Quebec's fundamental values and cultural heritage in all the policies and laws of the province.

Bill 195, which attracted the most public attention, would have, among other things, required newcomers to Quebec, whether from Canada or abroad, to acquire Quebec citizenship as a precondition for running for office in provincial, municipal, or school board elections, making a donation to a political party, or submitting a petition to the National Assembly. To be granted Quebec citizenship one would have to demonstrate first "an appropriate knowledge of the French language" as well as "an appropriate knowledge of Québec and of the responsibilities and advantages of citizenship" and take an oath of loyalty to the people of Quebec swearing to observe its laws and comply with its constitution. Bill 195 would have also modified Quebec's Charter of Rights and Freedoms to specify that its interpretation and application must be done "with due regard for the historical heritage and fundamental values of the Québec nation and, in particular, the importance of ensuring the predominance of the French language, protecting and promoting Québec culture, guaranteeing equality between women and men, and preserving the secularity of public institutions." Finally, it would have introduced stricter measures both to ensure the compliance of enterprises of fifty employees or more with the obligation to obtain a francization certificate and force small and medium-size enterprises of twenty-five to fifty employees to submit to the process of francization.

As private members' bills from an Opposition party, Bills 195 and 196 had very little chance of going anywhere past their formal tabling in the legislature. All political observers agreed the move was primarily meant as a tactic for the PQ to regain the favour of old-stock French Canadian Quebecers and re-appropriate its traditional political monopoly on national identity, lost earlier in the year to Mario Dumont's effective, chest-thumping defence of "Quebecness" against practices of reasonable accommodation. If indeed the idea was to draw attention to the party, it certainly worked. Bill 195 in particular triggered a storm of controversy well fuelled by the ongoing reasonable accommodation debate. Both the Liberals and the ADQ rejected it flat out, legal scholars denounced it as discriminatory and unconstitutional, a protest letter written by a graduate student at the Université de Montréal gathered more than 1,000 signatures in less than two days, labour movement leaders condemned it, and several commentators, including some sovereignists close to Marois, severely criticized it.[27] Whether it paid off politically, though, is not entirely clear. A public opinion poll conducted by Léger Marketing for the French-language daily *Le Devoir* during the first week of November revealed that barely one in four Quebecers (23 per cent) thought Marois's initiative was on target; 39 per cent believed it should be modified to conform with the Canadian and Quebec Charters of Rights and Freedoms, while another 27 per cent dismissed it without reservation (11 per cent offered no opinion) (Kathleen Lévesque, *Le Devoir*, 7 Nov.). A month later, another Léger Marketing poll, commissioned this time by PQ adviser Jean-François Lisée, reported that nearly two in three Quebecers supported the idea of a Quebec constitution upholding Quebec's fundamental values, and three in four did not object to forcing immigrants to demonstrate their knowledge of French in order to exercise the right to vote or seek public office.[28] There are undoubtedly important segments of the Quebec population who share the spirit of Bill 195 and its underlying focus on upholding the French language and French Canadian heritage as Quebec society's defining parameters, but the PQ did not quite succeed in leveraging the uninhibited identity concerns expressed through the reasonable accommodation debates by "old-stock" Quebecers into an unmitigated groundswell of support for its identity bill.

Still as the year ended with Marois standing as Quebec's most trusted political leader and the PQ constantly doing better in the polls, one can assume that Bill 195 did have some impact in the party's improving fortunes. The well-known *Gazette* columnist Josée Legault has suggested that "tactically speaking [Bill 195] did achieve three things. One was to

27 Lysiane Gagnon, "Sovereigntists under pressure," http://www.vigile.net/Sovereigntists-under-pressure, accessed 26 June 2011.

28 Mario Girard, "Plus de 60% des Québécois souhaitent que leur province se dote d'une constitution interne qui affirmerait ses valeurs," http://www.vigile.net/Les-Quebecois-veulent-une-constitution-interne, accessed 26 June 2007.

cast Marois in the classic role of the defender of Quebec's interests … Second, it mobilized those PQ members who, with no referendum in sight, are content with Marois's more traditional form of nationalism. Third it helped to polarize the debate, not on sovereignty this time, but on nationalism" (*Gazette*, 9 Nov.).

On the flip side, Bill 195 reconfirmed in the mind of anti-sovereignists and anti-nationalists the conviction that the PQ is the party of a narrowly ethnocultural – some even say tribal and racist – French Canadian vision of Quebec society (Don Martin, *National Post*, 25 Oct.; Henry Aubin, *Gazette*, 25 Oct.; Presse canadienne, 25 Oct.). Despite the few political points Marois has scored with Bill 195 in the short run, her proposal may well have undone decades of work on the part of civic nationalists to convince detractors of Quebec nationalism that it is in fact inclusive, pluralistic, and encompasses all who live in the province of Quebec regardless of their origin, culture, or length of residence.

In trying to remobilize nationalist forces around French Canadian heritage, identity, and non-negotiable social norms and values rather than the political goal of sovereignty, Marois has in a way gone back to a fundamental rule of successful nationalist movements: without a clear, strong, and widely shared sense of collective self, the likelihood of getting millions of disparate individuals to act in unison towards a common political goal is small. But that sense of collective self is not something that can be engineered or forced upon people. Bill 195 has probably opened the way to two possible outcomes, both of which may prove to constitute additional, intractable hurdles towards the dream of an independent Quebec. One will be to enhance the sentiments of alienation and exclusion Quebecers who do not partake of the French Canadian cultural heritage are bound to experience; without their being imbued with great sympathy for that heritage, without their feeling some sense of belonging – in other words, without their unconditional support – any future referendum on Quebec sovereignty is unlikely to favour the yes side. The result of the past two referendums is quite clear on this score. The second foreseeable outcome will be a marked increase in the tension already apparent during the public discussions over Bill 195 between ethnic and civic nationalists. It is probably safe to bet that the opposition to Marois's identity bill voiced from within the PQ and the ranks of people close to the sovereignty movement portends internal discord. The history of the Quebec nationalist/sovereignist movement has shown on several occasions that Quebec nationalists can be their own worst enemies.

Up in the air ...

On 1 January few political observers, if any, would have guessed that the year ahead would have unfolded the way it did. In the minds of almost everyone, Jean Charest's government was already dead; André Boisclair and the PQ seemed poised to succeed him; and Mario Dumont was hardly showing on anyone's radar. By year end, Jean Charest and his Liberals were still in power, albeit in a considerably weaker political position following the election, and rising in voter satisfaction; the PQ, under the new leadership of Pauline Marois, had dusted itself off from the spectacular tumble in took in the election and was picking up steam again; and the glow surrounding Dumont after his amazing electoral performance was starting to wear off as doubts about his judgment and the ability of his team to govern began to emerge.

What would come next was anybody's guess as pretty much everything was up in the air. Polls taken late in the year showed the Liberals and the PQ almost neck and neck (at around 30 to 32 per cent) and the ADQ trailing five to six percentage points behind, not enough for any party to win a majority government. No new major policy initiative seemed to be in the offing. As the commission on reasonable accommodation concluded its hearings in mid-December the furore over identity concerns and the national question, which monopolized virtually everyone's attention through the year, was likely to abate somewhat in the months to come, but it will probably remain prominent on the public agenda. At the end of 2007 Quebec finds itself in a strange place, unclear as to the lay of the land, unsure as to where the next shifts might come from or whether indeed there will be shifts.

RICHARD WILBUR

New Brunswick

Shawn Graham's first legislative session as premier

Five months after the last House prorogued, the new Liberal government finally launched its first legislative session on 6 February when Lieutenant Governor Herménégilde Chiasson presented the throne speech. Most importantly in terms of events and reactions during the rest of the year, it referred to two studies that had already begun their work since their creation a month earlier. The Self-Sufficiency Task Force was co-chaired by Francis McGuire, president of the Moncton-based Major Drilling and a key adviser to former premier Frank McKenna, and Giles Lepage, former president of La Mouvement des caisses populaires acadiennes. Their views on how the province could achieve self-sufficiency by 2020 had already received wide media coverage since they began public consultations on 16 January, and their report, based on seven discussion forums held throughout the province, was promised by mid-April. The other study was the Commission on Post-Secondary Education, co-chaired by Rick Miner, president of Seneca College and former vice president of the University of New Brunswick in Saint John, and Jacques L'Ecuyer, vice president of the Université de Québec. Underscoring the self-sufficiency theme (a phrase repeated nineteen times) the throne speech emphasized three key concerns: energy, education, and economic development. Although it ended on the environmental issue, there were no specific promises other than one to remain "good environmental stewards" and to present a climate action plan within the year.

Graham's first test as premier came on 5 March when voters in Moncton East selected the successor to Bernard Lord, who resigned days after the general election. They returned the riding to the Liberals by choosing Chris Collins by a wide margin. If voters could have anticipated finance minister Victor Boudreau's first budget, introduced 13 March, the vote might have been different. Despite Premier

Graham's promise to the contrary, Boudreau imposed across-the-board increases to personal income taxes plus a 1 per cent hike in the general corporation tax – the first such increases since 1994. Small business taxes, which were expected to drop by 1 per cent, instead were increased to 5 per cent, which would add $35 million to the provincial treasury, while a 1 per cent hike to the general corporation tax would add another $17 million. The $6.6 billion budget would see a 5.7 per cent increase in the education budget, pushing it to $875.6 million. The Hospital Services' budget increased by $127 million, or 6.6 per cent, for a final total of $2.1 billion. An additional $13.7 million would be needed for the government's plan to establish a single provincial ambulance system, replacing a private system run by several independent operators. Premier Graham defended the tax increases, saying he had no choice but to break his word because he did not know the true state of the province's finances until a later independent auditor predicted a projected deficit of $400 million. University of New Brunswick (UNB) economics professor David Murrell called the tax increases "retrogressive" because they unfairly penalized those who could least afford them (*New Brunswick Telegraph-Journal*, 15 March). John Williamson, federal director of the Canadian Taxpayers' Federation, thought the Graham government had "just thrown away a prime tool to attract people and businesses to locate and stay in New Brunswick," a view supported by the Conservative Opposition leader Jeannot Volpe.

By 20 May, the fifty-fifth day of the current session, the legislature had debated and voted on budget estimates for ten of the twenty-six government departments. The notable exception was education, whose minister, Kelly Lamrock, said he would wait until the release of an independent policy review before tabling his estimates. On 5 July the House rose after the longest recorded legislative session in the province's history – seventy-nine days. The government passed all seventy-four bills it introduced. These included changes to the Ombudsman and Child and Youth Advocate Acts allowing greater access to information, banning children under 14 years old from riding ATVs, a climate change action plan establishing targets for emission reductions, and changes to the Elections Act establishing fixed dates for all future elections. They will be held on the fourth Monday in September in the fourth year following an election; in the case of a minority government, the premier could set an earlier date. The government decided against a recommendation of a Commission of Legislative Democracy calling for a public plebiscite to decide on some form of proportional representation.

Setting policy by task forces

Judging by the headlines and the space the Irving-owned daily press gave to government-created task forces during the year, political observers might well have wondered what if anything was going on in the provincial legislature, especially since any coverage of its deliberations was usually relegated to the inner pages. From mid-January through to May, the front and editorial pages were dominated by the hearings of the Self-Sufficiency Task Force, which released its thirty-five-page report on 8 May. As the front-page summary noted, "there were no surprises … All the major [ninety-one] recommendations were well covered in the three earlier discussion documents released by the commission" (*New Brunswick Telegraph-Journal*, 8 May). For New Brunswick to be self-sufficient in twenty years, a modern childcare system "is mandatory." To meet the government's goal as a major energy exporter, there had to be a twenty-year strategic plan for power sales to the United States, an investment into the opportunities for a clean coal-fired plant at Belledune, and a removal of barriers to increased cogeneration, wind, and tidal energy. It recommended a 25 per cent increase in the yield from Crown forest land by 2026 and a 10 per cent cut in the amount of Crown land set aside for conservation – a suggestion immediately challenged by environmental as well as private forestry groups. As co-chairman Francis McGuire put it, "the approach is very Keynesian … You are going to have to finance it" (ibid.). Noting what the task force regarded as a cautious civil service and a bureaucracy increasingly working in silos, McGuire recommended the appointment of a deputy minister to oversee the program's implementation and a system of performance bonuses that could increase salaries by 25 per cent. Since the federal government had refused to contribute $500 million as its share of the cost, McGuire said the province had no choice but to keep working on the vision. Less than a month later, in the first response to the report, the government announced it would use an $8 million trust fund established by the previous Lord administration to create 750 more day-care spaces. It added that this would be a one-time expenditure.

The future of New Brunswick's overall education system became a hot topic in February when the president of the Université de Moncton, Yvon Fontaine, claimed the Education Act protected the institution from any cost-cutting measures, a possibility raised by Dr Rick Miner, co-chair of the Commission on Post-Secondary Education, who warned that access, cost efficiencies, and satellite campuses (a key aspect of the Moncton institution's province-wide mandate) were all issues being considered by the commission. A discussion paper published 10 March raised more concerns with warnings that "the college system may need greater differentiation, while the university sector might benefit from closer collaboration" (*New Brunswick Telegraph-Journal*, 10 March). By April Premier Graham, in an attempt to ease mounting concerns, affirmed that his alma mater, St Thomas University, was in no danger of being dismantled or merged. When Education Minister Lamrock finally presented his department spending estimates on 1 June, it included $10 million to implement some of the many recommendations of the MacKay Report on classroom inclusion, and three days later he tabled a thirty-seven-page plan involving more than 130 programs, strategies, and committees to improve New Brunswick's education system, which consistently ranked far below the Canadian average. By mid-September, the post-secondary commission regained the spotlight when it released its report calling for replacing two of the Université de Moncton's northern campuses in Shippagan and Edmundston as well as converting University of New Brunswick in Saint John to a polytechnic centre. It proposed that the government create a post-secondary education commission responsible for quality control, assessment, data collection, and analysis as well as a review of strategic plans and oversight of credit transfers. A presidents' council would act in an advisory role for the commission. The polytechnics would combine a university campus with one or several community college campuses with each sector teaching courses interchangeably.

The reactions were immediate and overwhelmingly negative. The president of the Université de Moncton said scrapping the existing system would betray the legacy of Louis Robichaud, who acted on the only other post-secondary study, headed by John Deutsch in the 1960s, which also had recommended the establishment of the UNB campus in Saint John and moving St Thomas University from Chatham to Fredericton. On 17 September more than 1,700 students demonstrated outside the Saint John office of Ed Doherty, minister of post-secondary education, training, and labour, who was supported by four colleagues, including three from the Saint John area. He assured them that in his reading of the report, "an undergraduate university degree will always be possible here in Saint John" (ibid., 18 Sept.). Later that day, both Miner and his co-chair Jacques L'Ecuyer were booed and heckled as they handled questions and criticisms from about 500 gathered at a local hotel. In Fredericton, on the eve of his first anniversary, Premier Graham told a news conference that the status quo was not an option: "This will be a year that presents some challenges. I have no illusions that it will be an easy road" (ibid.). Two days later, Dr John McLaughlin, president of the University of New Brunswick, told the *Telegraph-Journal* editorial staff that while he supports change, it was vital for the Saint John campus to continue to offer full liberal arts programs. On 15 October the Association of Atlantic Universities reported that UNB's overall enrolment for 2007–8 had dropped 5.6 per cent, or 664 students, the sharpest decline in the entire region. Two days later, Premier Graham announced the formation of a new working group made up of the presidents of the province's four universities. His colleague Ed Doherty repeated earlier assurances that UNB–Saint John, the site of a proposed polytechnic, would continue to have "a university presence," adding that it would be up to the new working group to suggest ways to achieve this as well as how to still "combine the strengths of the university and community college" (*Daily Gleaner*, 18 Oct.). On 29 October Yvon Fontaine, Université de Moncton president, said that providing university courses throughout the entire community college system as suggested by Commission on Post-Secondary Education would weaken the entire system. He told the Moncton Rotary Club that New Brunswick "doesn't need new polytechnic institutions or a duplication of efforts at community colleges" (*New Brunswick Telegraph-Journal*, 30 Oct.).

Meanwhile the education minister, Kelly Lamrock, had opened a potential Pandora's box in late July when he appointed James Croll, a UNB education professor, and Patricia Lee, chairwoman of District 16 Education Council in Miramichi, to examine French second-language programming and submit their recommendations early in 2008. He admitted "there will likely be some resistance from parents," adding that "everything is open. The only boundary on them is the goal of having bilingual graduates [which] is not open for debate" (ibid., 24 July). Noting that New Brunswick is Canada's only official bilingual province, he said a complete review was needed because of the fact that at present only 35 per cent of high school graduates were bilingual, just half the target figure. In the past "too often the curriculum was left unchanged for fear of political debate over bilingualism." He would not shy away from tough debates or become a victim of political interference. The commission was given a "tight schedule" to report to the minister by February or March, which he said would allow full debate and Cabinet response "in time to begin changing the system in September." By November, the anticipated debate was well underway with concerns being expressed by Walter Lee, president of the Canadian Parents for French in New Brunswick, that his group was being "marginalize[d]" and that "we fully expect the review to call for the elimination of early immersion" in the first grade (ibid., 15 Nov.).

The post-secondary scene became even more involved on Boxing Day when the president of St Thomas University, Dr Michael Higgins, sent an email to his faculty association announcing that its members, both full- and part-time staff, were locked out as a result of a breakdown in contract talks that had been going on for weeks.

More electricity rate hikes

In June 2006, the Public Utilities Board had approved a 9.6 per cent hike, which the then premier Bernard Lord rejected and instead imposed an 8 per cent cap that translated into an average rate of 6.9 per cent. On 7 February, NB Power officials confirmed rumours that it would be applying for a new increase that could hit double digits. For the next few weeks, speculation continued as the utility prepared its case based on ever-rising fuel costs and a government edict that it had to balance its books. On 19 April, David Hay, CEO of NB Power, confirmed that it would ask for a 9.6 per cent interim increase, which he said was necessary to cover the shortfall caused by the 8 per cent rate cap imposed the previous year. The next day Jack Keir, the energy minister, said the government would spend over $30 million in energy efficiency programs and another $7 million to help low-income families. The latter move would mark the first time since 1989 that the Family and Community Services would raise the amount offered in its monthly heating allowance. On 23 April the minister was joined in Moncton by the head of the Energy Efficiency and Conservation Agency to explain the government's plans to offset the negative effects of the increases. On 1 June the Utilities Board unanimously approved the 9.6 per cent interim increase, citing the lack of evidence presented by interveners at a public hearing a few days earlier. On 23 August, the board ordered NB Power to reduce its interim rate hike to 6.4 per cent as a result of the $338 million it had received from the Orimulsion settlement reached earlier in the month after a prolonged legal battle with Venezuela's state-owned oil company, which had cancelled a long-term delivery agreement. The new rate would remain in place until 31 March 2008 or until the board ruled on the interim rate during hearings scheduled to begin in November.

While homeowners worried about how high their winter electricity bills would be, even more numerous motorists now had to watch gasoline pumps each Thursday morning to see what changes, if any, there were. On 1 February energy minister Jack Keir released details of changes to the gas regulations imposed seven months ago. By knowing the price weekly instead of waiting two weeks, he said this would "mimic more the market" and as a result companies would not lose money for two weeks if prices jump in between.

Another vehicle-related issue, insurance, continued to be debated, especially by lawyers frustrated by ruling imposed by the former Conservative government which capped claims at $2,500 for pain and suffering resulting from vehicle accident injuries. The Liberal justice minister, T.J. Burke, said the cap would remain despite calls for reform by provincial lawyers. In September, a provincial judge admitted she would have awarded a crash victim $30,000 but was restricted by law to the lower figure.

The uneven economic picture

After repeated rumours, Irving Oil Ltd. moved a big step closer to building a second refinery estimated to cost $7 billion. In late January a company spokesman said that the projected size, with a proposed capacity of 300,000 barrels a day, necessitated finding another partner, particularly one that could guarantee a crude oil supply. An application has been filed for an environmental impact assessment, and if improved, the facility could be up and running by 2012. Irving Oil already owns 95 per cent of the estimated 600 acres near the existing Irving Canaport deepwater terminal at Red Head, and negotiations were underway with landowners for the remaining 5 per cent. It was estimated that the huge project would create about 5,000 construction jobs and 1,000 permanent ones plus many more in related business opportunities (*New Brunswick Telegraph-Journal*, 25 and 26 Jan.). On 1 June the National Energy Board approved a 145-kilometre pipeline route from the Irving-owned Canaport Liquefied natural gas terminal, and early in September the Irvings announced the building of a third LNG tank that would involve twelve months' work; two other tanks have already been completed.

Slightly east of Saint John, near Sussex, officials of the Potash Corporation of Saskatchewan announced in mid-July that it would spend US$1.6 billion on a second mine that would generate 140 new jobs. Once environmental impact assessments have been approved, construction would take about four years, and once completed the provincial government would collect a total of over $330 million in royalties over the next twenty years (*Daily Gleaner*, 24 July).

The Liberal government's much-publicized goal to make Saint John the region's energy hub received an additional boost with a mid-May announcement by Westjet that this was a key factor in its decision to establish regular daily flights to Toronto from the Saint John terminal – a service already made available by Air Canada out of Moncton and Saint John.

A government announcement in mid-November that the minimum wage would be raised by 50¢ to $7.75 got mixed reactions. A spokesman for the Canadian Federation of Independent Business, Dan Kelly, said many small operators would not be able to afford the increase, the third since October 2006. The managing director of a Saint John food bank, noting the sharp rise in clients, said the increase would relieve some of their financial stress. On the other hand, a researcher for the provincial self-sufficiency task force noted that in terms of real dollars, New Brunswick's minimum wage in 1975 was $8.90.

Another measuring stick for the economy was provided by the population numbers released by Statistics Canada in December. They show a slight drop in the historic outflow to other provinces. In fact the overall population grew by 1,100 – the first gain since 1991. However, a total of 10,605 left the province between 2001 and 2006 and in this same period there was a steady drop in francophone numbers. For the first time this group has fallen to below a third of the total population; it was also aging more rapidly than the anglophone sector.

French New Brunswick's image was not helped by the collapse of the Caisse populaire de Shippagan, in the heart of the Acadian Peninsula. It had been placed under supervision of Credit Union Central in 2004, and in March when it held its first annual meeting in three years, it revealed a deficit of $33.7 million and an asset drop from $291 million in 2004 to $192 million in 2007. The provincial superintendent of credit unions announced a bailout totalling $60 million, to take effect 1 June, an amount underwritten by the provincial treasury. In response to Conservative requests for explanations, a government official said the deal had to go through to avoid an even higher liquidation price tag of $86 million.

Call centre workers in Fredericton and Bathurst got bad news in August when they tried to open the doors to their workplace at Connect North America. They were locked out. About 350 in Fredericton and 75 in Bathurst lost their jobs and were told to wait to be contacted. The firm received $300,000 in Atlantic Canada Opportunities Agency (ACOA) grants between 1992 and 1995 and another $170,000 from 2002 to 2005 in the form of wage reimbursements under the Workplace Expansion Program. In January the CEO of Enterprise Greater Moncton released the results of a survey of nineteen of the city's thirty-two call centres. All told, they contributed $423 million in wages in 2006 despite an employee turnover rate of over 40 per cent. The pay scale was 11 per cent lower than similar jobs elsewhere in Canada. Early in November finance minister Victor Boudreau announced the lifting of a provincial ban on casinos, opening the door for one only at a centre to be selected by the private developers. The one-only stipulation did not deter New Brunswick's fifteen First Nations communities from revealing plans to go ahead with a big casino resort project, to be operational by 2010. Currently, eight First Nations have gambling revenue sharing agreements with the province, and in 2006 they got back $7.5 million.

The sagging natural resource sectors

About the only good news about New Brunswick's once robust forestry sector came in January when the Port of Saint John shipped its first load of lumber to the United Kingdom since 1993. The supplier was a long-time Fredericton lumberyard which unfortunately would be bankrupt and closed within the year. In June 600 workers at the UPM-Kymmene in Miramichi learned they would have no jobs after August. A month earlier the same firm closed its mill in nearby Blackville. This news came just days after the Weyerhaeuser Company announced that it would not be reopening its oriented strand board mill also at Miramichi, closed since February; another 140 people were affected. The company blamed weak markets and a high Canadian dollar. A government move to provide a two-year $16 million property tax aid package to offset a 10.6 per cent power hike had little or no effect. In August 175 workers at the Juniper sawmill, owned by Fraser Papers, learned they would be laid off for at least a year. In September Fraser announced a temporary closure of its Plaster Rock sawmill. The biggest closure of all came in November when 350 people at the Dalhousie paper mill, which had been operating for seventy-eight years, were abruptly told by owners AbitibiBowater Inc. that it would be permanently closed in January. On the same day, 29 November, the government announced a $10–20 million loan to save 250 jobs at the AV Cell Inc. pulp mill at Atholville, near Campbellton. In mid-December, the Finnish owners of the UPM paper mill at Miramichi confirmed its permanent closure because of the rising dollar. They would maintain operations of a sawmill in Bathurst and continue to control 1.26 million cubic metres of Crown land. Three days after the closure news, the company announced a deal to spend $1.7 billion to build three new mills in Russia.

New Brunswick's lobster fishery was faring no better. A report issued by the Fisheries Resource Conservation Council warned that the industry must make "serious changes" to survive (*New Brunswick Telegraph-Journal*, 5 July). It said that larger vessels were threatening the species' ability to regenerate its numbers. One region that has seen the sharpest catch decline is along the Northumberland Strait between New Brunswick and PEI. A rare positive sign was the sharp increase in sardine herring in the Bay of Fundy. The biggest buyer and processor, Connors Bros Ltd. at Blacks Harbour, had to increase its operation hours to handle the catches from local weirs.

On the environmental front

An eight-year fight to preserve 1,150 hectares of marshland making up the Musquash estuary just west of Saint John was finally won in January with a joint federal-provincial announcement that it would become New Brunswick's first marine protected area. In March local MP and veteran affairs minister Greg Thompson joined Premier Graham and local dignitaries to announce that Ottawa would spend $26.6 million as its share in the long-delayed task of cleaning up Saint John Harbour within the next five years. In September Thompson was in Fredericton to unveil a compensation package of $20,000 for each one providing proof of permanent health damage after being sprayed with Agent Orange at CFB Gagetown in 1966–7. Government officials expect the final payment figure could reach $96 million, based on department estimates that 4,500 veterans and civilians could qualify before the application deadline is reached in April 2009.

Another long-standing issue involving the replacement of the Petitcodiac Causeway at Moncton reached a milestone in August when the minister of supply and services, Roly MacIntyre, revealed plans to build a 280-metre bridge, something demanded by the Petitcodiac Riverkeepers, a citizens' group pressing for that option since 2005. Opponents to any change have argued that their properties, located around an artificial lake above the causeway, would decrease in value and the river's current would erode their land. An environmental impact study dismissed their concerns. The bridge is not expected to be completed for another eight years.

In March, energy minister Jack Keir said the government had reached an agreement with a Calgary-based firm, Vector Wind Energy Inc., to construct a 21-megawatt wind farm near Dorchester. He said it would generate enough electricity to supply 3,700 homes when it went online next year. In June, environment minister Roland Hache outlined the government's green plan committed to reduce greenhouse gas emissions to 1990 levels by 2012. Environmental groups welcomed the news but noted that the sixty-four-point plan did not place emission caps on the province's largest polluters and neglected to consider the implications posed if and when a second Irving refinery is built in Saint John.

Beaverbrook gallery wins bitter legal battle

After one of the longest and costliest court battles in New Brunswick history, retired Supreme Court justice Peter Cory delivered his 114-page verdict on 26 March. The Fredericton Beaverbrook Art Gallery would keep possession of the majority and the most valuable of 133 paintings that have been on display ever since Lord Beaverbrook presented them when he opened the gallery in 1959. Although the Beaverbrook UK Foundation, whose members include Beaverbrook's grandson, Maxwell Aitken III, immediately filed an appeal, observers as well as officials of the gallery were confident that the decision would be upheld. In October Judge Cory rejected arguments from foundation attorneys that no costs should be awarded and instead ordered the foundation to pay the gallery $4.88 million in legal costs, a record for New Brunswick. The dispute, which began in 2004, proved a boon to the gallery as the resulting publicity boosted the annual patronage from 22,000 to 41,000 and increased membership from 700 to over 1,000.

The fall legislative session

Considering the amount of information released after the end of the spring legislative session, it left many, including this long-time observer, wondering why it was not released earlier. For example, it had been more eighteen months since the Crown corporations and government departments had been given their customary scrutiny by the Standing Committee on Public Accounts. When they finally began their deliberations, the committee members, including Conservative MLAs, found themselves examining the 2005–6 financial period, when the Tories were in power (*New Brunswick Telegraph-Journal*, 30 July). As it turned out, their scrutiny was not covered by the media. Meanwhile, Premier Graham continued to turn to outside experts. On

20 September he revealed that Jean-Guy Finn, a former senior civil servant, would write what he called "the most important report on local government" since the Byrne Commission's report in 1962, which set the stage for Louis Robichaud's historic Equal Opportunity program (ibid., 21 Sept.). Three days later, yet another government report was released: the findings of the task force headed by Donald Savoie of the Université de Moncton on the right-to-information and privacy law. The total cost of the task force was $18,758 – far below its original estimate of $150,000. Among its forty-three recommendations was the need to reshape the thinking inside the government apparatus to emphasize disclosing information instead of finding ways to block it from public view. Specifically it would have such commonly sought information as expense accounts of ministers and senior civil servants be made available on the province's Web site. A statement from the premier's office said the government would respond to the recommendations in the upcoming legislative session.

The throne speech, released to the media the day before it was delivered, promised a balanced budget, targeted property tax relief for low-income and senior homeowners, and several new initiatives to improve literacy, early childhood development, and wellness. As the Tory Opposition leader Jeannot Volpe noted, two goals emphasized in the much-vaunted self-sufficiency agenda, namely a new health plan and changes to the post-secondary education system, "were both largely glossed over, a point acknowledged by Premier Graham who said they were still to be finalized" (ibid., 28 Nov.).

A more revealing moment came 11 December when finance minister Victor Boudreau unveiled a $486 million capital budget that focused on upgrading the highway system, taking up $325 million of the total. A week later, Education Minister Lamrock announced plans to spend $41.6 million which would include funds to build two schools with help from the private sector, one in Moncton and the other in Rexton, the premier's home constituency. He added that if these partnering projects go over budget, the private builder would pay. Tom Mann of the NB Public Service Union voiced his group's strong opposition, pointing to two earlier public-private efforts involving Greenarm Schools Ltd., which, as noted by the former attorney general, had cost the province $1.3 million more than if the government had financed them alone. Lamrock admitted this but added that "private bidders can mean more affordable schools built quicker" (ibid., 17 Dec.). When health minister Mike Murphy introduced his department's capital estimates two days later, he defended opposition objections to $8 million as part of a three-year $30 million addition to the Saint John Regional Hospital. The chair of the Atlantic Health Science Corp., Paschal Chisholm, noted that when the facility was built in the early 1980s, it was designed for 25,000 patients compared to 60,000 today, making it the busiest in the province.

PETER E. BUKER

Prince Edward Island

Prince Edward Island's economy fared well in 2007, although prospects for agriculture were dire. The provincial government changed in May 2007 from twenty-three Conservatives and four Liberals under Pat Binns to twenty-three Liberals and four Conservatives under Robert Ghiz.

Economy

In 2007 PEI's economy expanded 2.4 per cent and the provincial GDP was estimated to be $4,538 million.[29] Personal income grew an estimated 4.3 per cent to $3,915 million. The All-Items Consumer Price Index rose 1.8 per cent. Total employment was 69,300 people, and the average unemployment rate was 10.3 per cent. The population estimate was 138,627* as of 1 July. In 2006–7 PEI had 695 international immigrants. In terms of annual changes by major economic measures: total investment increased 14.1 per cent to $943.7 million; tourist expenditures increased 4.4 per cent to $354.3 million; the value of total fish landings declined 2.9 per cent to $166.8 million; retail trade was up 7.7 per cent to $1,628.9 million; total farm cash receipts declined 3.4* per cent to $364.0 million – and the news media was describing "a crisis in agriculture"; island manufacturing shipments decreased to $1,431.6 million or by 3.9 per cent; and exports declined 4.2 per cent to $802.8 million. The public sector accounted for 28.3 per cent of total island employment.

Provincial total revenue was $1,230.5 million in the fiscal year 2006–7 – 5.2 per cent higher than the previous year. Provincial tax revenues increased 4.0 per cent to $739.2 million, while total federal transfers accounted for 38.6 per cent of the total revenue. Total provincial

29 Revised numbers (indicated by asterisks) by Statistics Canada, November 2008; all other statistical data are from the PEI Provincial Treasury's *34th Annual Statistical Review 2007*, June 2008.

government expenditures rose 3.2 per cent to $1,206.6 million, giving a surplus in the operating fund for 2006–7 of $23.9 million. By the end of the 2006–7 fiscal year provincial net debt had increased to $1,312 million. In December Standard and Poor's Ratings Services changed the province's credit rating on long-term borrowing from A stable to A positive.

Fiscal events

The provincial government released *A Guide to Watershed Planning on PEI* on 18 January as a resource for watershed groups; the PEI Environmental Advisory Council had five public consultation meetings on protecting water resources and managing watersheds throughout January and February. The province declared 8–14 July "Aquatic Invasive Species Awareness Week." In early July, the PEI Aquaculture Alliance's Island Oyster Growers Group received funding to research ways to manage invasive species on oyster aquaculture farms. At the end of July, the province announced a joint funding initiative for the island aquaculture industry to develop and assess approaches to manage invasive tunicates. Late in the year, PEI's fisheries minister sought continued federal support to deal with the threat of invasive species to the aquaculture industry as well as funding to expand that industry. The second International Invasive Sea Squirt Conference brought industry representatives and leading experts in tunicates from ten countries to a meeting in Brudenell in October. The Department of Environment, Energy and Forestry investigated two fish kills in the Tryon and Dunk Rivers mid-July. The department also held island-wide clinics in November and December to test well water for nitrates as part of a strategy to address the issue of high nitrate concentrations.

As of April there were 8.4 physician vacancies in PEI. The Ministry of Health announced in October the creation of a Health Care Recruitment and Retention Secretariat to coordinate human resource needs in health care. In December the provincial government announced an agreement with Dalhousie University's Faculty of Medicine to develop a Family Medicine Residency Program to address the doctor shortage in PEI. In a November agreement, the PEI government increased the number of seats designated for Islanders at the Memorial University Faculty of Medicine in Newfoundland from the existing two to four in 2009 and up to six in 2011.

The Department of Health released *Cancer Trends in PEI: 1980–2006* on 15 March. Overall cancer rates were 10 per cent higher for men and 8 per cent higher for women relative to Canadian averages. The Binns government announced in February a province-wide drug information system to record all prescription drugs dispensed; the computerized pharmacy network would connect pharmacists, physicians, and authorized health-care professionals with medication profiles for all patients. Beginning 1 June the Department of Health resumed its annual collection of dead birds, testing for West Nile Virus; no tests had detected the virus in the past. In July Heather Morrison was designated as the chief health officer for PEI, working part-time with Lamont Sweet, who formerly held that position and who began working half-time as the deputy chief health officer. A program to immunize Grade 6 girls against human papillomavirus (HPV) was launched in island elementary schools. In December the PEI Radon Project was announced to collect PEI-wide baseline data for radon levels. Over 500 tests were planned for 100 public facilities to determine if radon levels were within federal guidelines.

On 29 June the $2.1 million expansion of the Charlottetown Airport was officially opened and, on the same day, Delta Airlines began offering non-stop service to Boston for the summer. Starting 15 December Air Canada offered year-round service between Charlottetown and Toronto four days a week.

The Eastern Kings Wind Farm began commercial operation 29 January. The $13.5 million National Research Council of Canada Institute for Nutrisciences and Health – a research and commercialization hub for PEI's bio-resources sector – opened 16 February. New provincial grants of $400 to $1,000 annually for post-secondary students attending the University of Prince Edward Island (UPEI), Holland College, and la Société Éducative were announced in July.

Politics and the legislature

The fourth session of the sixty-second General Assembly convened 3 April and dissolved 30 April with the election writ. A controversial amendment to the Police Act was passed, but not proclaimed, to appoint a police commissioner to investigate complaints against the police; as well, the Election Act was amended to set fixed dates for provincial elections.

The year 2007 was the first where Sunday shopping – a contentious issue – was allowed from Victoria Day weekend until 24 December. This was also the first year that daylight saving time was changed to stretch from the second Sunday in March until the first Sunday in November.

On 29 January the conflict of interest commissioner ascertained that provincial treasurer Mitch Murphy had no conflict of interest but had contravened the Conflict of Interest Act over Murphy's shareholding in Murcan Construction. In February Pat Binns initiated discussions to replace the provincial museum storage facility with a new building in Murray River. Liberal MP Joe McGuire, MP for Egmont riding since 1988, and minister for the ACOA from 2003 to 2006, announced in March his intention to not offer in the next election. In March Darlene Bernard was re-elected chief of the Lennox Island First Nation.

In April Pat Binns appointed former PEI chief justice Armand DesRoches chair of the premier's Task Force on Nitrates.

The provincial election was held 28 May, the Liberal Party winning 23 seats and the Progressive Conservative Party 4 seats. The breakdown of votes province-wide were thus: Liberals 52.9 per cent; Progressive Conservatives 41.4 per cent; Green Party 3.0 per cent; NDP 2.0 per cent; and independent 0.7 per cent. Voter turnout was 83.84 per cent. Thirty-three-year-old Liberal leader Robert Ghiz was re-elected in his district of Charlottetown-Brighton with 60.2 per cent of the vote. Six Progressive Conservative Cabinet ministers were defeated; eight of the nine Binns government ministers ran for office again in the twenty-eight-day campaign. Former premier Pat Binns was one of four Progressive Conservatives elected. Robert Ghiz was sworn in 12 June as premier, along with ten ministers and the government House leader.

The first session of the sixty-third General Assembly sat 6 July 2007 to elect Speaker Kathleen Casey and make other key provincial government appointments; it was adjourned the same day; the Assembly reconvened 16 October, with provincial treasurer Wes Sheridan giving a budget that maintained most commitments made by the previous Binns government, and sat until 2 November. A legislative amendment to protect Canadian Forces reservists' jobs while on duty and an amendment to freeze residential property tax assessments at the 2007 level until 2009 were passed. MLAs' base salaries were raised from $36,689 plus a $12,000 tax-free expense allowance to $62,500 with no allowance.

The thirty-first Conference of New England Governors and Eastern Canadian Premiers was held 25–26 June in Roseneath. In August the province established the Office of Energy Efficiency to provide one-stop shopping for energy-reducing programs and services. On 29 August the Ghiz government announced an open, public call for participation in over seventy of the island's agencies, boards, and commissions to promote government transparency and fair appointments.

Pat Binns was named Canada's ambassador to Ireland 30 August. A by-election held 15 October in his former riding of Belfast–Murray River was won by Liberal Charles McGeoghegan.

The Ghiz government announced 6 September that it would not proceed with legal action, initiated by the Binns government, against Canada's Department of Fisheries and Oceans challenging their constitutional power in the PEI fishery. Later, in October, PEI's fisheries and aquaculture minister, Allan Campbell, protested fisheries and oceans minister Loyola Hearn's decision to allow the use of mid-water trawls to fish herring in the Gulf of St Lawrence despite evidence it destroyed fish stocks.

National and PEI provincial government representatives and native-Canadian leaders signed the tripartite New Canada/Prince Edward Island/Mi'kmaq Partnership Agreement on 1 December.

In December PEI's only hog plant, the Natural Organic Food Group (NOFG), sought provincial support for approximately $2 million in operating costs on top of millions of public and private funding already received. The PEI government refused to give more money, the plant was placed in receivership, and the province's auditor general was called upon to examine the government-NOFG relationship. On 9 December a $12 million financial aid package funded by the three Maritime provinces and the federal government was given to Atlantic beef plant cooperative in Borden-Carleton – the region's only federally inspected beef-processing plant.

Other events

In March Shauna Sullivan Curley, deputy minister of the Department of Education, was awarded the 2007 Lieutenant Governor's Award for Excellence in Public Administration. The 2007 recipients of the Order of Prince Edward Island were William MacLean of Wilmot, Ray Murphy of Stratford, and Helen Robbins of Montague. Kathleen Eaton, chief librarian at the Confederation Centre Public Library, received the Excellence in Public Service Award given by the Institute of Public Administration of Canada. His Royal Highness Prince Edward, Earl of Wessex, visited PEI on 13–14 October; he serves as colonel-in-chief for the Prince Edward Island Regiment (RCAC). World-renowned PEI visual artist Hilda Woolnough died 11 December at age 73. Retired PEI senator Eileen Rossiter died on 20 January at the age of 77. Former PEI Supreme Court justice Charles R. McQuaid died 24 May at age 90. Former provincial minister Elmer MacFadyen died 17 August at age 64. Internationally renowned musician and PEI resident Doug Riley died 28 August at age 62.

The pop music group Aerosmith played to an estimated 33,000 people 21 July in Charlottetown – the largest concert in PEI history.

Charlottetown hosted several conferences: from 18 to 21 January, the Annual Canadian Presiding Officers' Conference; in September the eighty-ninth annual meeting of the Uniform Law Conference of Canada; and 23–28 September the eighth International Conference and Workshop on Lobster Biology and Management.

The inaugural "*Tour de* PEI," a women's cycling tour sanctioned by the Union Cycliste Internationale, was raced 10–14 June. Thirty-two-year-old Jennifer Alexander, a Halifax native with Type 1 diabetes, completed a double-crossing of the Northumberland Strait 26 July. PEI sent eighty-two athletes and coaches to the twelfth biennial "International Island Games" held in Rhodes, Greece, from 30 June to 6 July. The second "Making the Connection Legends of Golf" featuring golf stars Vijay Singh and Mike Weir was played 30 July at Crowbush Cove.

Compass, PEI's CBC Television's evening newscast, was restored to a one-hour program 19 February. A ceremony of provincial and RCMP officials was held 1 May celebrating the seventy-fifth anniversary of RCMP policing on PEI. Eight island estuaries were identified as experiencing anoxic conditions. In September police reopened the unsolved nineteen-year-old murder case of Byron Carr. The autumn saw controversy about the consolidation of parishes and planned closures of PEI Roman Catholic churches; Church officials planned to reduce the number of parishes from over fifty to seventeen.

ROBERT G. FINBOW

Nova Scotia

It was a year of political continuity as the minority government of Premier Rodney MacDonald managed to survive with the help of Opposition leaders who were not eager to go back to the polls. However, the government's popularity dipped amidst small scandals, errors, and policy reversals. The NDP emerged as a legitimate threat to win power, with growing support outside Halifax. The Liberals elected a new leader to begin their reconsolidation as a credible Opposition. The economy performed in mediocre fashion outside metropolitan Halifax, with a few technology and offshore projects producing optimism. Relations with Stephen Harper's federal Conservatives were tense as the province faced a choice of equalization formulas that put offshore oil revenues in question.

Politics

The Conservative government of Rodney MacDonald continued a slow decline in support as it was dogged with a series of minor embarrassments. The premier seemed likeable but directionless, changing positions on issues like Sunday shopping, regulation of gas prices, and taxation on heating oil depending on public opinion. Nonetheless, there was no serious challenge to his leadership and the party endorsed him at its convention despite a decline in the polls.

Human resources minister Ernie Fage resigned in January for a second time when he was charged with leaving the scene of an accident after he rear-ended another vehicle. The incident had been captured on camera by a witness who reported it to the police. Fage was suspended from the Tory caucus while the charges were dealt with; the Opposition queried why staff seemed to know about the accident before Premier MacDonald. Fage paid for the repairs to his government-leased car, but taxpayers were out $3,282.66 for repairs to the victim's vehicle. Fage was later convicted and fined, had his licence suspended, and was expelled from caucus (*Chronicle Herald*, 2 Feb., 19 Dec.).

The government faced questions over its provincial business mentorship program, in which immigrants paid a private firm $130,500 to provide employment placements of at least six months to learn about the work environment and business opportunities in the province. The plan was set up by Premier MacDonald when he was the province's first immigration minister. The company running the plan, Cornwallis Financial, suggested the government had imposed a higher fee than it proposed. The government terminated the program and its contract with Cornwallis after criticisms of the high fees. The government suggested that other provinces charged more for similar programs and denied that the untendered contract had been designed to benefit Cornwallis, which was the first private firm to run such a program (ibid., Dec. 12). Federal authorities had expressed concerns that immigrants received too little for their fees, often paid into investment plans that did not give them equity. Cornwallis sued the province to recover interest on funds that had accumulated by the termination of the contract. The government replaced minister of immigration Carolyn Bolivar-Getson in a shuffle that the premier claimed had nothing to do with the scandal. The legislature's public accounts committee and auditor general investigated the program and tendering process (*Daily News*, 27 Nov.). The Opposition complained about the government's failure to release documents as the investigation continued.

The NDP continued its moderate image under leader Darrel Dexter and sought to expand its electoral base. The party focused on rural issues to push support beyond its urban base, having picked up more rural ridings than ever in the 2006 election. Dexter focused on preservation of agricultural land and promotion of farm products to prevent rural families from having to abandon operations because of rising costs and declining profits. He proposed a Buy Nova Scotia program to ensure supermarkets, restaurants, and government institutions carried local produce and that exports were clearly identified as Nova Scotian in origin. The party spoke in support of declining fishing communities, which needed government help to survive and thrive. Similarly the party sought to ensure that manufacturing capacity in small towns was not lost to closures or takeovers and sympathized with Amherst gas retailers facing low price competition in nearby New Brunswick (*Chronicle Herald*, 11 June). Dexter emphasized the importance of rural emergency services, which had problems attracting and retaining medical personnel; he suggested incentives to rectify this shortage. Dexter stressed job creation, childcare, rural broadband access, and other policies to keep young people in smaller towns. The party held its retreat in Digby with outreach to hear from social sectors in that rural community.

The impact of these efforts was substantial, as even rural newspapers previously hostile to the NDP as an "urban protest splinter party" now praised this "solid political party with down-to-earth, sensible and achievable policies" (*Kentville Advertiser*, 13 Feb.). The NDP took the lead in the polls before its June annual meeting, where policy moderation continued on issues like minimum wages; the NDP maintained support near 40 per cent in December. The NDP held a metro seat in an October by-election; the Conservative candidate embarrassed MacDonald by claiming that the district would receive nothing from government for electing an NDP MLA (*Chronicle Herald*, 3 Oct.).

The Liberals moved on from their poor election showing, selecting Annapolis MLA Stephen McNeil as their new leader. In an April vote, McNeil defeated three candidates – Colchester mayor Mike Smith, party organizer Kenzie MacKinnon, and Halifax Clayton Park MLA Diana Whalen. In her convention speech, Whalen felt forced to defend her electability as a female premier, but she lost by only 68 votes to McNeil on the second ballot, after the two other candidates threw their support to her. McNeil presented an energetic young presence and sought to establish the party's policy credentials in several areas, including anti-poverty measures like increased minimum wages, affordable housing, training, legal aid, and job placement. McNeil suggested that rising crime was linked to poverty and that the root causes must be addressed alongside stronger law enforcement. Some questioned whether his training in appliance repair was suitable for the province's top political job, but he defended his outsider status and noted that many had underestimated him in past campaigns.

Legislature

The legislature convened twice early in the year, for five days in January for a special session to deal with unfinished bills and for a brief eighteen-day session in March. The government wanted to avoid opportunities for a defeat, while the Liberals focused on their leadership race. The special January session – during which the Fage story broke – dealt mainly with the incomplete issue of campaign finance reform, as the province moved to ban corporate and union contributions. Among the important measures passed in the spring were the new Environmental Goals and Sustainable Prosperity Act, which set targets for electricity from renewable energy sources, garbage diversion, and wilderness conservation. The premier suggested this indicated the government's "green" credentials, but ecology groups stressed the importance of follow-up and implementation to meet the targets within the ten-year time frame.

In response to court decisions and a human rights complaint, Nova Scotia joined other provinces in ending mandatory retirement at age 65; this was despite concerns raised by employers, including universities and school boards, about the inflated costs of keeping senior, high-salaried employees on the job longer. Some 5 per cent of the provincial civil service was approaching the previous retirement age. A private member's bill moved by Liberal leadership candidate Diana Whalen received royal assent, providing for fairness in user fees charged to residents by the province. The government also put in place $120 million in additional appropriations approved by Cabinet to cover the previous year's commitments for universities, the 2011 Canada Winter Games, and other programs. This was despite past criticism of this practice by the auditor general, Roy Salmon, who believed all such spending should go to the House for approval.

African Canadian MLA Percy Paris claimed racism was still a problem in the legislature; the Speaker reviewed tapes and transcripts and indicated he found no evidence of the problem. Paris also suggested the chilly climate for non-white MLAs had improved after his comments. Later the Assembly greeted Haitian-born Michaëlle Jean, who became the first governor general to speak to the provincial House. The House passed an Act to Celebrate the 250th Anniversary of Democracy in Nova Scotia, as the province would soon celebrate its status as the first site of responsible government in British North America. The legislature also established a "medal of bravery" to recognize persons who risked their life or safety to protect others.

At the eleventh hour planning for the provincial budget was overshadowed by the choice Nova Scotia had to make between a new equalization formula, which provided more money up front, or sticking with the Atlantic Accord, which promised future returns if offshore revenues boomed. The province opted to take more revenues now while complaining and challenging Ottawa for forcing this choice. The decision garnered an added $157 million for the province in the current year. Critics suggested the budget, due only days after the federal budget imposed this choice, should be delayed, but the government proceeded on schedule with a view, some claimed, to putting a budget in place before a provincial Liberal leader was selected.

The budget was less ambitious on new commitments than MacDonald's election promises but included added personal tax exemptions, increased allowances for social assistance recipients, an energy rebate program for poor families, a tuition freeze, a harmonized sales tax (HST) rebate on tours and conventions, $50 million for recreation upgrades, and $10 million for rural broadband access. With $440 million in new revenues from taxes and transfers, the minister of finance projected a surplus of $118.4 million, up some $44.9 million from 2006–7, with space for up to $100 million to make debt reduction payments. The government was forced to delay promised new spending for lack of revenues. These included pharmacare for low-income families, a disabled persons allowance, and a healthy living tax credit. With no party keen to force another vote, the $7.9 billion spending plan was approved unanimously. NDP leader Dexter criticized the budget's lack of vision and inconsistency but conceded that voters did not want a return to the polls; the budget left important issues out but contained enough to warrant NDP support since it addressed party concerns such as a tuition freeze, reduced taxes on heating oil, a volunteer firefighters tax credit, and a local purchasing promotion. The Opposition suggested the budget vote was not a measure of confidence, but the premier claimed it showed such support.

The fall session began with a throne speech which promised public-private partnerships for infrastructure and services, highway improvements, and a new department of the environment. The House met for sixteen days, with thirty-two measures passed. The government outlined priorities like educating to compete, environmental protection, highway upgrades, health and safety promotion, and reduced wait times for medical and hospital services. Legislation targeted street racing and speeding, with measures like traffic light cameras to catch dangerous drivers; imposing fines for driving while using cell phones or texting devices; measures to prevent law breakers from making money from their crimes; human rights improvements to cover racial and religious harassment; and permission for class-action lawsuits. A mental health court was created to deal more effectively and sensitively with accused persons with mental illnesses. An additional 250 police officers were to be hired at a cost of $65 million. The province pledged to spread high-speed Internet to all communities by 2009. Other bills sought to improve municipal governance and make it easier to conduct business. Nova Scotia marked the ninetieth anniversary of the Halifax explosion with a measure to honour victims and commend the aging survivors of the worst disaster in Canadian history.

In the minority setting, Opposition initiatives also made it to the books, including protection of holidays for retail employees, a ban on smoking in vehicles when children are passengers, and an end to uneven school board lunch supervision of children. The Opposition supported measures to protect pensions for workers of closed businesses and extend collective bargaining rights to part-time, contract, and seasonal government workers. The Opposition did not agree to prevent health services from interruptions by strikes, threatening to defeat the government should it treat this as a confidence measure. The government had hoped to replace strikes with binding arbitration or mediation but avoided a confrontation by not calling the issue to a vote. Opposition MLAs took issue with government plans to fund infrastructure, including roads and hospitals, via public-private partnerships even though such plans previously led to cost overruns.

The NDP and Liberals wanted legislation to prevent clear-cutting from being a common practice in forestry. Most woodlots were now harvested by clearing large areas. An NDP bill would make clear-cuts the exception, while the Liberals sought to ban harvesting of trees and mining in provincial game sanctuaries. The government countered that the forestry harvest was sustainable because of government support for replanting and that clear-cuts should be allowed to continue even in sanctuaries. The Liberals wanted to cut gas taxes and get rid of the price regulation system, which had not prevented closures of rural stations, with twenty-six more shutting during the past year. Cynics noted that the legislators still sat fewer days than in any other province, despite a 22 per cent increase in salary and spending allowances.

The economy

There were some positive signs in the provincial economy. Job numbers were up in mid-year especially in services like education, finance, real estate, hotels, and leisure. Despite gains in housing prices, new construction numbers were down 12 per cent. Resumption in paper production at Stora Enso helped boost employment numbers. Gas production was up, and additional development at Deep Panuke and spin-off petro-chemical projects promised future benefits. Overall employment was disappointing outside metro Halifax, and increased gas production of some 13 per cent was the main bright spot. Other manufacturing sectors were in decline, with the closure of the Moir's chocolate factory in Dartmouth, the Trenton railcar works, and the Maple Leaf poultry packing plant in the valley. Aerospace firms did expand to work on defence contracts for Canadian helicopter and US fighter jets. And financial services companies added capacity and employment in Halifax (*Atlantic Report*, Fall 2007, 14).

A slump in US demand for lumber as its construction sector slowed meant reduced demand, with exports off by 26 per cent from 2006. This meant closures or layoffs for some large sawmills in the province.

Exports benefited from Stora's resumption of paper shipments to customers south of the border; demand for the specialized glossy paper produced at the mill helped drive the sale of Stora to NewPage corporation, based in Ohio. Overall gains were modest as consumer confidence and construction trailed other parts of Canada. By year's end, employment was up only 1.3 per cent versus 2.3 per cent in other provinces. Renewable energy showed modest growth with increased electricity output by wind farms and renewed consideration of tidal power potential, especially in the Bay of Fundy, which features the world's highest tides. Local contractors continued to benefit from offshore-related projects, including construction of offshore platforms and provision of pipeline materials. Secunda Marine, which operated offshore support vessels, was sold to a Texas buyer, a subsidiary of McDermott International Inc. There was hope for expansion in the future given the buyer's interest in using the skilled workforce in offshore oil- and gas-related projects.

The port of Halifax suffered some decline as companies pulled out or diverted cargos to Montreal. Tourism revenues were up slightly, although the high dollar discouraged US visitors. The biotechnology sector reported positive results as innovative products designed in the province began to reach markets, including new treatments for diabetic foot pain and incontinence; breakthroughs in immunotherapy and blood-testing and test vaccines for diseases like cancer were also in the works. General Dynamics planned to open a new software support centre near Dartmouth, while Atlantic Windows planned a new production centre in Amherst. In manufacturing, Michelin invested more in the province's tire plants with provincial assistance, aided by a favourable ruling on its pension obligations (*Chronicle Herald*, 26 Dec.).

The province's Utility and Review Board approved a rate increase of 4.8 per cent for Nova Scotia Power, adding to the already high costs of power in the province, already among the highest in the country. The premier joined others in criticizing the decision in light of the high salaries that top Nova Scotia Power executives were receiving and suggested these be factored into any future rate decisions. The company defended the seven-figure salaries (with additional benefits) as "fair" (ibid., 4 April). The premier mused about a resumption of uranium exploration and mining and even the possibility of a nuclear power plant, to reduce the province's reliance on dirty coal. In his estimation, safety practices in civilian nuclear sectors had improvised sufficiently to reopen the issue, although there were no immediate plans. The NDP restated its opposition to the use of nuclear energy and mining of uranium, which posed environmental dangers.

The government launched a Web site to tout the virtues of life in the province in an effort to attract Maritimers back home to work; the site mocked "delusions" of a better life in Alberta's cities and was designed to attract returnees given labour shortages in skilled fields caused by outmigration to better-paying jobs in the booming oil industry. This tactic raised the ire of the province's farmers who had been rebuffed in their search for more assistance based on fiscal constraint. Provincial hog farmers especially continued to struggle and demonstrated at the legislature to pressure government for additional short-term bridging assistance until longer-term programs could assist them; debt loads were making it impossible for most farmers to keep their operations afloat (ibid., 7 Jan.). Controversy also swirled over findings that lottery retailers won at a rate ten times greater than others players. The province examined the Atlantic Lottery corporation, run jointly with neighbouring provinces, to determine if there was a problem; the NDP called for a ban on purchases of lottery tickets by vendors, at least at their own establishment.

Intergovernmental relations

Relations with Ottawa were coloured by the sudden federal decision to alter the equalization system. Provincial politicians were critical of Ottawa's proposed revisions to equalization, which would force the province to choose between the Atlantic Accord that guaranteed no clawbacks on offshore royalties or a more lucrative short-term arrangement that would pay the province more for the first two years but risked losing future benefits if offshore revenues escalated. This was considered a betrayal of Prime Minister Harper's pre-election pledge to both respect the accord and exclude fossil fuel revenues from equalization calculations altogether. The federal government employed a divide-and-conquer strategy, negotiating separately with Nova Scotia despite the similar concerns of Newfoundland and Saskatchewan. Provincial finance officials claimed the province would lose substantially from these changes with losses of $50–200 million in the next two fiscal years. Some federal Conservative MPs from the province mused about voting against the budget in Parliament unless the deal with Nova Scotia was respected (ibid., 8 May). Cumberland MP Bill Casey voted against the government on the issue and then was forced to leave the governing caucus and sit as an independent.

Having urged Casey to dissent, the province now distanced itself. The premier expressed open reluctance to combat Ottawa on the offshore accord for fear of harming relations on important issues such as infrastructure investments for the Atlantic Gateway and other initiatives. The Opposition pushed him not to settle for less than was agreed in the accord. Opposition MLAs tried to force the federal minister responsible for the region, Peter MacKay, to testify before the provincial public accounts committee, but he refused. After first suggesting the deal had not been touched, Harper again made a side agreement to resolve the issue, pledging to make the province the main beneficiary of offshore development and promising Nova Scotia $230 million more in equalization payments by 2019. The premier defended this undocumented accord which was only contained in an exchange of letters and in "technical amendments" to the Budget Implementation Act. But while it did not fully restore the 2005 accord, this agreement promised a solution to the long-standing "crown shares" dispute between the province and Ottawa which could bring extra revenues (*Daily News*, 22 Oct., 13 Nov.).

The province continued to collaborate on other issues, welcoming a $48 million infusion of federal funds to cut health-care wait times for instance. This infusion was desperately needed as more rural hospitals endured shortages of physicians and were forced to close emergency wards frequently for lack of staff. The province joined its Atlantic neighbours in pressing for early commitment for federal funds to assist in construction of the Atlantic Gateway initiative, which would fund port upgrades in Halifax and highway improvements in Prince Edward Island and New Brunswick. The federal government wanted to stick to a memorandum of understanding which promised this funding, which could also cover pipelines, airports, and cruise-ship facilities, in two years' time; the province continued planning for this initiative with federal agencies. The province held hearings on proposed reforms to the federal Fisheries Act, which could concentrate harvesting and processing in a few large firms. Among notable cuts was federal support for the Pearson Peacekeeping Training Centre in Cornwallis, where officers from other countries were trained in one of Canada's signature specialties, peacekeeping.

The province, Ottawa, and Mi'kmaq leaders signed a Framework Agreement in February to begin to clarify power sharing and implement Supreme Court decisions respecting the treaty rights of Nova Scotia's First Nations communities. The 1999 Supreme Court Marshall decision affirmed Mi'kmaq Aboriginal and treaty rights including access to hunting, fishing, and foresting to sustain a living. The Framework Agreement specified what issues need to be addressed going forward to rectify past aberrations of treaty rights, including natural resources, land tenureship and stewardship, community governance, and effective provision of modern services. Eleven of the thirteen Mi'kmaq communities signed the agreement, while discussion with the other two continued. Negotiators were hopeful for flexibility and dealt with concerns respecting resource access including moose hunting, lobster harvesting, and forestry. The province's Tripartite Forum brought Mi'kmaq, federal, and provincial officials together to address non-treaty matters, including education, health, economic development, culture, and heritage. Mi'kmaq leaders condemned Ottawa's refusal to support the UN Declaration on the Rights of Indigenous Peoples; Canada was one of only four countries not to support the declaration.

Halifax suffered a setback when the city and provincial governments decided to end their bid for the 2014 Commonwealth Games. Supporters had promoted the games for its contribution of legacy facilities including housing, a multi-use complex, and a large stadium to attract major events or professional sports franchises. Critics charged that the benefits were exaggerated, while costs were underestimated and would inevitably escalate. The decision to abandon the bid led to finger pointing, with bid officials arguing they had not been given enough time to finalize costs and that politicians had ignored potential spin-offs. Opponents accused the bid committee of withholding information which prevented a full assessment of costs and benefits and criticized high costs for consultant and professional services (*Chronicle Herald*, 22 Dec.) The province and city chastised Ottawa for failing to offer more funds to support the bid. Concerns about the bid process, other government contracts, and consultants' fees prompted creation of a municipal auditor general for the province's cities and towns.

Meanwhile the Nova Scotia government asked the courts to dismiss a suit by Cape Breton Regional Municipality which claimed the province violated the charter guarantee for equalization by allegedly underfunding this city. The province denied this, pointing out the larger contributions for Cape Breton versus some other municipal districts. A conference board report showed Halifax trailed all other major cities in Canada in transfers from provincial and federal governments (ibid., 9 Feb.). Municipalities complained that the cap program, designed to protect homeowners from sudden property tax hikes, had become too generous at the expense of local budgets, but the province refused to alter this policy. The province and its municipalities signed a seven-year agreement to reduce local payments for corrections and housing, to free up funds to restore infrastructure, but cities complained it was insufficient.

PETER NEARY AND MELVIN BAKER

Newfoundland and Labrador

The year 2007 began in Newfoundland and Labrador with political shocks and surprises. On 4 January Premier Danny Williams (Humber West) announced the departure from Cabinet of the transportation and works minister and minister of Labrador affairs, John Hickey (Lake Melville), "pending further information on a review currently being done by the Auditor General … into constituency allowances" (Executive Council, *News Release*, 4 Jan.). Four days later Auditor General John L. Noseworthy submitted separate reports to House of Assembly Speaker Harvey Hodder (Waterford Valley) on double-billing by Hickey and Progressive Conservative member of the House Assembly (MHA) Kathy Goudie (Humber Valley) in the amounts of $3,770 and $3,818 respectively. On the same day Hickey was returned to Cabinet. According to Williams there had been "no intentional wrong doing" and the double-billing problem that had arisen could be traced to "carelessness, poor book keeping and most significantly, a serious lack of processes and controls in the House of Assembly" (ibid., 8 Jan.).

On 17 January veteran Tory member Jim Hodder (Port au Port) resigned his seat for health reasons. Two days later Goudie resigned her seat, and it was reported that NDP member Randy Collins (Labrador West) would vacate his in mid-February. Williams immediately called by-elections – for 8 February in the districts of Kilbride (vacated by former minister Ed Byrne on 1 January), Ferryland (vacated by former finance minister Loyola Sullivan on 29 December 2006), and Port au Port and for 12 February in Humber Valley. The Cabinet was now also reorganized, with Tom Osborne (St John's South) and Ross Wiseman (Trinity North) shifting portfolios and Shawn Skinner (St John's Centre) joining the administration.

On 31 January, during the by-election campaigns, the auditor general submitted his annual report. It showed that, in 2004, the House of Assembly's Internal Economy Commission had voted to increase constituency allowances by $2,875 and had, in effect, arranged matters so as not to draw attention to the favourable change made on behalf of members. No receipts had been required for the additional payments, which Williams and PC MHA Elizabeth Marshall (Topsail), a commission member and former auditor general, had declined to accept but which had been made to their legislative colleagues. This further revelation about the House of Assembly accounts provoked fresh public outrage, the more so because of the hard stand the government had taken in negotiations with public-sector workers the same year. In response, Williams, who had facilitated the scrutiny of Assembly financial affairs by the auditor general, who had previously been constrained in this regard, announced on 2 February that he would ask the PC members of the commission to move that constituency allowances in the current year be reduced by the amount of the additional payment made.

In the round of by-elections on 8 February the government easily held the three districts contested. But in the voting on 12 February, Liberal Dwight Ball ultimately prevailed in Humber Valley. The final vote in a season of by-elections was held on 13 March in Labrador West (Randy Collins had resigned on 14 February). In this contest the Conservatives took the seat from the NDP in a four-way split.

The future of Canada's complex equalization program was also much in the news at the beginning of 2007, with attention focusing on the 2006 report of a panel chaired by former Alberta deputy treasurer Al O'Brien. It recommended a revised equalization formula that would include 50 per cent of provincial revenue from non-renewable resources – a plan anathema to Williams. He insisted that Prime Minister Stephen Harper had promised Newfoundland and Labrador that the calculation of the province's share of equalization would never take resource revenue into account, while maintaining all the benefits of the 2005 revised Atlantic Accord negotiated with the government of Paul Martin. On 23 January Williams said in Saskatoon that the O'Brien report was "flawed" and constructed on "arbitrary principles" (*National Post*, 24 Jan.). Moreover Harper had promised in two election campaigns and in four letters not to follow the course of action recommended by the O'Brien study: "I'm still prepared to give him the benefit of the doubt," Williams said of the prime minister. "I think he will deliver on his promise." But on 2 March the *Globe and Mail* reported that an exchange of letters about equalization between Williams and Harper had set Ottawa on a "pre-election collision course" with the province.

Against this backdrop, the budget introduced in the House of Commons on 19 March by finance minister Jim Flaherty evoked an angry response from Williams. The federal decision on equalization was twofold. A province could either continue under the existing formula or join in a revised, enriched scheme, which would take account of non-renewable resource revenue (either at 50 per cent or 100 per cent, depending on the preference of the province) and cap payments to prevent equalization-receiving provinces from achieving greater per capita fiscal capacity than provinces that did not benefit from the scheme. Under this arrangement, Newfoundland and Labrador could avoid having its non-renewable resource revenue included in its equalization calculation, avoid a cap, and keep the benefits of the Atlantic Accord – but at the cost of not being eligible for the enriched equalization payments proffered in the revised formula. Williams immediately denounced the federal plan and advised the people of the province not to vote Conservative in the event of a national election. A promise that had been made had been broken – "a breach of trust," resulting in "a very sad day" for Canada (Executive Council, *News Release*, 20 March).

Williams followed up on 28 March with a national newspaper advertising campaign that cost about $250,000. When the federal government countered with its own media advertising blitz, he declared the effort an insult to "the intelligence and integrity of the people of Newfoundland and Labrador" (*National Post*, 4 April). His campaign against Ottawa's action won support ("Danny's got a point") from the St John's *Telegram* (21 March), but it met a hostile reception in the national press. On 24 March the *Globe and Mail* pointed out that, thanks to equalization, in 2007–8 Newfoundland and Labrador would have a per capita fiscal capacity of $500 more than Ontario. And whereas Newfoundland and Labrador had spent $8,567 per capita on program expenditures in 2005–6, Ontario, the lowest-ranked province, had managed only $5,975 per capita. All this proved that Newfoundland and Labrador was "the big winner in the equalization sweepstakes." On 29 March John Ivison wrote in the *National Post* that Williams was "rapidly becoming the Hugo Chavez of the Rock, blaming Ottawa for every misfortune from rural poverty to Newfoundland fog."

Caught in the middle of the battle royal now raging were the province's three Conservative MPs – fisheries and oceans minister Loyola Hearn (St John's South–Mount Pearl), Norman Doyle (St John's East), and Fabian Manning (Avalon). With the four Newfoundland Liberal MPs egging Williams on, their position proved decidedly uncomfortable, although Doyle had made it known before the budget that he would not run again. Both Williams and Liberal Opposition leader Gerry Reid (Twillingate and Fogo) called on the Conservative MPs to put province ahead of party, but caucus solidarity prevailed. On 4 May, with Flaherty reported to be negotiating a sidebar deal with Nova Scotia to keep that province under the new equalization formula, Williams told a Toronto audience that his advice to voters across Canada in the event of a federal election could be summed up in the acronym "ABC" – "Anybody But Conservative" (*National Post*, 4 May). The Harper government – the premier had shortly before publicly referred to the prime minister by the diminutive "Steve" – was untrustworthy and had a "propensity to provide misleading and inaccurate information to further their own interests." After the Newfoundland Conservative MPs voted with the majority, on 13 June, in support of the government in the final Commons vote on the budget, Williams said that his skin "crawled" at their action (*Telegram*, 14 June).

On 24 April, in the midst of this uproar, the fourth session of the forty-fifth General Assembly began in St John's, with the fourteen-page, single-spaced Speech from the Throne extolling the virtues of a proud, responsible, and self-reliant province. The people of Newfoundland and Labrador were "proud nationalists" who believed that only by affirming their identity could they realize the "goal of economic equality within the federation" (http://www.exec.gov.nl.ca/thronespeech/2007/speech2007.htm). "Our people are ready to take charge of our future," the lieutenant governor proclaimed, "and, under My First Minister's leadership, our province will achieve self-reliance by becoming masters of our own house." The *National Post* was decidedly unimpressed and in a hard-hitting 26 April editorial ("Maîtres chez Newf") claimed that "[i]f only Newfoundland and Labrador could export its Premier's melodramatic rhetoric, the province would be Canada's richest, instead of its poorest." Writing in that paper two days later, Williams asserted, "It's not separation we crave, but respect – the kind of respect that comes from within." On 5 May the *Post* called him "Newfoundland's bumptious blowhard," but in the same issue columnist Don Martin ventured that Williams had "become the Rock face of East Coast politics" and that "his electoral opponents … [were] to be pitied as future campaign roadkill."

On 26 April the budget speech was delivered in the Assembly by finance minister Tom Marshall (Humber East). In a document full of pre-election good news, he reported a revised surplus of $76 million for 2006–7 ($6.2 million had been predicted) and laid out plans for 2007–8 that forecast revenue of $5,632.1 million and net expenses of $5,566.4 million for a surplus of $261.2 million. On the revenue side, the province's three offshore oil projects (Hibernia, Terra Nova, and White Rose) were expected to deliver more than $1.25 billion in 2007–8.

This fiscal performance made possible income and other tax reductions billed as the "largest tax cut in the history of the province" (Finance, *News Release*, 26 April). Included in the speech was the controversial news that the government would work with the Board of Regents of Memorial University to grant Sir Wilfred Grenfell College, Memorial's Corner Brook campus, "full university status and a separate executive, senate and budget while maintaining a common Board of Regents" (http://www.budget.gov.nl.ca/budget2007/speech.htm).

Legislation passed during the session included acts relating to sustainable development, certified public accountants and chartered accountants, the reorganization of Newfoundland and Labrador Hydro, and the creation of a provincial energy corporation with a broad mandate for investment and development. To facilitate the end of mandatory retirement in the province, various amendments were made to the Human Rights Code and to four pension acts. On 13 June a bill – the House of Assembly Accountability, Integrity and Administration Act – was introduced to carry out the recommendations of Chief Justice Derek Green, who, amidst public uproar about the financial affairs of the Assembly and the conduct of some members, had been commissioned in the summer of 2006 to give an opinion on how best to reconcile the autonomy of the legislature with the requirement of public accountability in relation to its affairs. His report, *Rebuilding Confidence: The Report of the Review Commission on Constituency Allowances and Related Matters*, was delivered on 4 June. It contained thirteen chapters and, as Schedule I, the bill introduced on 13 June. In the event, the draft bill, which was accepted by the government and endorsed by the Opposition parties, breezed through the Assembly with only minor amendment and, on 14 June, the day the Assembly adjourned, was given assent. Through foresight and careful management, Williams had adroitly closed a difficult file.

At the last sitting of the session, the Assembly also bade farewell to five members – four Liberals and Speaker Hodder – who had decided not to run in the forthcoming election, scheduled, by 2004 statute, for 9 October. In July charges arising from the constituency spending investigations that had triggered the Green report were brought against Liberal MHA Wally Andersen (Torngat Mountains). Subsequently charges were laid against Jim Walsh, a former Liberal minister; Randy Collins, former New Democrat MHA; Ed Byrne, former Tory leader, Cabinet minister, and deputy premier; and former House of Assembly director of financial operations Bill Murray. On 14 September Auditor General Noseworthy submitted a searching review of House of Assembly constituency allowance claims from 1989–90 to 2005–6. This comprehensive document ignited yet another media feeding frenzy. In a report submitted on 17 September Noseworthy found that the government had received "good value" for its $15 million investment in a fibre-optic deal that had become a cause célèbre in 2006 (http://www.ag.gov.nl.ca/ag/special/2007FibreOptic/FibreOpticReport2007.pdf).

Other government actions and initiatives in 2007 included the launch of a provincial immigration strategy; the implementation of the second part of a program to curb video lottery terminal (VLT) addiction; the release of a Northern Strategic Plan for Labrador; and the launch of a Forestry and Agrifoods Agency. In January the report of the Electoral District Boundaries Commission, chaired by retired Court of Appeal justice John O'Neill, was made public. The same month lawyer John F. Roil was appointed to conduct a review of a proposal by Mount Pearl for a boundary change in its favour vis-à-vis St John's (he advised against). In June, after anguished public debate about the accuracy of test results, it was announced that Justice Margaret A. Cameron would undertake a Judicial Commission of Inquiry on oestrogen and progesterone receptor testing for breast cancer patients. In October the Transportation Safety Board of Canada released its final report into the September 2005 capsizing of the *Melina and Keith II*, in which four crew members lost their lives. In October also the province announced an ex gratia payment of $750,000 to Ronald Dalton, who had been wrongly convicted of murder and had spent eight years in prison awaiting appeal.

Public appointees in 2007 included Gillian Butler (Supreme Court judge); Annie Evans, Nunatsiavut (Provincial Advisory Council on the Status of Women); Jane Fitzpatrick (executive director, Human Rights Commission); Gilbert Dalton (chair, Board of Regents, Memorial University); Jean K. Madill (president of the College of the North Atlantic); Len Simms (chairperson and CEO, Newfoundland and Labrador Housing Corporation); and Megan Davis Williams (interim director, the Rooms Provincial Art Gallery). In January Ross Reid resigned as deputy minister to the premier. On 25 January, less than a month after resigning from the provincial Cabinet, Loyola Sullivan was appointed Canadian ambassador for fisheries conservation. Following the surprise resignation of former Liberal Cabinet minister Charles Furey, effective 1 May, Paul Reynolds was named chief electoral officer and commissioner of members' interests. In October – breaking with long-established practice – Bishop Martin William Currie of the Roman Catholic diocese of Grand Falls was named archbishop of St John's while retaining his existing responsibility. In December former Tory Cabinet minister John Ottenheimer was named chair of the Board of Directors of Newfoundland and Labrador Hydro. Effective 31 December Axel Meisen resigned as president of Memorial University; vice president (academic) Eddy Campbell was named acting president effective 1 January 2008.

Economically, the 2006 pull-out of Chevron Corporation and its partners Exxon Mobil, Petro-Canada, and Norsk Hydro from negotiations with the province for developing the Hebron–Ben Nevis offshore oil field, at a price tag of about $6 billion, cast a long shadow in 2007. Combined with difficulty over the authorization of production at Hibernia South and the prospect of a new provincial energy plan (scheduled to be issued before the provincial election), this led to a great deal of hesitation and uncertainty – and industry criticism of the Newfoundland and Labrador authorities. On 17 January the province announced that it had not approved a Canada–Newfoundland and Labrador Offshore Petroleum Board (C-NLOPB) decision that would have opened up Hibernia South for production. Natural resources minister Kathy Dunderdale (Virginia Waters) said more information was needed before the province could make "an informed decision" on whether the change proposed, which the federal government approved, was in the public interest (Natural Resources, *News Release*, 17 Jan.). This action received wide coverage in the national financial press, much of it adverse, with Liberal Opposition leader Gerry Reid quoted as saying that the province did not "seem to be able to make a deal with anybody" (*Globe and Mail*, 18 Jan.).

On 1 February C-NLOPB posted a letter on its Web site defending its decision on Hibernia South and arguing that "as a general rule, delaying production erodes value, whereas accelerating production enhances value" (Natural Resources, *News Release*, 2 Feb.). This letter drew criticism from Dunderdale, who noted that representatives of the Hibernia Management Development Company (HMDC) had now agreed to give the government the additional information it was seeking before making a decision. In a news release dated 5 March the minister expressed disappointment that HMDC and Petro-Canada would appeal a court ruling that upheld the C-NLOPB right to specify research and development guidelines for companies operating offshore. On 28 March it was reported that a Chevron-led consortium was withdrawing the *Eirik Raude*, a rig specially equipped for deep-sea exploration, from exploration work in the Orphan Basin and relocating it to the Gulf of Mexico. This meant that for the first time in many years there would be no exploration in progress off Newfoundland.

Interviewed on 4 May by Claudia Cattaneo, the Calgary bureau chief of the *Financial Post*, Williams said that he remained optimistic that the Hebron–Ben Nevis deal could be completed. The province, he noted, had started out wanting an 8.5 per cent equity share but had scaled back to 4.9 per cent – a figure from which, along with a super-royalty tied to rising oil prices, it would not back down. Moreover, once the new energy plan was adopted, the province would want a higher equity share in future development projects. Accordingly, in hope of reaching a deal with Chevron and its partners, the plan, now in third draft, was being held back. In a follow-up feature article on "New-found problems," Cattaneo reported from St John's that the local business community "was feeling the pain" of the dispute between the premier and the oil companies, that housing prices had slumped badly, and that the province was losing to Alberta the skilled workers it would need to go forward (*National Post*, 5 May). In sum, the Newfoundland oil patch was stagnant. On 19 June, however, Williams made known that talks, albeit informal, had resumed with the Hebron–Ben Nevis partners following "a brief but necessary hiatus" (ibid., 20 June). In August a spokesperson for the government announced that formal negotiations had been resumed.

In the fishing industry a notable development during the year was the 12 April announcement of what would be done under the 2006 federal-provincial Fishing Industry Renewal Initiative. Ottawa committed to a program that included fleet rationalization, flexibility on vessel size, a more favourable treatment of capital gains, improved financial access, and a three-year, $19.5 million investment in fisheries science. The province's commitments included the introduction of a Processing Policy Renewal Strategy, an improved fisheries guarantee loan program, the creation of a Newfoundland and Labrador Seafood Marketing Council, and a three-year, $6 million research investment.

Ottawa and St John's were also active during the year in support of the annual seal hunt, which was hampered in 2007 by especially heavy ice conditions. In March Canada sent a delegation overseas to lobby the European Union, and the province launched a Web site to counter the efforts of seal-hunt opponents. In July a decidedly different note was struck after Ottawa announced a spending package for the British Columbia fishing industry. Acting fisheries and aquaculture minister Trevor Taylor (the Straits and White Bay North) now complained that the Newfoundland and Labrador industry was being short-changed in the Fishing Industry Renewal process and that Ottawa had not lived up to its commitment with respect to custodial management of fish stocks that straddled the offshore territorial limit. In October Fisheries

Minister Hearn hailed a new convention of the North Atlantic Fisheries Organization as opening the way for "a much better, stronger regional fisheries management organization" without impairing Canada's sovereignty within its 200-mile territorial limit – a view hotly contested by Liberal and NDP fisheries critics (*Telegram*, 29 Sept.).

The possible sale of Fishery Products International (FPI), the province's largest fish processor, was likewise prominent in the news in 2007. Complicating the proposed sale was the fact that, by law, no shareholder could own more than 15 per cent of the company and the province had to approve any deal. On top of all this, the company was deadlocked in negotiations with its plant employees represented by the Fish, Food and Allied Workers union. In March the government blocked a bid for the company by the Barry Group of Corner Brook, one of several prospective purchasers. But by May, pending government approval, the company had worked out a deal with High Liner Foods of Lunenburg, Nova Scotia, for the sale of its American assets and the plant at Burin, Newfoundland, and with Ocean Choice International (a division of the Penney Group of Companies owned by St John's businessman Ches Penney) for the sale of its other holdings. On 28 May, after a further round of negotiations, the government approved the proposed sale in principle and final agreement followed. Following the completion of its deal with High Liner and Ocean Choice, FPI set out to restructure itself as a publicly traded company known as FP Resources and listed on the Toronto Stock Exchange.

Change, much of it adverse, also proceeded apace in 2007 in the hard-pressed forestry sector. In March Abitibi-Consolidated and the Grand Falls–Windsor Local of the Canadian Energy and Paperworkers Union made an agreement whereby the company effected a saving of $10 million. In October Kruger announced the indefinite shutdown, effective 5 November, of the No. 1 paper machine at its Corner Brook mill, and bad news followed for Grand Falls–Windsor when newly merged AbitibiBowater announced a thirty-day review of its diverse operations that threatened a big local layoff. In the event, the central Newfoundland operation was spared in the downsizing plan the company announced on 30 November. But at year's end the future of the province's forestry industry remained problematic. Between 2003 and 2007 newsprint exports from the province declined from 781,000 to 594,977 tonnes.

By contrast, in his budget speech the finance minister had reported real provincial GDP growth of 1.8 per cent in 2006 and predicted 8.5 per cent for 2007, thanks to increased oil and other mineral exports.

These were impressive numbers, but the 2006 census, the first results of which were released on 13 March, was sobering. Whereas the population of Canada rose between 2001 and 2006 by 5.4 per cent, the population of Newfoundland declined by 1.5 per cent to 505,469. Newfoundland and Labrador, moreover, was one of only two provinces (the other was Saskatchewan) to lose population. Within the province, suburban areas around St John's – Paradise, Portugal Cove–St Philip's, and Torbay – showed robust population growth, and the city itself grew by 1.5 per cent. But other communities – Channel-Port aux Basques, Corner Brook, Happy Valley–Goose Bay, Labrador City, and Mount Pearl among them – showed declines. Labrador, which had lost 5.8 per cent of its population, was now one of the ten fastest-declining ridings in Canada.

In the wake of the annual spring session of the House of Assembly, July and August are usually quiet months politically in the province, but in 2007 the summer calm was broken on several occasions. On 27 July Memorial University chancellor and national Conservative heavyweight John Crosbie, incensed by public policy in relation to Grenfell College, accused the government of "political interference in the management of Memorial" (http://today.mun.ca/news.php?news_id=3126). On 1 August the southeastern part of the Island of Newfoundland was hit hard by Tropical Storm Chantal. Two days later Prime Minister Harper made an impromptu visit to the province to inspect the damage and support flood victims. His unannounced visit drew a rebuke from Williams, who complained that Harper had not had the "simple courtesy" of letting him know he was coming to the province (*National Post*, 4 Aug.).

On 23 August, with election day fast approaching, the premier grabbed national attention, confounded his business critics, and won many plaudits with the announcement that the government had reached an agreement with Chevron and its consortium partners for the development of the Hebron–Ben Nevis oil field, with its reserves of more than 700 million barrels. Under this arrangement, the details of which remained to be worked out, the province would invest $110 million in the project and have a 4.9 per cent equity stake. "Step by step," a triumphant Williams said, "we are becoming masters of our own house" (*London Free Press*, 23 Aug.). Claudia Cattaneo now wrote that "[o]bservers were hard-pressed to identify significant differences between the new deal and the one the two sides walked away from last year" – a point of view also trumpeted by *National Post* columnist Andrew Coyne (*National Post*, 23 and 25 Aug.). But the ebullient

Williams was having none of it. In a *National Post* article on 31 August he accused Coyne and Cattaneo of spreading "negativity" and doing "a disservice to the public interest."

On 11 September, at a glitzy news conference in the Johnson Geo Centre, St John's, the government released its much-heralded energy plan, *Focusing Our Energy*, which promised "self-reliance, prosperity and sustainable green energy solutions for the 21st century" (http://www.releases.gov.nl.ca/releases/2007/exec/0911n02.htm). The plan spelled out three principles – sustainability, control, and cooperation and coordination – and six goals. Specifically the plan committed the government to establishing "a policy to obtain a 10 per cent equity position in all future oil and gas projects requiring a Development Plan approval, where it fits our strategic long-term objectives."

On 17 September while basking in the glow of all this success, Williams called on Lieutenant Governor Edward Roberts and triggered the election. In the campaign that followed the PCs capitalized on their many advantages, not least the chartered jet in which the premier toured the province (smoked salmon and bakeapple cheesecake were served on board). By contrast Liberal leader Reid travelled by bus (only water and juice available) and NDP leader Lorraine Michael in a van. Following a televised leaders debate on 25 September, the St John's *Telegram* (1 Oct.) praised Michael for her "relatively quiet decorum" and criticized Williams and Reid for "endlessly trying to yammer over each other." All three parties produced comprehensive platforms and made them available on the Internet.

Both the Liberal Party and the NDP scrambled to find candidates, and when nominations closed on 29 September only the Conservatives fielded a full slate. Altogether 135 candidates were nominated – PC 48, Liberal 47, NDP 36, Labrador Party 1, non-affiliated 2, and undesignated 1 (Fred Wilcox in Virginia Waters). There were 38 women candidates – 15 NDP, 13 Liberal, and 10 PC. Following the death of Liberal candidate Dr Gerry Tobin on 1 October, the election in Grand Falls–Windsor–Buchans was rescheduled to 6 November (eventually there were fresh nominations, and the NDP, which had not previously named a candidate, now contested the seat). When Liberal candidate Clayton Hobbs withdrew from the race in Bonavista South, Roger Fitzgerald (PC) was elected by acclamation.

Of the 46 seats in play on election day the PCs carried 42. Only 3 Liberals survived the onslaught – popular incumbents Yvonne Jones (Cartwright–L'Anse au Clair), Kelvin Parsons (Burgeo–La Poile), and Roland Butler (Port de Grave). Williams ran strongly in Humber

West, and Lorraine Michael handily carried Signal Hill–Quidi Vidi against two female rivals. But, on a judicial recount, Gerry Reid lost by 12 votes to PC Derrick Dalley in the Isles of Notre Dame. Former Liberal leader Jim Bennett, who ran in St Barbe, was also defeated. The popular vote on election day was distributed as follows: PC 69.60 per cent (a provincial record), Liberal 21.68 per cent, NDP 8.49 per cent, Labrador Party 0.03 per cent, non-affiliated/undesignated 0.20 per cent. In sum, on an election-day turnout of 60.2 per cent, the Tories had dominated the province. Following the Grand Falls–Windsor–Buchans election, which PC candidate Susan Sullivan won easily (the Liberal candidate, who pulled out and then came back in, placed third), the final party standings were PC 44, Liberal 3, NDP 1. Eleven of those returned to the new House of Assembly were women – 9 PCs, 1 Liberal, and 1 NDP.

The premier was soon back trading punches with the prime minister. After Harper and Nova Scotia premier Rodney MacDonald appeared together in Ottawa on 10 October to announce agreement between the province and the federal government over equalization and offshore resource revenues, Williams denounced the prime minister for trying to set province against province: "I don't think Canadians can trust him. We will fight him all the way" (*National Post*, 11 Oct.). For his part, noting that Newfoundland and Labrador wanted "a new special equalization arrangement," Harper said on 11 October that the equalization formula had "to be the same for every province." Williams, he commented, had "a unique style of federal-provincial relations. Let me just put it that way" (ibid., 12 Oct.). The day before the Newfoundland and Labrador provincial election, the *Globe and Mail* had editorialized that Williams deserved re-election. But after his latest outburst against Ottawa, the *National Post* (12 Oct.) called him "a clown." Triumphant at home, Williams, as always, continued to play to mixed reviews in the national media, although in reality being underestimated in Toronto may have been a source of strength for him.

On 30 October the Cabinet was reorganized and five new faces added to it, including two rookie members of the House of Assembly. The Cabinet sworn in after the PC election victory in 2003 had fourteen members, but this total now rose to eighteen (thirteen men and five women). In announcing these changes the premier also made known that the new House of Assembly would not meet until well into 2008. On 1 November all but one (Elizabeth Marshall – PC Topsail) of the members duly returned to the forty-sixth General Assembly were sworn or affirmed into office in the House. Immediately thereafter, Roger

Fitzgerald was elected as Speaker. On 13 November, after his defeat in the Isles of Notre Dame was confirmed by judicial recount, Gerry Reid announced his resignation as leader of the provincial Liberal Party. This would take effect, he said, when the party executive chose an interim leader, and a general meeting the Liberals had scheduled for October 2008 would now be a leadership convention. Two days later it was announced that Yvonne Jones would be interim party leader at least until June 2008 (she would have to give way then if she decided to enter the October leadership race).

Having tidied up post-election business, Danny Williams exited for Brazil and a round of meetings with officials of Companhia Vale do Rio Doce, which, following its 2006 takeover of Inco, was the owner of the Voisey's Bay Nickel Company. Then, on 30 November, he met briefly, privately, and amicably in St John's with Harper, who was making a multipurpose visit to the province. On this occasion Williams advanced options for resolving the still-simmering dispute with Ottawa over equalization and the Atlantic Accord, but for the moment the two leaders "agreed to disagree" (*Globe and Mail*, 1 Dec.). In leaving his proposals for Harper's further consideration, Williams put a price tag of $10–11 billion on the loss to the province to 2020 under the existing equalization/Atlantic Accord arrangement, which had been unilaterally imposed. This, he ventured, was the sum that would have to be covered in one way or another in any settlement between the two governments. If matters did not work out with the federal government, Williams cautioned, his recommendation of "Anything But Conservative" would hold in the event of a federal election.

On 10 December Finance Minister Marshall announced that for the current year the province would opt into the same arrangement that Nova Scotia had with the federal government on equalization. This would produce $66 million more than the alternative arrangement open to Newfoundland and Labrador. But Williams was quick to point out that the rationale was "one year gain"; in the long run a "broken promise" would result in the province being "short changed by approximately $10 billion" (News Release, Executive Council, 12 Dec.). In his fall financial update, issued on 10 December, Marshall reported that, thanks mainly to the rise in oil prices since the April budget, the surplus for 2007–8 would be a whopping $881.8 million rather than the substantial $261.2 million initially forecast. More good news followed when the province completed an agreement between its new energy corporation and Husky Energy for the development of the White Rose expansion oil fields. In December, too, the province completed an infrastructure framework agreement with the federal government whereby Ottawa would contribute $430 million.

There were several developments of note during 2007 in the interaction of the province with its First Nations communities. In February the Newfoundland and Labrador Supreme Court denied an application to allow a class-action suit on behalf of over 7,000 individuals of Mi'kmaq descent not recognized under the Indian Act. But on 30 November Harper announced at St George's that an agreement had been reached between the government of Canada and the Federation of Newfoundland Indians (subject to ratification by federation members), whereby Mi'kmaq people in Newfoundland and Labrador would become eligible for various benefits under the Indian Act although not living on reserve. In April the federal and provincial governments announced joint funding of $18.6 million for the construction of a new school for the Sheshatshiu Innu First Nation. From 20 to 22 June, in Corner Brook, the Native Women's Association of Canada and the provincial government co-hosted the first-ever National Aboriginal Women's Summit.

With the Rooms in St John's now well established on the Canadian cultural landscape, the province had another considerable year of achievement in arts and letters. The 2007 offerings of the Provincial Art Gallery included an Anne Meredith Barry retrospective, an exhibition of work by the neglected artists Frances Jones (Bannerman) and Margaret Campbell Macpherson, and a comprehensive survey of the Labrador work of the nineteenth-century Canadian artist William Hind. In January well-known arts writer Joan Sullivan became the editor of the venerable *Newfoundland Quarterly*, and in March Kenneth J. Harvey was awarded the $15,000 Rogers Writers' Trust Fiction Prize for his 2006 novel *Inside*. In June tourism, culture and recreation minister Tom Hedderson (Harbour Main–Whitbourne) announced the establishment of the Status of the Artist Working Committee to assist the government in funding matters. Visual artist Pam Hall was named to chair the new group. Money flowed during the year from the province's Cultural Economic Development Program to various organizations, and in June Hedderson announced details of the government's plan for a $2 million celebration in 2010 to mark the 400th anniversary of the establishment of the first English colony in present-day Canada, at Cuper's Cove (now Cupids), Conception Bay.

Numbered in the province's 2007 necrology, near and far, were Ray Bellew (actor); Augustus Brennan (educator); Iain Bruce (classicist and academic administrator); Elison Bugden (Corner Brook businessman); John Douglas Eaton (vice president of student affairs at Memorial

University); Gladys Groves Copeland (Bonavista benefactor); Richard Greene (lawyer and MHA); Alastair A. Macdonald (English professor and poet); Hilda (Batten) Menchions (survivor of the 1919 shipwreck of the SS *Ethie*); Ransom Myers (fisheries biologist); John O'Mara (broadcaster); Dermot O'Reilly (of the folk group Ryan's Fancy); Apinam Pone (Innu justice advocate); Garfield Pynn (business professor); Ian Rusted (founding dean of the Memorial medical school); and Sam Andersen (first president of the Labrador Inuit Association). Among Canada's honoured 2007 fallen in Afghanistan were three gallant sons of Newfoundland and Labrador: Corporal Stephen Bouzane, Private Kevin Kennedy, and Sergeant Donald Lucas. On 15 February the province marked in sadness the twenty-fifth anniversary of the sinking of the offshore oil rig *Ocean Ranger*. The entire crew of eighty-four was lost in an event that reverberates through the modern history of the province.

The year 2007 was a year of intense political activity in Newfoundland and Labrador and of bitter conflict between St John's and Ottawa. At the centre of events was the media-savvy Williams. Long known as "Danny Millions," in 2007 he also acquired the moniker "King Danny" (*Globe and Mail*, 18 Sept.). Ten years after production had started at Hibernia, the province was on an economic roll and, although the fishery and forest industries continued to struggle and overall unemployment remained high, there was evidence of spreading prosperity and burgeoning enterprise. In February Fortis of St John's completed the takeover of Terasen Gas of British Columbia. The handiwork of Fortis president and CEO Stan Marshall, this deal highlighted the growing sophistication, ambition, and reach of the Newfoundland business community. In November the Conference Board of Canada reported that Newfoundland and Labrador would lead the provinces in percentage of economic growth in 2008. And in December Statistics Canada, releasing national July–October population numbers, reported population growth in the province, which was now well on its way to "have" status in Canada and experiencing transformative change. What the long-term constitutional, political, social, and demographic effect of this would be was now much discussed.

On 20 December John Crosbie was named to succeed Edward Roberts as lieutenant governor. With Crosbie headed for Government House and Danny Williams in the premier's office in the Confederation Building, Newfoundlanders and Labradorians had much to look forward to in 2008.

Obituaries

ANDERSON, DORIS (2 March, age 85). *Chatelaine* magazine editor (1957–77), columnist, leading Canadian women's rights activist, chancellor of the University of PEI, Companion of the Order of Canada.

APPEL, BLUMA (15 July, age 86). Philanthropist who founded the Canadian Foundation for AIDS Research.

ASH, BOBBY (20 May, age 82). Actor and star of *The Uncle Bobby Show*.

AVISON, MARGARET (31 July, age 89). Poet, Griffin Poetry Prize winner, and Officer of the Order of Canada.

BELL, RICHARD (17 June, age 61). Musician, played with the Band and Janis Joplin.

BOSS, WILLIAM "BILL" (17 October, age 90). Journalist, Second World War correspondent for the Canadian Press.

BOUCHER, ANDREE (24 August, age 70). Mayor of Quebec City.

BOWERMAN, TED (20 December, age 77). Former NDP Cabinet minister in Saskatchewan.

BRADSHAW, RICHARD (16 August, age 63). Conductor for the Canadian Opera Company.

CALLWOOD, JUNE (14 June, age 82). Journalist, social activist, a founder of Casey House, Companion of the Order of Canada.

CAMPBELL, ARCHIE (17 April, age 65). Ontario Justice who led inquiry into the SARS crisis.

CAMPBELL, ELAINE (11 August, age 82). Co-writer of the *Anne of Green Gables* musical.

CHEVRIER, DON (17 December, age 69). First television commentator for the Toronto Blue Jays.

CROUSE, LLOYD (28 April, age 88). Former lieutenant governor of Nova Scotia and member of the House of Commons.

CURNOCK, RICHARD (8 February, age 84). Stratford stage actor.

DANBY, KEN (23 September, age 67). Realist painter.

DANIELS, STAN (6 April, age 72). Emmy-winning screenwriter, director, and producer.

DICKSON, ROBERT (19 March, age 62). Poet, author, professor, and winner of the Governor General's Literary Award.

DOHERTY, DENNY (21 January, age 66). Musician, songwriter, and member of the Mamas and the Papas.

DURELLE, YVON (6 January, age 77). Professional boxer.

FRANCA, CELIA (19 February, age 85). Founder of the National Ballet of Canada.

FRANCIS, LLOYD (20 January, age 86). Former speaker of the House of Commons.

GAUDAUR, JAKE (4 December, age 87). Former commissioner of the Canadian Football League.

GAUVIN, JEAN (7 June, age 61). Former minister of fisheries in New Brunswick.

GOULET, ROBERT (30 October, age 73). Singer.

HEBERT, JACQUES (7 December, age 84). Senator, journalist, and writer.

HILLIER, JAMES (15 January, age 91). Scientist and developer of the first electron microscope.

HUGHES, E.J. (5 January, age 93). Landscape painter.

HUTT, WILLAIM (27 June, age 87). Classical stage actor.

ISFELD, CAROL (15 August, age 68). Created the Izzy Doll, distributed by peacekeepers to children worldwide.

JOE, RITA (20 March, age 75). Mi'kmaq poet, songwriter, and Member of the Order of Canada.

KNIGHT, KEITH (22 August, age 51). Actor.

LAMER, ANTONIO (25 November, age 74). Former chief justice of the Supreme Court of Canada.

LANCASHIRE, DAVID (15 September, age 76). Journalist, first North American to report from mainland China following the 1949 revolution.

LARKIN, RYAN (14 February, age 63). Animator and inspiration for Academy Award–winning animated short *Ryan.*

LA SALLE, ROCH (20 August, age 79). Politician and former Cabinet minister under Brian Mulroney.

LE DAIN, GERALD (18 December, age 83). Former Supreme Court of Canada justice.

LIBA, PETER (21 June, age 67). Former lieutenant governor of Manitoba.

MACFADYEN, ELMER (17 August, age 64). Politician, former Cabinet minister in Prince Edward Island.

MAXWELL, LOIS (29 September, age 80). Actor, played Miss Moneypenny in fourteen James Bond movies.

MCKEAG, WILLIAM JOHN "Jack" (23 August, age 79). Former lieutenant governor of Manitoba.

MIRVISH, ED (11 July, age 92). Owner of Honest Ed's discount store and the Royal Alexander and the Princes of Wales Theatres in Toronto, philanthropist, Officer of the Order of Canada.

MISTAKEN CHIEF, STEPHEN (4 April, age 84). Last surviving Second World War veteran from the Blood Reserve.

MORAWETZ, OSKAR (16 June, age 90). Classical music composer.

MORRISSEAU, NORVAL (4 December, age 75). Painter and Member of the Order of Canada.

O'REILLY, DERMOT (17 February, age 64). Celtic singer-songwriter and producer.

OSTASHEK, JOHN (10 June, age 71). Former leader of the Yukon Party.

PETERSON, OSCAR (23 December, age 82). Jazz legend, Companion of the Order of Canada.

PINSENT, CHARMION KING (6 January, age 81). Actor and member of the Straw Hat Players.

POLLOCK, SAM (16 August, age 81). Former Montreal Canadiens general manager and vice president.

PROULX, MICHEL (14 January, age 67). Quebec Court of Appeal judge.

RASKY, HARRY (9 April, age 78). Oscar-nominated documentarian.

READ, JEANI (21 December, age 60). Journalist.

RIEL, MAURICE (20 July, age 85). Canadian senator.

RILEY, DOUG (27 August, age 62). Arranger, record producer, composer, pianist, and organist.

ROBERTS, JOHN (30 March, age 73). Former Liberal Cabinet minister under Pierre Trudeau.

ROSSITER, EILEEN (20 January, age 77). Second woman appointed to the Senate from Prince Edward Island.

RULE, JANE (27 November, age 76). Novelist and non-fiction writer.

SALTZMAN, PERCY (15 January, age 91). First person to appear on Canadian English-language television.

SAUDER, WILLIAM (19 December, age 81). Former chancellor of the University of British Columbia.

SHULEMSON, SYD (25 January, age 91). Canada's most decorated Jewish soldier from the Second World War.

SOMERS, BRETT (15 September, age 83). Actor, singer, and comedian.

STEEN, VINCE (3 February, age 65). Former Cabinet minister in the Northwest Territories.

SWART, MEL (27 February, age 87). Former NDP MLA in Ontario.

THORKELSON, SCOTT (19 May, age 49). Former member of the House of Commons.

TOLKIN, MEL (26 November, age 94). Comedy writer, *Your Show of Shows* and *Caesar's Hour.*

VENNE, JAMES MILES (28 November, age 89). Former chief of Saskatchewan's Lac La Ronge Indian Band (LLRIB), First Nations' advocate, and businessman.

WESLOCK, NICK (27 October, age 89). Amateur golfer and member of Canada's Sports Hall of Fame.

WILSON, BERTHA (30 April, age 83). First woman appointed to the Supreme Court of Canada, Companion of the Order of Canada.

WILSON, PERCY DWIGHT (9 May, age 106). Canada's second-last surviving veteran of the First World War.

Election tables

Saskatchewan 26th Provincial General Election 7 November 2007

Political party	Votes received (Valid)	Percentage of popular vote	Candidates elected
Saskatchewan Party	230,671	50.92	38
New Democratic Party	168,704	37.24	20
Saskatchewan Liberal Party	42,585	9.40	0
Green Party	9,128	2.01	0
Progressive Conservative Party of Saskatchewan	832	0.18	0
Western Independence	572	0.13	0
Saskatchewan Marijuana Party	517	0.11	0
Total	453,009	100.00	58

Source: Elections Saskatchewan

Quebec 38th National Assembly Election 26 March 2007

Political party	Votes received (Valid)	Percentage of popular vote	Candidates elected
Parti libéral du Québec/Quebec Liberal Party	1,313,664	33.08	48
Action démocratique du Québec	1,224,412	30.84	41
Parti Québécois	1,125,546	28.35	36
Green Party	152,885	3.85	0
Québec Solidaire	144,418	3.64	0
Parti marxiste-léniniste du Québec	2,091	0.05	0
Bloc pot	1,564	0.04	0
Christian Democracy Party	1,548	0.04	0
Independents	4,490	0.11	0
Total	3,970,618	100.00	125

Source: Directeur général des élections du Québec

Ontario 39th Provincial Election 10 October 2007

Political party	Votes received (Valid)	Percentage of popular vote	Candidates elected
Ontario Liberal Party	1,869,273	42.3	71
Progressive Conservative Party of Ontario	1,398,806	31.6	26
New Democratic Party	741,465	16.8	10
Green Party of Ontario	354,897	8.0	0
Family Coalition Party of Ontario	35,702	0.8	0
Ontario Libertarian Party	9,249	0.2	0
Freedom Party of Ontario	3,003	0.1	0
Communist Party of Canada (Ontario)	1,603	0.0	0
Party for People with Special Needs	502	0.0	0
Ontario Provincial Confederation of Regions	446	0.0	0
Reform Party of Ontario	354	0.0	0
Republican Party of Ontario	272	0.0	0
Independents	8,326	0.2	0
Total	4,423,898	100.00	107

Source: Elections Ontario

Northwest Territories 21st General Election 3 September 2007

District	Votes received	Percentage of valid votes	Candidate elected	Candidates defeated
Deh Cho	acclaimed		Michael McLeod	
Frame Lake	389	56.05	Wendy Bisaro	Chris Johnston Jeff Groenewegen
Great Slave	336	43.58	Glen Abernethy	Doug Ritchie Christopher Hunt Beaton MacKenzie Mark Bogan
Hay River North	514	60.83	Paul Delorey	Vince McKay
Hay River South	423	50.72	Jane Groenewegen	Greg McMeekin Marc Miltenberger
Inuvik Boot Lake	acclaimed		Floyd Roland	
Inuvik Twin Lakes	306	53.78	Robert C. McLeod	Denise Kurszewski
Kam Lake	489	79.51	Dave Ramsay	Brad Enge
Mackenzie Delta	303	50.33	David Krutko	Mary Joanne Clark Donald Robert

Continued

(Continued)

District	Votes received	Percentage of valid votes	Candidate elected	Candidates defeated
Monfwi	579	53.17	Jackson Lafferty	Henry Zoe
Nahendeh	548	61.30	Kevin A. Menicoche	Arnold Hope Bob Hanna Keyna Norwegian
Nunakput	266	40.92	Jackie Jacobson	Vince J. Teddy Eddie T. Dillon Calvin P. Pokiak
Range Lake	564	72.59	Sandy Lee	Ashley Geraghty
Sahtu	acclaimed		Norman Yakeleya	
Thebacha	531	44.81	J. Michael Miltenberger	Peter Martselos Jeannie Marie-Jewell
Tu Nedhe	252	52.72	Tom Beaulieu	Steve Ellis Raymond Simon Bobby J. Villeneuve Andrew Butler James W. McPherson
Weledeh	522	43.07	Bob Bromley	Andy Wong Jonas Sangris Carol Morin
Yellowknife Centre	430	46.09	Robert Hawkins	Sue Glowach Ben McDonald Bryan Sutherland
Yellowknife South	539	61.46	Bob McLeod	Amy Hacala Garett Cochrane

Source: Elections NWT

Index of names

Index of subjects

FSC
www.fsc.org
MIX
Papier | Fördert
gute Waldnutzung
FSC® C083411

Kolibri 360 GmbH
Ferdinand-Jühlke-Straße 7
99095 Erfurt, Deutschland
produktsicherheit@kolibri360.de